MARVEL MASTERWORKS

PRESENTS

THE AVENGERS

VOLUME 9

REPRINTING
THE AVENGERS NOS. 11–20

STAN LEE • JACK KIRBY • DON HECK

MARVEL MASTERWORKS

VOLUMES AVAILABLE

VOLUME 1: THE AMAZING SPIDER-MAN NOS. 1–10
& AMAZING FANTASY NO. 15

VOLUME 2: THE FANTASTIC FOUR NOS. 1–10

VOLUME 3: THE X-MEN NOS. 1–10

VOLUME 4: THE AVENGERS NOS. 1–10

VOLUME 5: THE AMAZING SPIDER-MAN NOS. 11–20

VOLUME 6: THE FANTASTIC FOUR NOS. 11–20

VOLUME 7: THE X-MEN NOS. 11–21

VOLUME 8: THE INCREDIBLE HULK NOS. 1–6

VOLUME 9: THE AVENGERS NOS. 11–20

VOLUME 10: THE AMAZING SPIDER-MAN NOS. 21–30
& ANNUAL NO. 1

VOLUME 11: THE X-MEN NOS. 94–100
& GIANT-SIZE NO. 1

THE AVENGERS

Written by: Stan Lee
Co-plotted by: Jack Kirby (Issue Nos. 14–16)
Co-scripted by: Larry Lieber and Paul Laiken (Issue No. 14)
Breakdowns by: Jack Kirby (Issue Nos. 14–16)
Penciled by: Don Heck (Issue Nos. 11–15, 17–20) Dick Ayers (Issue No. 16)
Inked by: Chic Stone (Issue Nos. 11, 14) Dick Ayers (Issue Nos. 12–13, 16–19)
Mike Esposito (Issue No. 15) Wally Wood (Issue No. 20)
Colored by: Mark Chiarello (Issue Nos. 11–15) Bob Sharen (Issue Nos. 16–18)
Michael Rockwitz (Issue No. 19) Steve Buccellato (Issue No. 20)
Lettered by: Sam Rosen (Issue Nos. 11, 12, 14, 17) Art Simek (Issue Nos. 13, 15, 16, 18–20)
Art restoration by: Michael Higgins

CREDITS

Editor in Chief: Tom DeFalco
Special Projects Editor: Bob Budiansky
Editor: Gregory Wright
Assistant Editors: Sara Tuchinsky, Evan Skolnick
Book Design: Lillian Lovitt
Logo Design: Ken Lopez
Dust Jacket Frame: Sandy Plunkett with Tom Palmer

PRINTED IN THE UNITED STATES OF AMERICA   ISBN 0-87135-595-7

MARVEL MASTERWORKS

CONTENTS

Introduction by Stan Lee . . . . *vi*

"The Mighty Avengers Meet Spider-Man"
   The Avengers #11, December, 1964 . . . . *1*

"This Hostage Earth"
   The Avengers #12, January, 1965 . . . . *22*

"The Castle of Count Nefaria"
   The Avengers #13, February, 1965 . . . . *43*

"Even Avengers Can Die"
   The Avengers #14, March, 1965. . . . . *64*

"Now, By My Hand, Shall Die a Villain"
   The Avengers #15, April, 1965 . . . . *85*

"The Old Order Changeth"
   The Avengers #16, May, 1965. . . . . *106*

"Four Against the Minotaur"
   The Avengers #17, June, 1965 . . . . *127*

"When the Commissar Commands"
   The Avengers #18, July, 1965. . . . . *148*

"The Coming of the Swordsman"
   The Avengers #19, August, 1965 . . . . *169*

"Vengeance is Ours"
   The Avengers #20, September, 1965 . . . . *190*

MARVEL MASTERWORKS

INTRODUCTION

BY STAN LEE

Y'know the toughest part of writing about the Avengers? It's trying to remember who they are!

Since our titanic little team was formed, way back in the dark ages of the early Sixties, it seems that virtually every Marvel hero (and some hero/villains) have been Avengers at some time or other. In fact, one of my own biggest frustrations is the fact that I myself never got the chance to pick up the gavel and yell, "Avengers Assemble." I'm probably the only civilian left!

Anyway, I think you're in for a treat once you struggle through my obligatory intro and get to the heavy stuff on the exciting pages ahead. But, before turning you loose, I'd like to start with a confession.

Having written countless comic book yarns since the late Thirties, you can probably imagine how difficult it is for me to remember the older ones. (I even have trouble remembering the newer ones, but let that be our secret). Thus, writing these introductions has been a rare treat for me because since I don't remember those older yarns, I've had to reread them for the first time in years so that I'll know what I'm writing about—and let me tell you—I *love* 'em!

There's something about stories which involve a team, like the Avengers or the X-Men, which really grabs me. I think it's because there's so much opportunity for interesting characterization. Just think, when you have a lot of characters, all inter-relating to each other in story after story, there are so many things a writer can do to introduce conflicts, jealousies, romances, tensions, almost all the emotions and social crises that we encounter in our day-to-day existence. Working with a team gives us such a broad spectrum of plot potential, such a colorful palette of possibilities for a comic book creator to dip into.

For example…

As our series runs on, Steve Rogers grows increasingly dissatisfied with his lot in life. He feels that he's the only member of the team who has no additional private-life identity. He's not an industrialist like Tony Stark, or a scientist like Henry Pym and certainly not a part-time god like Don Blake. So, as a running sub-plot, we find him applying to Col. Nick Fury to become an agent of S.H.I.E.L.D., because he doesn't want to feel like a free-loader with the Avengers footing all his bills. And wait'll you see the sacrifice he makes in a later yarn, in order to save his fellow teammates!

We also have a situation wherein teenaged Rick Jones wants to be a full-fledged Avenger but is considered to be too young. And one of my favorite oddities, where Spider-Man becomes an Avenger—well, sort of! I'll let you see how it all shakes out. Then there's the time the Avengers offer a full membership to Prince Namor, the

MARVEL MASTERWORKS

INTRODUCTION

Sub-Mariner, with an unexpected result.

Of course, one of the best things about a team such as ours is the villains they have to fight. Obviously, when you've got a mighty menage of multi-powered mega-heroes you can't merely have them battling litterbugs and jay-walkers. So, one of our prime concerns is creating fiendish foes who are powerful enough to give them a real battle. Now I'll let you judge for yourself if we managed to succeed. Here's a startling sample of the burgeoning baddies our costumed cavorters will be tackling on the pages that follow…

Kang, the deadly descendant of Dr. Doom! The murderous Mole Man, teamed with the reprehensible Red Ghost! Count Nefaria, head of the malevolent Maggia! Baron Zemo! The Executioner! The Enchantress! The Black Knight! The Mysterious Melter! The Minotaur! The Red Commissar! The Swordsman! The Mandarin!

And that's not to mention such extra added attractions as the Watcher, the Hulk, the Aliens, Dr. Svenson, the Scarlet Witch, Quicksilver and Robo-Spidey! (Yes, Robo-Spidey! It'll all be clear to you once you get into the story)!

All the sagas in this issue were drawn by one of the true talents of Marvel's early days, the dynamic and dashing Don Heck. In a few cases, which are so labeled on the title pages, some had layouts supplied by Jack Kirby. Some stories were inked by Chic Stone and some by Dick Ayers, while one each was embellished by Wally Wood and Mike Esposito. They're all suitably credited on the title pages, so you won't be confused! Except for one instance (the story "Even Avengers Can Die"), all were scripted by yours truly. (I suppose I just couldn't bring myself to write about an Avenger dying. I mean, hey, these cats are like family to me!)

Well, I've rattled on long enough. There's a world of adventure waiting on the pages ahead, so let's get to it. I can't bear the thought of hearing the ringing summons, "Avengers Assemble!" and finding that we haven't shown up!

EXCELSIOR!

Stan

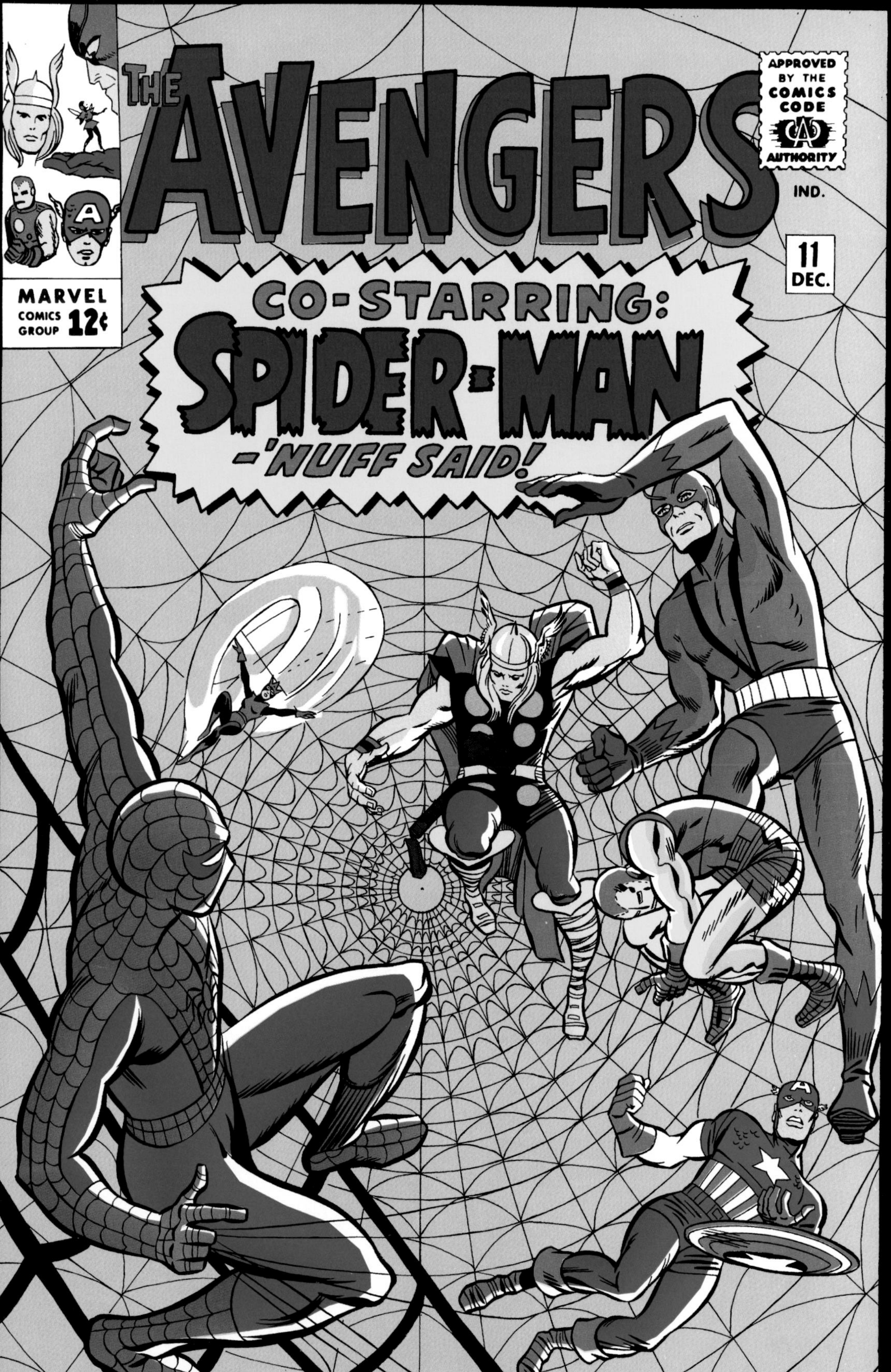

THE AVENGERS
APPROVED BY THE COMICS CODE AUTHORITY
IND.
11 DEC.
MARVEL COMICS GROUP 12¢
CO-STARRING: SPIDER-MAN -'NUFF SAID!

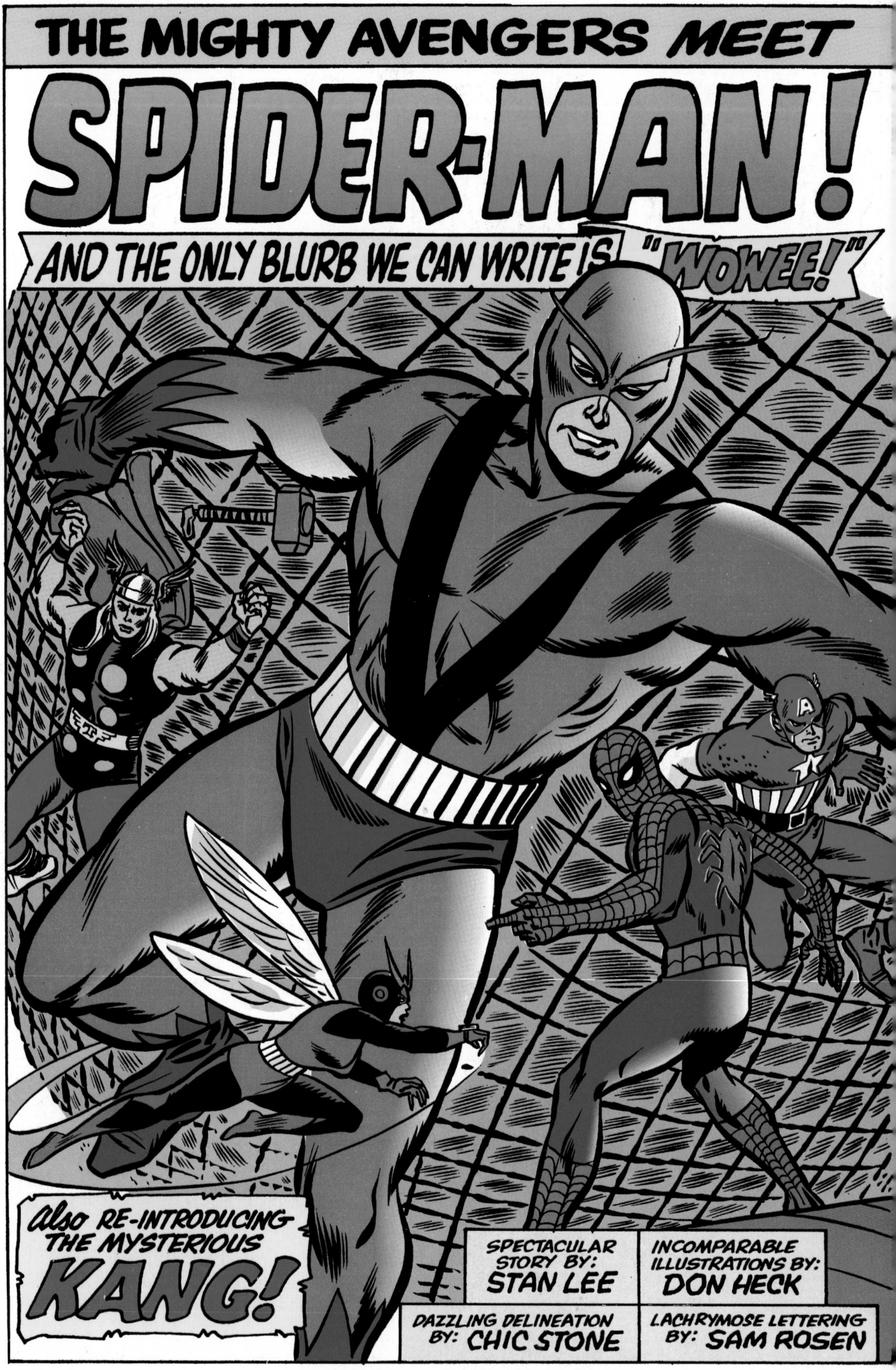
THE MIGHTY AVENGERS MEET
SPIDER-MAN!
AND THE ONLY BLURB WE CAN WRITE IS "WOWEE!"
also RE-INTRODUCING THE MYSTERIOUS KANG!
SPECTACULAR STORY BY: STAN LEE
INCOMPARABLE ILLUSTRATIONS BY: DON HECK
DAZZLING DELINEATION BY: CHIC STONE
LACHRYMOSE LETTERING BY: SAM ROSEN

THE BIGGEST PROBLEM IN TELLING ANY TALE IS... WHERE TO BEGIN? *THIS* TIME WE START WITH THE FLASHING OF A SIGNAL LIGHT IN *GIANT-MAN'S* LAB...

OH, *NO!* NOT *NOW!*

THOR SPEAKING! AS CHAIRMAN OF THE *AVENGERS* FOR THIS WEEK, I SUMMON YOU TO A SPECIAL MEETING IMMEDIATELY! THAT IS *ALL!*

HEY... *WAIT!* HOLD ON, *CURLY!* I'M RIGHT IN THE MIDDLE OF A DELICATE EXPERIMENT! HOW ABOUT...?

REQUEST DENIED! THERE CAN BE NO EXCEPTION! *AVENGERS* BUSINESS ALWAYS TAKES PRIORITY! OVER AND OUT!

I SHOULD HAVE HAD MY *HEAD* EXAMINED WHEN I LET THEM TALK ME INTO JOINING THEIR LITTLE SEWING CIRCLE! THAT LONG-HAIRED SQUARE HAS ALL THE CHARM OF A RUSTY DOORKNOB!

NOW THAT YOU GOT *THAT* OFF YOUR CHEST, LET'S GO! YOU KNOW YOU WOULDN'T MISS A MEETING FOR *ANYTHING!*

AND SO, WITHIN MINUTES...

I HAVE A DISTRESSING ANNOUNCEMENT TO MAKE! YOU'VE ALL HEARD OF THE ALLEGED DEATH OF OUR GOOD FRIEND, TONY STARK*, WHOSE HOME WE USE FOR OUR HEAD-QUARTERS!

WELL, SINCE STARK'S DEATH, OUR FELLOW AVENGER, IRON MAN, HAS BEEN *MISSING!*

IT'S PRETTY EASY TO FIGURE OUT, MR. CHAIRMAN! IRON MAN WAS STARK'S FRIEND AND BODY-GUARD! THERE'S NO DOUBT IN MY MIND THAT HE'S TRACKING DOWN CLUES TO THE *MURDERER* OF STARK... IF IT *WAS* MURDER!

PERHAPS! BUT WHY HAS HE NOT SUMMONED *US* TO ASSIST HIM!?

WE "MERE MORTALS" HAVE A CODE OF HONOR AND DUTY WHICH YOU MAY FIND HARD TO UNDERSTAND, THOR!

I'LL GO ALONG WITH GIANT-MAN! I'M SURE THAT THE GOLDEN AVENGER WANTS TO DO THIS JOB *ALONE*... AS A MATTER OF PRIDE!

HENCE, I MOVE THAT WE SUSPEND ALL OPERATIONS FOR TWENTY-FOUR HOURS AS A MARK OF RESPECT TO THE LATE TONY STARK, WHOSE HOME WE NOW OCCUPY!

I *SECOND* THE MOTION!

* SEE TALES OF SUSPENSE #61... STAN.

IRON MAN

THANKS FOR YOUR SUPPORT, CAP... BUT I'D LIKE TO *AMEND* YOUR MOTION...

I FEEL THAT STARK HIMSELF WOULD WANT US TO CONTINUE ...TO STAY ON DUTY IN CASE WE'RE NEEDED!

SO I MOVE INSTEAD THAT WE VOTE *IRON MAN* A TEMPORARY LEAVE OF ABSENCE... UNTIL HIS MISSION IS DONE!

I *SECOND* GIANT-MAN'S MOTION!

YOU'RE OUT OF ORDER, RICK! YOU HAVE NO VOTING PRIVILEGE WITH THE *AVENGERS* AS YET!

HOWEVER, ONCE AGAIN I AGREE WITH THE MASTER OF MANY SIZES! IF THE CHAIR WILL PERMIT, I WITHDRAW MY MOTION AND SECOND GIANT-MAN'S!

2.

IT IS SO MOVED AND SO CARRIED! IRON MAN IS GRANTED A TEMPORARY LEAVE OF ABSENCE AND THE AVENGERS REMAIN ON ACTIVE DUTY! I HEREBY DECLARE THIS MEETING ADJOURNED!

WHY DOES THAT REMARK ALWAYS SEEM TO BE A SIGNAL FOR YOU TO PUT ON FRESH LIPSTICK, LITTLE LADY?

EVERY REMARK IS A SIGNAL FOR A GIRL TO FRESHEN HER LIPSTICK, BIG BOY!

AND PLEASE DON'T SPEAK TO ME RIGHT NOW, OR I MIGHT SMUDGE IT!!

THE CHAIRMAN OF OUR NEXT REGULARLY SCHEDULED MEETING WILL BE CAPTAIN AMERICA, ACCORDING TO OUR PLAN OF ROTATION! AND SO, I NOW YIELD THE GAVEL!

BUT, LITTLE DOES MIGHTY THOR SUSPECT THAT THE ENTIRE MEETING HAS BEEN MONITORED... BY A FANTASTIC ELECTRONIC DEVICE FROM THE FAR FUTURE!

AND NOW WE TURN OUR ATTENTION TO THE ONE KNOWN AS KANG... AS HE STANDS BEFORE A VIEW-SCREEN IN THE YEAR 3,000... HIS HEART FILLED WITH STARK HATRED!

I'VE WAITED PATIENTLY FOR MY CHANCE TO STRIKE BACK AT THE ACCURSED AVENGERS... AND AT LAST IT HAS COME!*

FOR, WITHOUT THE POWER OF IRON MAN, THEY ARE NOW AT THEIR WEAKEST FIGHTING STRENGTH!

* SEE AVENGERS #8...STAN.

BUT, I SHALL NOT BATTLE THEM IN PERSON! I AM TOO WISE... TOO CAUTIOUS FOR THAT! WITH ALL THE KNOWLEDGE OF THE FAR FUTURE AT MY DISPOSAL, IT WILL BE A SIMPLE MATTER FOR ME TO FIND ANOTHER TO WAGE MY BATTLE!

BUT I MUST TAKE CARE TO AVOID THE MISTAKES OF THOSE WHO TRIED BEFORE ME! FOR I HAVE WITNESSED SOME OF THOSE BATTLES FROM HERE IN THE FUTURE!

"ZEMO, AND HIS MASTERS OF EVIL CAME CLOSEST TO DESTROYING THE AVENGERS BY USING WONDER-MAN!* BUT THEY MADE ONE FATAL MISTAKE..."

"THEY FAILED TO REASON THAT WONDER-MAN HIMSELF MIGHT TURN AGAINST THEM!"

*SEE AVENGERS #9...STAN.

I MUST BE FAR MORE CLEVER! THE ONE I USE MUST BE TOTALLY INCAPABLE OF EVER BETRAYING ME! HE MUST BE COMPLETELY LOYAL TO KANG!

AND THERE IS ONLY ONE SUCH CREATURE WHO FULFILLS THAT REQUIREMENT... AND THAT IS... A ROBOT!

3.

JUST AS MY ANCESTOR, *DR. DOOM*, IS THE GREATEST ROBOTIC CREATOR OF THE 20TH CENTURY, SO AM *I* THE GREATEST OF *MY* CENTURY! BUT, BEING OF THE *FUTURE*, MY TALENTS ARE EVEN FAR GREATER THAN *HIS*!

IT WOULD BE A SIMPLE MATTER FOR ME TO MAKE EXACT REPLICAS OF THE MOST POWERFUL VILLAINS OF ALL TIME, AND LET THEM ATTACK THE AVENGERS *TOGETHER*!

BUT, THERE IS THE EVER-PRESENT DANGER THAT THEY MIGHT END UP FIGHTING AMONG *THEM-SELVES*, OR GETTING IN EACH OTHER'S WAY!

NO! I SHALL USE BUT *ONE* ROBOT TO DEFEAT THE AVENGERS! ONE WHOM THEY WILL *HAVE* TO TRUST! YET... ONE WITH ENOUGH POWER AND CUNNING TO BE ASSURED OF *SUCCESS!* AND I *KNOW* THE ONE!

I HAVE KEPT A VIDEO-TAPE FILE ON HIM FOR MONTHS... BECAUSE HIS UNIQUE POWER *INTERESTS* ME! I'LL PLAY THE TAPE BACK NOW! *AHHH...* THERE HE IS!

SO FAR AS I HAVE BEEN ABLE TO TELL, *SPIDER-MAN* HAS EVER BEEN A *LONER!* AND, THERE IS LESS REALLY *KNOWN* ABOUT HIM THAN ALMOST ANY OTHER COSTUMED ADVENTURER!

HE SHALL BE THE *PERFECT* CHOICE!

I MUST NOW LIST ALL OF HIS AMAZING POWERS...

...AS WELL AS STUDY AVAILABLE RECORDS OF HIS PREVIOUS BATTLES, TO LEARN TO DUPLICATE HIS FIGHTING STYLE...

...AND HIS STRONGEST WEAPON... HIS POWERFUL, EVER-CHANGING *WEB*— *THAT* I MUST BECOME THOROUGHLY FAMILIAR WITH!

4.

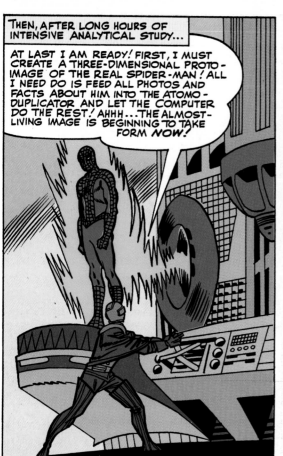

THEN, AFTER LONG HOURS OF INTENSIVE ANALYTICAL STUDY...

AT LAST I AM READY! FIRST, I MUST CREATE A THREE-DIMENSIONAL PROTO-IMAGE OF THE REAL SPIDER-MAN! ALL I NEED DO IS FEED ALL PHOTOS AND FACTS ABOUT HIM INTO THE ATOMO-DUPLICATOR AND LET THE COMPUTER DO THE REST! AHHH...THE ALMOST-LIVING IMAGE IS BEGINNING TO TAKE FORM NOW!

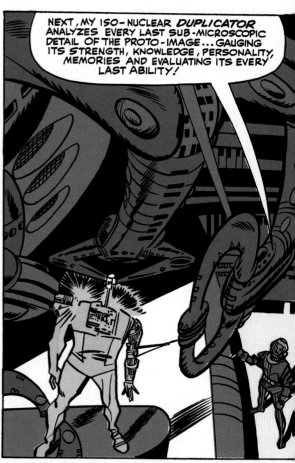

NEXT, MY ISO-NUCLEAR DUPLICATOR ANALYZES EVERY LAST SUB-MICROSCOPIC DETAIL OF THE PROTO-IMAGE...GAUGING ITS STRENGTH, KNOWLEDGE, PERSONALITY, MEMORIES AND EVALUATING ITS EVERY LAST ABILITY!

THEN, THE FINAL PHASE BEGINS! USING AUTOMATED DEVICES WHICH NEED NO HUMAN CONTROL, THE DUPLICATOR SOON CREATES AN EXACT DUPLICATE OF THE INTENDED SUBJECT...POSSESSING EVERY ABILITY OF THE ORIGINAL...BUT ANSWERABLE ONLY TO ME!

TO ONE FROM THE 20TH CENTURY, THIS MIGHT SEEM INCOMPREHENSIBLE! BUT, TO A MASTER OF SCIENCE HERE IN THE YEAR 3,000, IT IS MERELY CHILD'S PLAY!

WHAT IS YOUR NAME?

I..AM.. SPIDER-MAN!

GOOD! NOW, THE PROTO-IMAGE SHALL VANISH AND ONLY YOU SHALL REMAIN!

THEN, AFTER CAREFULLY GIVING THE LIFELIKE-LOOKING ROBOT THE MOST MINUTE INSTRUCTIONS, KANG SENDS HIM TO THE 20TH CENTURY BY THE MERE FLICK OF AN ELECTRONIC SWITCH...

AND, SO BEGINS ANOTHER IN THE UNIVERSALLY ACCLAIMED SERIES OF MIGHTY MARVEL MASTERWORK BATTLES!

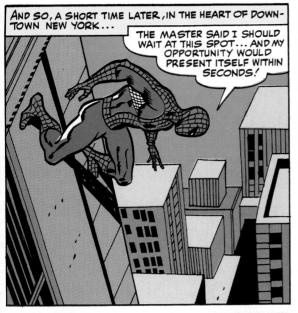

AND SO, A SHORT TIME LATER, IN THE HEART OF DOWN-TOWN NEW YORK...

THE MASTER SAID I SHOULD WAIT AT THIS SPOT... AND MY OPPORTUNITY WOULD PRESENT ITSELF WITHIN SECONDS!

THEN, IT *HAPPENS!* AS CAPTAIN AMERICA LEAVES ONE OF HIS REGULARLY-SCHEDULED VISITS TO RICK JONES' *TEEN BRIGADE* HEADQUARTERS, A BAND OF HOODLUMS ATTACKS HIM!

HEADS UP, MEN! *THIS* TIME YOU PICKED THE WRONG PIGEON!

FIGHTING WITH HIS CUSTOMARY SKILL AND VIGOR, CAP HAS NO WAY OF KNOWING THAT HE IS BATTLING CLEVER *ROBOTS*, SENT INTO THE PAST, AS THE ROBOT SPIDER-MAN WAS, BY *KANG* HIMSELF!

AH! *THIS* IS WHAT THE MASTER ARRANGED! NOW TO CARRY OUT THE CLEAR-CUT INSTRUCTIONS GIVEN TO ME BY *KANG!* FIRST, I CREATE A TYPICAL SPIDER'S WEB...

AND THEN, I DROP IT CAREFULLY OVER THE OTHER LIFELIKE ROBOTS...

WHAT'S *THAT??*

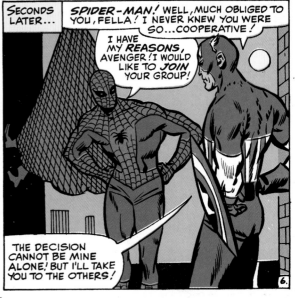

SECONDS LATER...

SPIDER-MAN! WELL, MUCH OBLIGED TO YOU, FELLA! I NEVER KNEW YOU WERE SO...COOPERATIVE!

I HAVE MY *REASONS*, AVENGER! I WOULD LIKE TO *JOIN* YOUR GROUP!

THE DECISION CANNOT BE MINE ALONE! BUT I'LL TAKE YOU TO THE OTHERS!

6.

SHORTLY THEREAFTER, AT *AVENGERS H.Q.*....

SPIDER-MAN!

IS *THIS* WHY YOU SUMMONED US, CAP?? WHAT'S *HE* DOING HERE?

I'D BETTER ZIP UP TO FIGHTING SIZE... JUST IN CASE!

YOU JUST WANT TO SHOW OFF THOSE DREAMY BICEPS, BLUE-EYES!

THERE'S NO NEED FOR ALARM! SPIDER-MAN WANTS TO *JOIN US!*

A MOST LAUDABLE AMBITION! BUT WE DO NOT ACCEPT ANY STRANGER MERELY BECAUSE HE POSSESSES SOME POWER OR OTHER! THERE ARE CERTAIN TESTS... AND A PERIOD OF TRIAL!

I DON'T *TRUST* HIM! EVERYTHING *ABOUT* SPIDERS MAKES MY WASP-INSTINCT TINGLE WITH HATE AND LOATHING!

I WAS WARNED TO EXPECT SUCH A RECEPTION! NOW TO RESORT TO PHASE TWO OF THE MASTER'S PLAN!

VERY WELL! I CAME TO TELL YOU WHERE TO FIND *IRON MAN*... FOR HE NEEDS YOUR HELP! BUT, IF YOU AREN'T INTERESTED...!

WHAT??!

YOU KNOW WHERE IRON MAN IS... AND HE *NEEDS* US!??

HALT! WE WISH TO DISCUSS THIS MATTER FURTHER!

FORGET IT, PAL! I KNOW WHEN I'M NOT WANTED!

THE THUNDER GOD SAID... *HALT!*

WHOOM!

7.

LOOK, LONG HAIR... I DON'T *LIKE* HAVIN' HAMMERS TOSSED AT ME!

YOU MAY BE A REAL WING-DOOZY WITH YOUR OWN TEAM, BUT UNTIL I'M ONE OF YOU, YOU'RE JUST ANOTHER GUY NAMED JOE TO ME... SAVVY?

A NOBLE OF ASGARD FINDS NO HUMOR IN SUCH REMARKS, INSOLENT ONE! PERHAPS A LESSON IN MANNERS MIGHT NOT BE AMISS!

SIMMER DOWN, AVENGER! WE HAVE *IRON MAN* TO THINK OF!

VERY WELL! FOR THE SAKE OF THE MISSING ONE, I SHALL STAY MY WRATH!

WELL, GOODY GUM-DROPS!

OKAY, NOW I'LL TELL YOU WHERE IRON MAN IS... BUT *NOT* 'CAUSE YOU SCARED ME INTO IT! ONLY TO PROVE I KNOW WHAT I'M TALKING ABOUT!

I WAS SWINGIN' AROUND THE ROOFTOPS THE OTHER NIGHT, LIKE A GOOD LITTLE SPIDER-MAN SHOULD, WHEN I SAW A GUY WITH A NUTTY-LOOKING MASK, ACCOMPANIED BY A 6½ FOOT TALL CREEP AND A GORGEOUS BLONDE DOLL HUSTLE HIM INTO A HELICOPTER!

ZEMO! WITH THE EXECUTIONER... AND THE EN-CHANTRESS! WE SHOULD HAVE *GUESSED!*

HOW *EASY* THIS IS! ONLY THE BRILLIANT *KANG* WOULD HAVE THOUGHT TO GIVE ME THE ABILITY TO SPEAK IN THE SAME VERNACULAR AS THE *REAL* SPIDER-MAN!

AS THEY PREPARED TO FLY OFF, I HEARD THE MASKED ONE GIVE THEIR DESTINA-TION! IT WAS THE *TEMPLE OF TIROD*, IN MEXICO!

AND, YOU DID NOT COME TO US *IMMEDIATELY*?!! WHAT MANNER OF MAN *ARE* YOU??

EASY, THOR! HE WAS UNDER NO OBLIGATION!

VERY WELL! OUR FIRST CONCERN IS TO OUR MISS-ING AVENGER! BUT, WHEN WE RETURN, I SHALL HAVE MORE TO SAY TO SPIDER-MAN!

OH, HAPPY DAY! I'LL COUNT THE SECONDS TILL WE MEET AGAIN, BIG MOUTH!

NO *WONDER* THEY ARE SO UNIVERSALLY RENOWNED! LOOK AT THE *SPEED* WITH WHICH THEY BLAZE INTO ACTION!

TOO BAD THEY DO NOT SUSPECT THEY ARE MERELY RACING TO... THEIR *DOOM!*

AVENGERS ---AWAAAY!

8

9

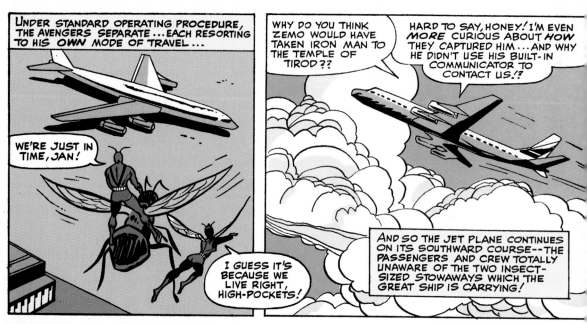

UNDER STANDARD OPERATING PROCEDURE, THE AVENGERS SEPARATE...EACH RESORTING TO HIS *OWN* MODE OF TRAVEL...

WE'RE JUST IN TIME, JAN!

I GUESS IT'S BECAUSE WE LIVE RIGHT, HIGH-POCKETS!

WHY DO YOU THINK ZEMO WOULD HAVE TAKEN IRON MAN TO THE TEMPLE OF TIROD??

HARD TO SAY, HONEY! I'M EVEN *MORE* CURIOUS ABOUT *HOW* THEY CAPTURED HIM...AND WHY HE DIDN'T USE HIS BUILT-IN COMMUNICATOR TO CONTACT US!?

AND SO THE JET PLANE CONTINUES ON ITS SOUTHWARD COURSE--THE PASSENGERS AND CREW TOTALLY UNAWARE OF THE TWO INSECT-SIZED STOWAWAYS WHICH THE GREAT SHIP IS CARRYING!

FINALLY...

THIS IS THE PLACE, JAN... LET'S GO!

HANK! WAIT! FOR HEAVEN'S SAKE, YOU BIG GOOP! *YOU CAN'T FLY!*

YOU DIDN'T THINK I'D FORGET A THING LIKE *THAT*, DID YOU, HON?

I'M IN CYBERNETIC CONTACT WITH A NEARBY FLYING ANT RIGHT *NOW!*

NEXT TIME *WARN ME*, HANDSOME.! AFTER ALL... YOU'RE THE ONLY LITTLE *ANT-MAN* I'VE GOT!

I'D *BETTER* BE, HONEY! LOOK... THERE'S THE TEMPLE OF TIROD *NOW!*

NO SOONER DO THEY LAND THAN HANDSOME HANK ONCE AGAIN ZIPS UP TO HIS POWERFUL 12-FOOT SIZE, WHILE THE LOVELY JAN CHANGES TO HER NORMAL FIVE FEET PLUS OF BREATH-TAKING BEAUTY...AND THEN...

GO SLOWLY, SWEETIE! THERE'S NO TELLING WHAT WE'LL FIND IN HERE....!

THERE'S NO SIGN OF OL' SHELL-HEAD, SO FAR!

THAT'S IT, UNSUSPECTING FOOLS! LITTLE DO YOU DREAM THIS ENTIRE TEMPLE HAS BEEN CONVERTED INTO A GIGANTIC *TRAP*...FOR THE *AVENGERS!*

9.

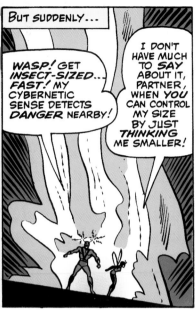

BUT SUDDENLY...

WASP! GET INSECT-SIZED... FAST! MY CYBERNETIC SENSE DETECTS DANGER NEARBY!

I DON'T HAVE MUCH TO SAY ABOUT IT, PARTNER, WHEN YOU CAN CONTROL MY SIZE BY JUST THINKING ME SMALLER!

I WAS RIGHT! LOOK... A LIGHT BEAM!

WHERE IS IT COMING FROM ??

FROM ME, YOU TWO DOOMED FOOLS!...FROM YOUR FRIENDLY NEIGHBORHOOD SPIDER-MAN!

HOW DID YOU GET HERE SO QUICKLY?

I HAVE SECRET METHODS YOU CAN'T EVEN BEGIN TO SUSPECT!

KANG CAN MOVE ME ANYWHERE BY MANIPULATING HIS MASTER CONTROL PANEL BACK IN THE 30TH CENTURY!

I KNEW WE SHOULDN'T HAVE TRUSTED HIM! NOW HE'S TRYING TO TRAP US... WITH THAT GRANITE BLOCK!

WASP!! EXECUTE MANEUVER 4-A! ON THE DOUBLE... BUT CAREFUL!

THEN, COMBINING HER WASPISH FLYING SPEED WITH HER POWERFUL MINIATURIZED "WASP'S STING", THE FABULOUS FEMALE LAUNCHES A SURPRISE ATTACK WHICH TEMPORARILY KNOCKS HER SEEMINGLY-GIGANTIC FOE COMPLETELY OFF BALANCE!

MMM...THIS HURTS YOU A LOT MORE THAN ME, YOU DOUBLE-DEALING DECEIVER!

GOOD WORK, JAN! IT LOOKS AS THOUGH YOUR FIRST IMPRESSION OF SPIDER-MAN WAS THE CORRECT ONE!

LOOK OUT! BEHIND YOU... HE RECOVERED FASTER THAN WE EXPECTED!

10.

11

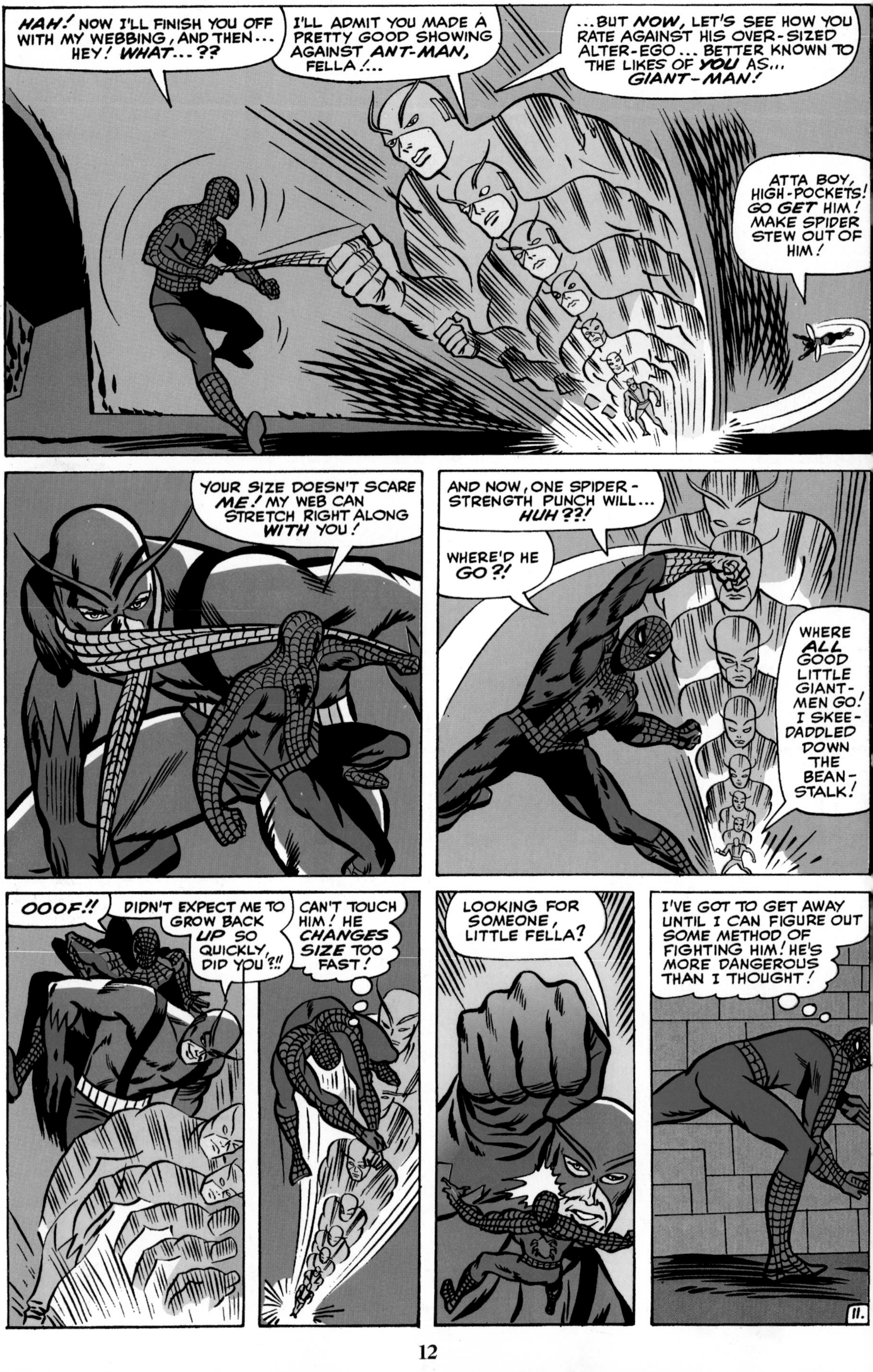
HAH! NOW I'LL FINISH YOU OFF WITH MY WEBBING, AND THEN... HEY! WHAT...??
I'LL ADMIT YOU MADE A PRETTY GOOD SHOWING AGAINST ANT-MAN, FELLA!...
...BUT NOW, LET'S SEE HOW YOU RATE AGAINST HIS OVER-SIZED ALTER-EGO... BETTER KNOWN TO THE LIKES OF YOU AS... GIANT-MAN!
ATTA BOY, HIGH-POCKETS! GO GET HIM! MAKE SPIDER STEW OUT OF HIM!
YOUR SIZE DOESN'T SCARE ME! MY WEB CAN STRETCH RIGHT ALONG WITH YOU!
AND NOW, ONE SPIDER-STRENGTH PUNCH WILL... HUH??!
WHERE'D HE GO?!
WHERE ALL GOOD LITTLE GIANT-MEN GO! I SKEE-DADDLED DOWN THE BEAN-STALK!
OOOF!!
DIDN'T EXPECT ME TO GROW BACK UP SO QUICKLY, DID YOU?!!
CAN'T TOUCH HIM! HE CHANGES SIZE TOO FAST!
LOOKING FOR SOMEONE, LITTLE FELLA?
I'VE GOT TO GET AWAY UNTIL I CAN FIGURE OUT SOME METHOD OF FIGHTING HIM! HE'S MORE DANGEROUS THAN I THOUGHT!
11.

YOU WON'T ESCAPE THAT EASILY, MISTER!

I'VE READ A LOT ABOUT SPIDER-MAN'S EXPLOITS...BUT SOMEHOW HE DOESN'T FIGHT WITH THE VERVE AND DARING I'D HAVE EXPECTED OF HIM! HE SEEMS DIFFERENT... IN SOME STRANGE WAY!

BUT, WHILE GIANT-MAN IS PHILOSOPHIZING...PERHAPS ON THE VERGE OF GUESSING THE ROBOT'S SECRET...HIS ADVERSARY STRIKES!

HAH! I OUTSMARTED YOU THIS TIME, BIG BOY! YOU'RE CAUGHT!

AND THIS WEBBING IS ELASTICIZED!! IT WILL SHRINK RIGHT DOWN WITH YOU IF YOU TRY TO ESCAPE THAT WAY!

SO! THE WASP IS TRYING TO HELP HER TRAPPED PARTNER, EH?

WELL, A FLY SWATTER MADE OF FINE WEBBING WILL PUT YOU OUT OF ACTION FAST ENOUGH!

OHHH!

BUT, BEFORE THE BOGUS SPIDER-MAN CAN DO MORE THAN TEMPORARILY STUN THE VALIANT FEMALE AVENGER, THE MIGHTY THOR HURLS HIMSELF INTO THE FRAY...!

NO NEED TO BATTLE A GIRL, TREACHEROUS ONE! I WILL GIVE YOU CONTEST ENOUGH!

THE THUNDER GOD!!

IN HIS HASTE HE MISSED ME! IF I'M LUCKY, I CAN PUT HIM OUT OF ACTION BEFORE HE REGAINS HIS BALANCE!

THWOP!!

12.

I WAS A *FOOL!* HE RECOVERED AS QUICKLY AS IF A *GNAT* HAD STUNG HIM! HE'S TOO *STRONG* FOR ME... BUT PERHAPS I CAN *TAUNT* HIM INTO DEFEAT!

HOW COME YOU DON'T GET A *HAIRCUT,* CHUM? TELL ME...DO YOU PREFER BOBBY PINS, OR ORDINARY CURLERS?

DEFEND YOURSELF, VILLAIN!!

IT *WORKED!* YOU'RE MADDER THAN A HORDE OF HUNGRY HORNETS!

HAH! I WAS *HOPING* YOU'D THROW THAT THING!!

YOU FORGOT TO RECKON WITH MY *SPIDER SPEED*... AND THE FACT THAT I MIGHT *DODGE* YOUR HAMMER AND THEN *CATCH* IT WITH A DOUBLE-THICK *WEB NET!*

WHIPP!

I'VE *GOT* TO GET MY HAMMER BACK, BEFORE SIXTY SECONDS ELAPSE!!

HERE! THIS GRANITE BLOCK IS SOMETHING FOR YOU TO WRESTLE WITH!!

HAH! AGAIN YOU DIDN'T EXPECT ME TO MOVE SO FAST!! MY *WEBBING* CAUGHT THE BLOCK... AND IT'LL HURL IT RIGHT *BACK* AT YOU!!

TWANNNG!

13.

BUT, FIGHTING MAD, AND WITH ONLY A FEW SECONDS REMAINING BEFORE HE'LL TURN BACK TO HIS MORTAL IDENTITY OF DR. DON BLAKE, THE AVENGER FROM ASGARD CRASHES THROUGH THE MASSIVE GRANITE BLOCK AS THOUGH IT'S MADE OF PAPER...!

THOUGH I AM PLEDGED TO HARM NO MORTAL BEINGS... NEVER HAVE I BEEN SO SORELY TEMPTED TO *BREAK* THAT PLEDGE AS *NOW*!!

IT'S NOT THAT EASY, GOLDILOCKS! IN ORDER TO *HARM* ME YOU HAVE TO *CATCH* ME FIRST! AND MY HANDY LITTLE SPIDER WEBBING IS GONNA MAKE THAT MIGHTY TOUGH FOR YOU!

SEE WHAT I MEAN, LOUDMOUTH?

BAH!! NO MATTER *HOW* STRONG YOUR PUNY THREADS ARE, *THOR* CAN RIP THROUGH THEM AS IF THEY DO NOT EVEN *EXIST*!

RRRIP!

SKRAKKKK!

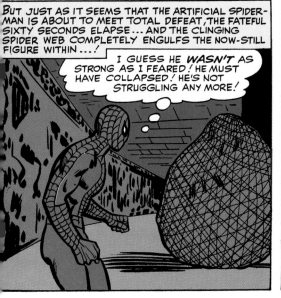

BUT JUST AS IT SEEMS THAT THE ARTIFICIAL SPIDER-MAN IS ABOUT TO MEET TOTAL DEFEAT, THE FATEFUL SIXTY SECONDS ELAPSE... AND THE CLINGING SPIDER WEB COMPLETELY ENGULFS THE NOW-STILL FIGURE WITHIN...!

I GUESS HE *WASN'T* AS STRONG AS I FEARED! HE MUST HAVE COLLAPSED! HE'S NOT STRUGGLING ANY MORE!

SO FAR KANG'S PLAN IS WORKING LIKE A *CHARM*! ONLY *CAPTAIN AMERICA* IS LEFT!

AND *HE'LL* BE EASY TO FINISH OFF! HE HAS NO SUPER POWERS AT ALL!

14.

BUT, THE SEEMINGLY VICTORIOUS "SPIDER-MAN" MIGHT NOT FEEL SO CONFIDENT IF HE KNEW THAT HE WAS BEING WATCHED BY *ANOTHER* PAIR OF COLD, ANGRY EYES... THE EYES OF THE LAST ONE HE WOULD EVER EXPECT TO MEET...!

AHH...PERFECT TIMING! HERE HE COMES *NOW!*

I GUESS I'M THE LAST TO ARRIVE! WONDER IF THEY'VE FOUND IRON MAN YET?

SAY! THAT LOOKS LIKE...IT *IS!* IT'S *SPIDER-MAN!*

HI, THERE!! WHAT ARE *YOU* DOING HERE? DID YOU SEE ANY OTHER AVENGERS IN THE AREA??

LOOK OUT!! WHAT ARE *YOU* DOING?? YOU'RE PUSHING THAT STONE SLAB RIGHT *DOWN* TOWARDS ME!!

ALTHOUGH TAKEN BY SURPRISE, CAP'S INSTINCTS ARE THOSE OF THE TRAINED GLADIATOR, AND HE LEAPS TO SAFETY WITH SPLIT-SECOND TIMING AND PRECISION....!

OUR FIRST SUSPICIONS WERE *RIGHT!* SPIDER-MAN IS OUR *ENEMY!*

THERE'S NO SIGN OF THE OTHERS! THAT LOOKS *BAD!!* SPIDER-MAN MUST HAVE TRAPPED *THEM,* TOO!

WELL, THE MIGHTY *AVENGERS* CAN *NEVER* BE TRAPPED!! NOT SO LONG AS *ONE* OF US REMAINS ALIVE...AND FREE!!

15.

THE FIRST THING TO DO WITH *YOU*, YOU HUMAN INSECT, IS TO GET YOU OFF YOUR PERCH!!

UHHHH!

BUT, HAVING BEEN ENDOWED WITH ALL THE AMAZING SPIDER POWERS OF THE *REAL* SPIDER-MAN, THE FANTASTIC DUPLICATE IS ABLE TO RECOVER HIS BALANCE IN MID-AIR AND LAND UPON HIS OPPONENT IN ATTACK POSITION!!

YOU WILL BE MY *EASIEST* VICTIM!!

JUST YOU *BELIEVE* IT, FELLA!

I'VE BEEN *WAITING* FOR A CHANCE TO DO THIS!!

WOC!

HE'S TOO BATTLE-WISE... TOO COURAGEOUS... TOO DANGEROUS! I'D BE A *FOOL* TO FIGHT HIM ON *HIS* TERMS! I'LL HAVE TO USE MY *WEBBING* AGAIN!

THWAP

AND, AS THE BLINDED AVENGER DESPERATELY TUGS AT THE STICKY WEBBING, A POWERFUL INHUMAN ARM LASHES OUT...!

FAREWELL, CAPTAIN AMERICA!

CAN'T *SEE*!! WEBBING'S COVERING MY EYES!! FALLING... FALLING...!!

EVEN THE GREAT C.A. CAN'T SURVIVE A HUNDRED-FOOT FALL! *KANG* WILL BE PLEASED!

16.

AND, STILL WATCHING FROM THE FUTURE, KANG *IS* PLEASED, UNTIL...

HAH! NONE OF THE DOOMED AVENGERS SUSPECTED I HAD PREVIOUSLY FILLED THE TOMB WITH AN ODORLESS *NERVE GAS* WHICH DULLED THE FIGHTING EFFECTIVENESS OF *ALL* OF THEM...BUT WHICH COULD NOT AFFECT A MERE *ROBOT!!*

WAIT! HAS MY ROBOT GONE *MAD?* WHY DID HE USE HIS WEB TO SAVE CAPTAIN AMERICA FROM A FATAL FALL??

PERHAPS HIS BUILT-IN INSTRUCTION CIRCUITS ARE FAULTY! I'LL HAVE HIM TURN THE DIAL WHICH WILL SEND ALL THE CAPTURED AVENGERS HERE TO THE *FUTURE* NOW...

A MENTAL COMMAND FROM MY MASTER IN THE FUTURE! I MUST TURN THE TIME-TRANSPORT DIAL, CONCLUDING MY TASK!

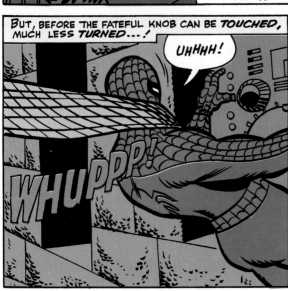

BUT, BEFORE THE FATEFUL KNOB CAN BE *TOUCHED,* MUCH LESS *TURNED...!*

UHHHH!

WHUPPP!

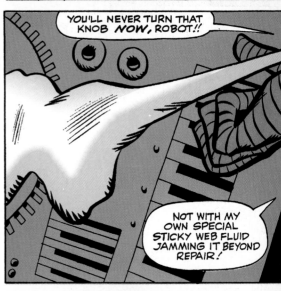

YOU'LL NEVER TURN THAT KNOB *NOW,* ROBOT!!

NOT WITH MY OWN SPECIAL STICKY WEB FLUID JAMMING IT BEYOND REPAIR!

ANOTHER ROBOT SPIDER-MAN!! BUT *WHY?* I WASN'T *TOLD* ABOUT YOU...!!

ROBOT, MY *FOOT!* YOU'RE LOOKIN' AT THE *REAL* THING, AND I'LL *PROVE* IT IN A MINUTE!

FIRST, I'LL SLAM THIS CONTROL BLOCK *SHUT* AGAIN, TO KEEP YOUR PRYING LITTLE FINGERS OUT OF TROUBLE!!

AND, A THOUSAND YEARS IN THE FUTURE, KANG GETS HIS FIRST SEVERE SETBACK...!

THE *REAL SPIDER MAN!!* HOW DID HE *LEARN* ABOUT US?? HE MUSTN'T WRECK MY BRILLIANT PLAN!! HE *MUSTN'T!!*

18

DID YOU THINK YOU COULD PROWL THE STREETS OF NEW YORK IMPERSONATING *ME* WITHOUT MY OWN SPIDER-SENSE WARNING ME OF YOUR PRESENCE ??

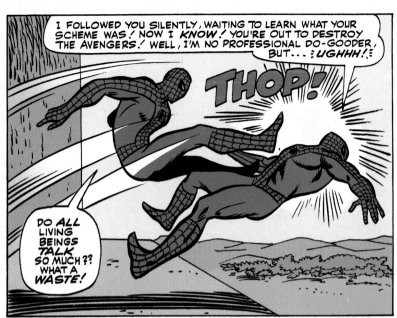

I FOLLOWED YOU SILENTLY, WAITING TO LEARN WHAT YOUR SCHEME WAS! NOW I *KNOW!* YOU'RE OUT TO DESTROY THE AVENGERS! WELL, I'M NO PROFESSIONAL DO-GOODER, BUT... UGHHH!

THOP!

DO *ALL* LIVING BEINGS *TALK* SO MUCH ?? WHAT A *WASTE!*

YOU *FORGET*, SPIDER-MAN... I WAS CREATED BY A *MASTER*.. AND GIVEN ALL THE POWERS, ALL THE STRENGTH WHICH YOU YOURSELF POSSESS!

WELL, YOU SURE HAVE A FORCE-FUL WAY OF *REMINDIN'* A FELLA!

WHUP!

JUST STAY WHERE YOU ARE, CHUM! I'M GONNA COME UP AND SEE WHAT MAKES YOU *TICK!*

WHISSSSS

BUT, THE AMAZING ROBOT, POSSESSING THE SPEED AND LIGHTNING-FAST REFLEXES OF HIS HUMAN COUNTERPART, SEIZES THE END OF SPIDEY'S WEBBING, AND...

NEVER! BEING A *ROBOT*, I AM FAR *SUPERIOR* TO ANY LIVING BEING!!

THINK SO? WELL, I'LL PROVE HOW *WRONG* YOU ARE!

REMEMBER... *I'M* THE ONE WHO *INVENTED* THESE LITTLE TRICKS!!

WHUP!

18.

WHOEVER YOUR "MASTER" *IS*, I SURE HOPE HE'S *WATCHING*!!

TRY TO LAND IN SOME OPEN AREA, ROBOT, SO I WON'T HAVE TOO MUCH TROUBLE PICKING UP THE PIECES!

BUT, AGAIN SPIDER-MAN HAS UNDER-ESTIMATED HIS MECHANICAL FOE...

I CAN SAVE MY-SELF JUST THE WAY *HE* WOULD DO IT! FIRST, I SHOOT OUT A THICK SPRAY OF WEB FLUID...

...WHICH SOLIDIFIES INTO *WINGS* IN A A MATTER OF SECONDS!

AND, ON THE TOWERING TOMB BELOW...

THIS IS GONNA BE *TOUGHER* THAN I THOUGHT!

IT'S LIKE FIGHTING *MYSELF*!!

HOW AM I GOING TO BEAT AN ENEMY WHO HAS EVERY ABILITY *I* HAVE??

HERE HE *COMES*! I'VE GOT TO THINK FAST...!!

SUDDENLY, UNEXPECT-EDLY...THE *REAL* SPIDER-MAN DROPS HIS "WINGS", MAKING A DEATH-DEFYING LUNGE IN MID-AIR..!

GOT YOU!!

TOO BAD YOU CAN'T LET GO OF *YOUR* LITTLE FLAPPERS, TOO, PAL... BUT *ONE* OF US HAS TO KEEP US IN THE AIR!!

AND, AS THE ROBOT'S ARTIFICIAL BRAIN TRIES TO FORMULATE A NEW PLAN...

I'VE GOT TO FIND HIS MAIN *CONTROL STUD* BEFORE WE LAND!! IT'S MY ONLY CHANCE!

19

AND THEN, THE AMAZING CRUSADER WHO IS ALSO A BRILLIANT TEEN-AGED SCIENCE MAJOR, *FINDS* WHAT HE'S SEEKING...

THERE! THIS WILL SHUT OFF ALL FUNCTIONING CIRCUITS, DEACTIVATING HIM!

NEXT, CREATING A 'CHUTE OF WEBBING, SPIDER-MAN WATCHES THE NOW INANIMATE MECHANICAL FIGURE PLUMMET EARTHWARD...

WHOEVER *DESIGNED* THAT THING IS A *GENIUS!* HE'D *HAVE* TO BE, TO TAKE ON THE MIGHTY *AVENGERS!*

BUT, EVEN A GENIUS CAN MAKE ONE MISTAKE!

A MECHANICAL BRAIN CAN BE FASTER, CONTAIN MORE MEMORY IMPULSES, MAKE NO MISTAKES, BUT...

...IT CAN NEVER REALLY *OUT-THINK* A HUMAN BRAIN!!

AND SO, THE TRIUMPHANT ADVENTURER SLOWLY FADES FROM SIGHT, UNAWARE THAT A PAIR OF PIERCING, THOUGHTFUL EYES HAD WITNESSED THE SWIFT, STARTLING BATTLE...

WE HAD BEEN BATTLING AN IMPOSTOR... A *ROBOT!!*

...AND THE *REAL* SPIDER-MAN SAVED US!!

MEANWHILE, INSIDE THE MYSTERIOUS TOMB, A THIN, DESPERATE HAND FINALLY REACHES ITS OBJECTIVE...

AT LAST! *AT LAST!*

AND, ONCE MORE, ONE OF THE MOST DRAMATIC CHANGES OF ALL TIME TAKES PLACE...

THOR LIVES AGAIN!

WITHIN SECONDS, THE MIGHTY THUNDER GOD GATHERS THE OTHER AVENGERS TOGETHER AS CAP DESCRIBES WHAT HE HAD SEEN...

... WE HAVE ONLY *ONE* FOE CAPABLE OF CREATING SO *PERFECT* A ROBOT..

IT CAN ONLY BE A MAN WITH ALL THE SCIENTIFIC MARVELS OF *THIRTY CENTURIES* AT HIS BECK AND CALL!

THAT MEANS...

...KANG!!

OF *COURSE!* IT CAN BE NO OTHER! EVEN *NOW* HE IS PROBABLY MONITORING THIS PLACE... SPYING ON US!

HEAR ME, MAN OF THE FUTURE! THE AVENGERS HAVE BEEN *WARNED!* NEXT TIME WE SHALL NOT BE TAKEN UNAWARE!!

AND, THOUGH SEPARATED BY A GULF OF A THOUSAND YEARS, THOR'S RINGING WORDS FALL UPON THEIR ARCH-FOE'S EARS LIKE THUNDERBOLTS!

IN VAIN!...IT WAS ALL IN VAIN! *STILL* THE AVENGERS LIVE...STILL THEY DEFY ME!

SLOWLY, THE MYSTERIOUS KANG TURNS, AND WALKS INTO THE SHADOWS, AS OUR ADVENTURE ENDS FOR NOW ...BUT...*ONLY* FOR NOW!

The End.

20.

THE AVENGERS

APPROVED BY THE COMICS CODE AUTHORITY

IND.

MARVEL COMICS GROUP 12¢

12 JAN

"THIS HOSTAGE EARTH!"

IN WHICH THE **MIGHTY AVENGERS** BATTLE TO SAVE THEIR BELOVED PLANET FROM A FATE SO DEADLY THAT NONE BUT THE MACABRE **MOLE MAN** COULD HAVE DEVISED IT!

A Marvel Tale OF MOST COMPELLING EXCELLENCE!

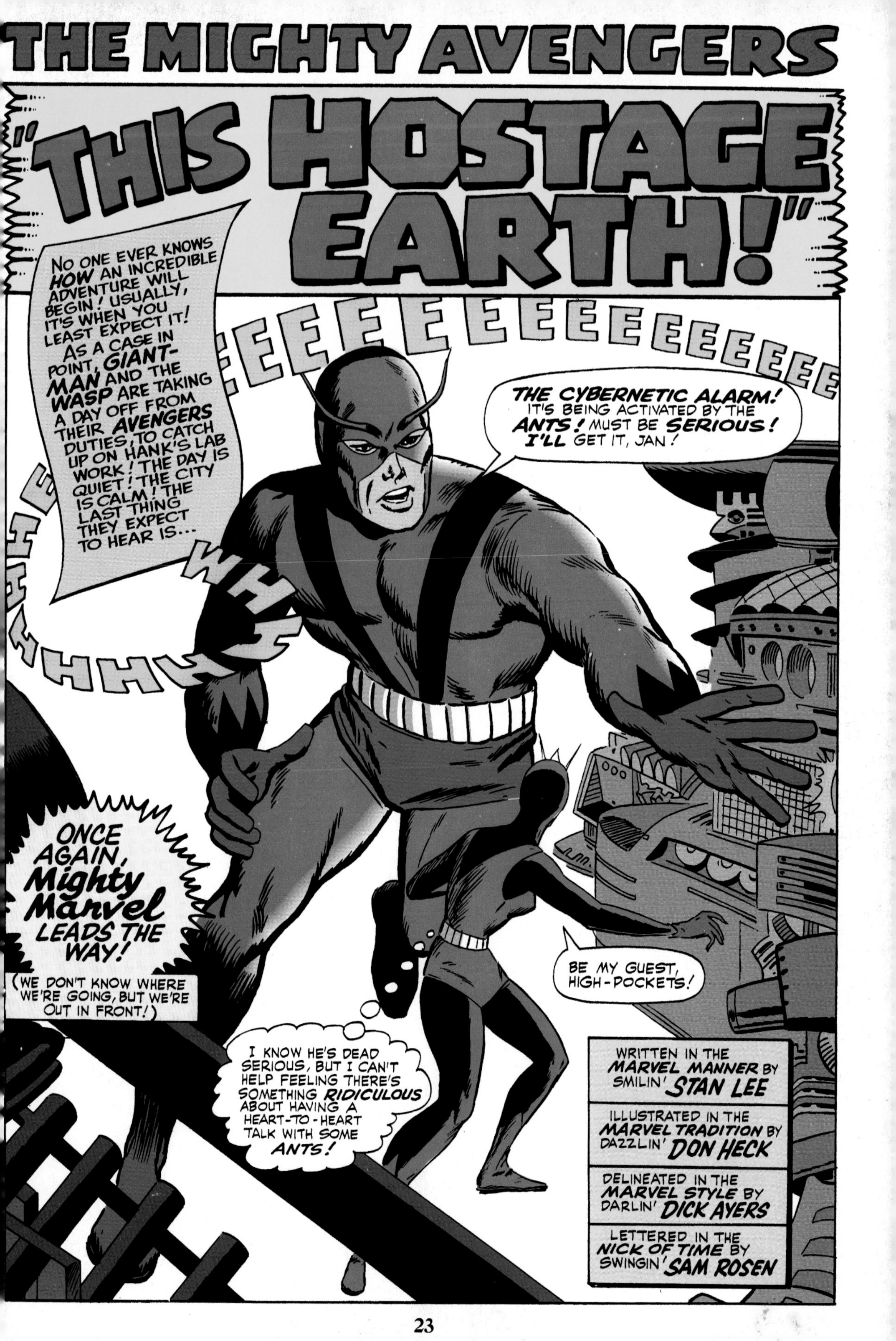
THE MIGHTY AVENGERS
"THIS HOSTAGE EARTH!"
NO ONE EVER KNOWS HOW AN INCREDIBLE ADVENTURE WILL BEGIN! USUALLY, IT'S WHEN YOU LEAST EXPECT IT! AS A CASE IN POINT, GIANT-MAN AND THE WASP ARE TAKING A DAY OFF FROM THEIR AVENGERS DUTIES, TO CATCH UP ON HANK'S LAB WORK! THE DAY IS QUIET! THE CITY IS CALM! THE LAST THING THEY EXPECT TO HEAR IS...
EEEEEEEEEEEEEEEE
WHEEEHHHHH
THE CYBERNETIC ALARM! IT'S BEING ACTIVATED BY THE ANTS! MUST BE SERIOUS! I'LL GET IT, JAN!
ONCE AGAIN, Mighty Marvel LEADS THE WAY!
(WE DON'T KNOW WHERE WE'RE GOING, BUT WE'RE OUT IN FRONT!)
BE MY GUEST, HIGH-POCKETS!
I KNOW HE'S DEAD SERIOUS, BUT I CAN'T HELP FEELING THERE'S SOMETHING RIDICULOUS ABOUT HAVING A HEART-TO-HEART TALK WITH SOME ANTS!
WRITTEN IN THE MARVEL MANNER BY SMILIN' STAN LEE
ILLUSTRATED IN THE MARVEL TRADITION BY DAZZLIN' DON HECK
DELINEATED IN THE MARVEL STYLE BY DARLIN' DICK AYERS
LETTERED IN THE NICK OF TIME BY SWINGIN' SAM ROSEN

AND, MANY LEAGUES UNDER THE SURFACE, WITHIN THE FRENZIED RECESSES OF A HIDDEN ANT HILL, THE ALARM IS REPEATED INCESSANTLY!

WHEEEE

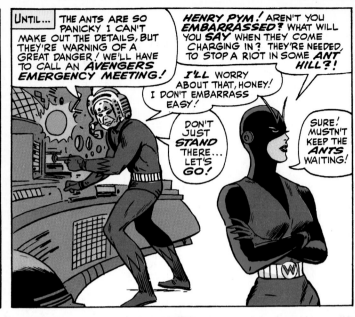

UNTIL... THE ANTS ARE SO PANICKY I CAN'T MAKE OUT THE DETAILS, BUT THEY'RE WARNING OF A GREAT DANGER! WE'LL HAVE TO CALL AN *AVENGERS* EMERGENCY MEETING!

HENRY PYM! AREN'T YOU *EMBARRASSED*? WHAT WILL YOU *SAY* WHEN THEY COME CHARGING IN? THEY'RE NEEDED, TO STOP A RIOT IN SOME *ANT HILL*?!

I'LL WORRY ABOUT THAT, HONEY! I DON'T EMBARRASS EASY!

DON'T JUST *STAND* THERE... LET'S *GO!*

SURE! MUSTN'T KEEP THE *ANTS* WAITING!

MOMENTS LATER, AFTER THE AVENGERS' *RED ALERT* HAS BEEN TRANSMITTED...

WHATEVER NEW MENACE CONFRONTS US SHALL NOT FIND *THOR* LACKING!

I FEEL LIKE AN OVERGROWN *KID*, USING THESE TRANSISTOR-POWERED ROLLER WHEELS, BUT THEY SERVE AS GENERATORS TO KEEP MY BUILT-IN BATTERIES FULLY CHARGED!

LUCKY I WAS NEARBY! JUST ANOTHER FEW ROOFTOPS TO HURDLE, AND I'LL BE THERE!

FINALLY, AT THE SUMPTUOUS TOWN HOUSE OF *TONY STARK*, WHICH SERVES AS AVENGERS H.Q...

I'LL COME RIGHT TO THE POINT! I RECEIVED A CYBERNETIC ALARM FROM A FRIGHTENED GROUP OF ANTS!

BOY, EVERYBODY'S A COMEDIAN! NOW TELL US THE *REAL* PROBLEM!

I *AM* TELLING YOU!

YOU HAVE THE *TEMERITY* TO SUMMON US BECAUSE SOME *ANTS* IN AN *ANT-HILL* ARE IN NEED OF ASSISTANCE? I KNOW NOT WHETHER TO FEEL *WRATH*... OR AMUSEMENT!

EASY, THOR! GIANT-MAN'S GOT A TEMPER, *TOO*... AND I WOULDN'T WANT TO SEE IT DIRECTED AGAINST *US!*

2.

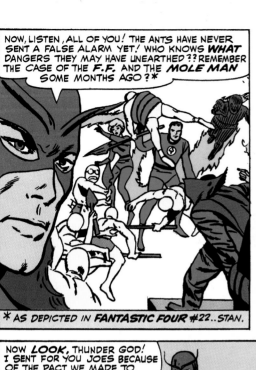

NOW, LISTEN, ALL OF YOU! THE ANTS HAVE NEVER SENT A FALSE ALARM YET! WHO KNOWS *WHAT* DANGERS THEY MAY HAVE UNEARTHED?? REMEMBER THE CASE OF THE *F.F.* AND THE *MOLE MAN* SOME MONTHS AGO?*

* AS DEPICTED IN *FANTASTIC FOUR* #22..STAN.

TO EMPLOY YOUR OWN VERNACULAR, YOU HAVE PULLED *THAT* ONE IN OUT OF LEFT FIELD!

DO YOU NOT RECALL THE RECORDS OF THE FANTASTIC FOUR'S *FINAL* BATTLE WITH THAT INSIDIOUS CREATURE? HE, AND HIS SUBTERRANEAN EMPIRE, WERE *DESTROYED* AT THAT TIME!*

*AS SHOWN IN F.F. #31...STAN.

NOW *LOOK*, THUNDER GOD! I SENT FOR YOU JOES BECAUSE OF THE PACT WE MADE TO FIGHT AS A *TEAM* WHENEVER POSSIBLE! BUT, IF YOU THINK I'M GONNA *BEG* FOR YOUR HELP, *FORGET* IT! I WAS DOING OKAY *BEFORE* I TEAMED UP WITH YOU, AND I'LL DO OKAY *WITHOUT* YOU!

DON'T BE RILED, BIG FELLA! THOR MEANT NO HARM!

NO ONE SPEAKS FOR *THOR!* I HAVE HEARD ENOUGH! THERE ARE MORE PRESSING MATTERS WHICH CONCERN ME!

AND THE *REST* OF YOU CAN *FOLLOW* HIM! I WOULDN'T TAKE ANY HELP *NOW* ON A BET! GO ON..CUT OUT!!

LET'S DO AS HE SAYS, BOYS! WE'LL COME TO *BLOWS* IF WE DON'T WATCH OUT!

BUT, THE MEETING YOU HAVE JUST WITNESSED WOULD HAVE ENDED QUITE DIFFERENTLY HAD THE MIGHTY AVENGERS KNOWN WHAT TRANSPIRED THOUSANDS OF LEAGUES BENEATH EARTH'S SURFACE SOME WEEKS AGO...

FASTER, YOU MINDLESS SUBTERRANEAN SLAVES! *FASTER!* MY MACHINE MUST BE COMPLETED *QUICKLY!!* I HUNGER FOR REVENGE!

3.

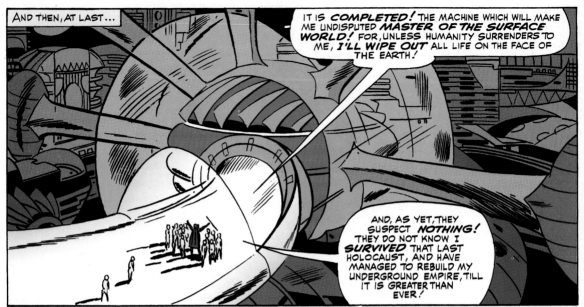

AND THEN, AT LAST...

IT IS *COMPLETED!* THE MACHINE WHICH WILL MAKE ME UNDISPUTED *MASTER OF THE SURFACE WORLD!* FOR, UNLESS HUMANITY SURRENDERS TO ME, *I'LL WIPE OUT* ALL LIFE ON THE FACE OF THE EARTH!

AND, AS YET, THEY SUSPECT *NOTHING!* THEY DO NOT KNOW I *SURVIVED* THAT LAST HOLOCAUST, AND HAVE MANAGED TO REBUILD MY UNDERGROUND EMPIRE, TILL IT IS GREATER THAN EVER!

ONCE I PULL THIS SWITCH, MY NEWLY COMPLETED *ATOMIC GYROSCOPE* WILL INCREASE THE SPEED OF THE EARTH'S ROTATION ON ITS AXIS! FASTER AND FASTER THIS PLANET WILL SPIN, UNTIL...

...UNTIL *I* STOP IT, ALL LIFE ON THE SURFACE WILL BE DESTROYED...WHILE *WE,* HERE AT EARTH'S CENTER, WILL BE SAFE, SECURE IN AN ARTIFICIALLY CREATED GRAVITY OF OUR OWN!

AT FIRST, THE MOTION WILL BE SLOW...NONE WILL NOTICE IT, EXCEPT THE SMALL LIVING CREATURES, SUCH AS *ANTS,* WHOSE ANT-HILLS WILL BE THE FIRST TO BE DESTROYED!

AND NOW THAT WE'VE CUED YOU IN, LET'S RETURN TO THE MASTER OF MANY SIZES AS HE PREPARES TO GO INTO ACTION ALONE...

BETTER PUT ON YOUR HEADGEAR, HONEY! WHAT WE HAVE TO DO NEXT CAN BE BEST ACCOMPLISHED IF WE SHRINK TO *ANT-SIZE!*

WHAT DO YOU MEAN *WE,* HANDSOME? I'VE GOT *OTHER* PLANS!

I'M DUE AT THE *HAIRDRESSER* IN FIFTEEN MINUTES!

I'M SURE A BIG STRONG AVENGER LIKE *YOU* DOESN'T NEED *HELP* TO VISIT SOME *ANTS!*

NOW JUST ONE COTTON-PICKIN' *MINUTE,* YOUNG LADY! ARE *YOU* WALKING OUT ON ME, *TOO?*

OH, STOP BEING SO *DRAMATIC,* HENRY PYM! AND FOR HEAVENS SAKE, REMAIN *ONE* SIZE, WILL YOU?

YOU *KNOW* HOW TEMPERAMENTAL *HAIR-DRESSERS* ARE!

4.

BUT, OF COURSE, IF YOU'RE GOING TO **SULK** ABOUT IT..!

FORGET IT, LADY! WE DON'T WANT TO KEEP YOUR HAIRDRESSER WAITING! I'LL SEE YOU AROUND!

HMMPH! AND THEY SAY **FEMALES** ARE HARD TO GET ALONG WITH!

A SHORT TIME LATER, A TINY FIGURE, TOO SMALL TO BE VISIBLE TO NORMAL-SIZED HUMAN BEINGS, ENTERS A HIDDEN ANT-HILL...

THIS IS WHERE THE CYBERNETIC ALARM ORIGINATED FROM!

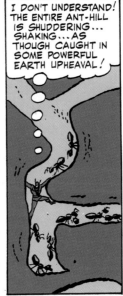

I DON'T UNDERSTAND! THE ENTIRE ANT-HILL IS SHUDDERING... SHAKING... AS THOUGH CAUGHT IN SOME POWERFUL EARTH UPHEAVAL!

AND THEN, SUDDENLY...

IT'S WORSE THAN I **THOUGHT!** THE ENTIRE STRUCTURE IS **COLLAPSING!**... I'M **FALLING!**

I'M DROPPING DOWN INTO A VAST, ALMOST BOTTOMLESS CHASM! MUST **STOP** MYSELF BEFORE IT'S TOO LATE! ONLY **ONE** WAY...!

LUCKILY, I CAN CONTROL MY SIZE **MENTALLY**... AND THIS IS THE TIME TO **DO** IT!

WHEW!... JUST **MADE** IT! QUICKLY INCREASING MY SIZE, I BROKE MY FALL BY PRESSING AGAINST THE SIDES OF THE PIT!

MINUTES LATER, BY CAUTIOUSLY LETTING HIMSELF DOWN TO THE BOTTOM WHILE GIANT-SIZED, THE GALLANT AVENGER FINDS...

THERE **IS** SOMETHING AFOOT DOWN HERE! I HEAR THE STEADY SOUND OF A GIGANTIC TURBINE... AND WHAT ARE THOSE STRANGELY COLORED LIGHT BEAMS SURROUNDING THE AREA?

I WAS **AFRAID** OF THIS! THEY'RE SOME SORT OF **DEFENSE** APPARATI! I CAN'T CRASH THROUGH!

BUT, A SHORT DISTANCE AWAY, THE COMMOTION REACHES THE EXTRA-SHARP EARS OF... THE **MOLE MAN!**

AN **INTRUDER** AT OUR GATES!

TO **ARMS**, MY SLAVISH ONES! **AFTER HIM!**

SEIZING A STRANGE, MENACING-LOOKING DEVICE, THE NEARLY BLIND ARCH-VILLAIN, EMPLOYING HIS AMAZING, RADAR-TYPE SENSE, LEADS HIS HORDE DIRECTLY TOWARDS HIS OVERSIZED INVADER!

IT MATTERS NOT THAT MY SUBTERRANEANS ARE VIRTUALLY MINDLESS... THEY FOLLOW ME TO THE DEATH!

5.

BUT POTENT AS HIS RADAR-SENSE IS, THE AWESOME SPEED AND POWER OF *GIANT-MAN* ARE A FORCE NEVER TO BE UNDER-RATED!

LOOKING FOR SOME-ONE, LITTLE FELLA??

SO! THE MOLE MAN *DOES* STILL LIVE! WAIT TILL THE *REST* OF THE AVENGERS LEARN... *OHHH!*

I *FORGOT* ABOUT THOSE BLASTED *SUBTERRANEANS* OF YOURS!!

GOOD WORK, MY DEVOTED SLAVES! KEEP ATTACKING THE ENEMY GIANT WITH YOUR PORTABLE BATTERING DEVICES!

BUT, IT'S LIKE A GROUP OF *GNATS* ATTACKING A *TIGER!* EFFORTLESSLY, THE TITANIC ADVENTURER SEIZES A HUGE STONE SLAB, WHICH HE USES AS A SHIELD....!

GO BACK TO YOUR BURROWS, BOYS! I DON'T WANT TO *HURT* ANYONE IF I CAN *HELP* IT!

HOWEVER, THE SUPPLY OF SUB-TERRANEAN WEAPONS SEEMS TO BE ALMOST *UNLIMITED!*

A *TANK!* WITH HEAVY ARTILLERY!

NOW *LOOK,* BOYS!! EVEN THOUGH I'M NOT OUT TO *HURT* ANYBODY, I DON'T INTEND TO BE USED FOR UNDERGROUND *TARGET PRACTICE,* EITHER!

WHAM!

BUT, EVEN A *GIANT'S* EYES CAN'T BE EVERYWHERE.!! SECONDS LATER, THE TWELVE-FOOT TITAN IS FELLED BY A BLAST FROM THE MOLE MAN'S STUN GUN....!

WRRUPP!

UHHH!

THERE! NOW *QUICK...* BIND HIM BEFORE HE RECOVERS!

6.

THEN, SECURELY TRUSSED WITH THIN, CONCENTRATED MULTI-STRAND CORDS, THE HELPLESS AVENGER IS BORNE INTO CAPTIVITY!

IT IS AN *OMEN!* I SHALL CONQUER ALL OF THE SURFACE WORLD JUST AS I HAVE CONQUERED *GIANT-MAN!*

NOT LONG AFTERWARDS, TELL-TALE SIGNS OF EARTH'S SPEEDED-UP ROTATION BEGIN TO BE NOTICED ON THE SURFACE..!

DO YOU FEEL THE BUILDING *SWAYING*... OR AM I *IMAGINING* THINGS?

IT'S *BUILT* TO SWAY A BIT IN HIGH WINDS... BUT I'VE NEVER NOTICED IT AS MUCH AS *THIS!*

MISS MAYHEW! WHY ARE THE PAPERS ON MY DESK TREMBLING THIS WAY??

I..I'M SURE I DON'T *KNOW,* SIR! ARE YOU...*FEEL-ING* ALL RIGHT??

WE'RE GETTING REPORTS FROM SEISMOGRAPHS ALL OVER THE WORLD, SIR! THEY SEEM TO BE GOING *MAD!*

OUR *OWN* INDI-CATORS ARE BEHAVING STRANGELY, TOO! SOME-THING *CATA-STROPHIC* IS HAPPENING FAR BENEATH THE SURFACE!

THE *LEANING TOWER OF PISA* HAS NEVER LEANED SO *FAR* BEFORE! THEY'RE TALKING OF ADD-ING *PROPS* UNDER IT!

AFTER ALL THESE YEARS! I WONDER *WHY!?*

ATTENTION! ATTENTION! POLICE EMERGENCY! CLEAR THE BRIDGE! IT IS IN DANGER OF SHAKING APART!

WHAT'S *HAPPENING* TO US?? WE'VE NEVER HAD EARTH TREMORS IN *NEW YORK* BEFORE!

AND, FINALLY... AT THE EAST SIDE MANSION OF TONY STARK ...

GIANT-MAN WAS *RIGHT!* WE SHOULD HAVE *LISTENED* TO HIM!

WE WERE SO BUSY MAKING WITH THE *WISE-CRACKS,* THAT IT NEVER OCCURRED TO US TO ASK WHAT *KIND* OF DANGER THE ANTS WERE WARNING US OF!!

MY HEART IS HEAVY WITH REMORSE! WE HAVE ACTED SHAMEFULLY TOWARDS OUR FELLOW AVENGER!

WELL, AS THIS WEEK'S ACTING CHAIRMAN, I PUT IT TO A VOTE! WHAT DO WE DO *NEXT??*

OUR *FIRST* TASK IS TO LEARN WHAT DANGER IS THREATENING US BENEATH THE SUR-FACE! PERHAPS *GIANT-MAN* HAS ALREADY SOLVED THAT RIDDLE!

I SAY WE BEGIN TO SEARCH FOR THE MASTER OF MANY SIZES AT *ONCE.!!*

7.

THERE'S NO ARGUMENT ABOUT FINDING HIGH-POCKETS! THE PROBLEM IS...*HOW*?

YOU CAN'T EXACTLY TAKE A *BUS* TO THE CENTER OF EARTH!

THERE *IS* A WAY!

REMEMBER OUR *IMAGE PROJECTOR*?

OF *COURSE*!!

IMAGE PROJECTOR?

WE USED IT IN THE PAST...IN OUR SEARCH FOR THE *HULK*!* IT WAS INVENTED BY TONY STARK! WATCH, CAP...IT WORKS LIKE *THIS*!

WASP, BE *CAREFUL*!!

DON'T WORRY.. I KNOW HOW TO USE IT!

*AS INTRODUCED IN *AVENGERS* #3..STAN.

NO NEED TO SLOW UP OUR TALE WITH LONG-WINDED EXPLANATIONS ...SUFFICE IT TO SAY THAT THE DEVICE OPERATES LIKE AN ULTRA-FREQUENCY T.V. SET, BEAMING THE SUBJECT'S IMAGE IN WHATEVER DIRECTION THE CIRCUITS ARE SET FOR.!! LIKE *THIS*...!

THOUGH MY REAL SELF REMAINS ON THE SURFACE, MY ETHEREAL *IMAGE* IS ZEROED IN TO FOLLOW THE TRAIL OF HANDSOME HENRY!

FINALLY, GUIDED AT THE SPEED OF LIGHT BY THE CYBERNETIC SIGNALS EMANATING FROM GIANT-MAN'S ANTENNAE, THE WASP REACHES...

THE MOLE MAN'S UNDERGROUND EMPIRE!! SO HE STILL *LIVES*! AND WE DARED TO LAUGH AT HANK!

ALERT THE GUARDS!! THERE IS *ANOTHER* AT THE GATES! I SENSE THAT *THIS* ONE IS A FEMALE!

DO THEY THINK A *GIRL* CAN SUCCEED WHERE *GIANT-MAN* HAS FAILED ??

BUT, BY THE TIME THE SUBTERRANEANS REACH THE SPOT, THE PROJECTO-IMAGE HAS RETURNED TO THE SURFACE...

I SHALL NOT WAIT FOR THE NEXT INTRUDER! NOW *WE* SHALL ATTACK *THEM*! YOU *HAVE* YOUR ORDERS! GO!

WITHIN SECONDS, A SKILLFUL SQUAD OF ARMED SUBTERRANEANS ENTERS A STRANGE, MOLE-LIKE MACHINE, AND BEGINS A SILENT, OMINOUS JOURNEY TO THE PLANET'S SURFACE...

SO OBEDIENT, SO LOYAL ARE THESE ALMOST MINDLESS DENIZENS OF EARTH'S CORE, THAT THEY WOULD PERISH RATHER THAN QUESTION A SINGLE COMMAND OF THEIR TYRANNICAL MASTER...THE SINISTER *MOLE MAN*!

MEANWHILE, BACK AT AVENGERS' H.Q...

NOW THAT WE *KNOW* OUR ENEMY, WHAT *GOOD* DOES IT DO? A PROJECTO-IMAGE HAS NO FIGHTING POWER! HOW DO OUR *REAL* SELVES REACH THE MOLE MAN??

IRON MAN! WHAT ABOUT THE NEW TRANSISTORIZED FOX-HOLE DIGGERS THE ARMY JUST ORDERED FROM TONY STARK??

SURE! EVEN *I* HEARD OF THEM!

I MUST BE *SLIPPING!* I INVENTED THEM *MYSELF*, AND FORGOT ALL ABOUT 'EM! THEY'RE JUST WHAT WE NEED!

YOU'RE *RIGHT*, CAP! ALL WE NEED DO IS HOOK THEM TOGETHER WITH A *BOOSTER* IN THE CENTER! I THINK *I* COULD HANDLE IT!

THEN WHAT ARE WE *WAITING* FOR? WE'VE GOT A *BUDDY* TO RESCUE!

SO *BE* IT! WE HAVE OUR BATTLE PLAN! WE STAND *UNITED!* THE *AVENGERS* WILL FIGHT AGAIN!!

BUT, AT THAT VERY SPLIT-SECOND...!

LOOK OUT! WE'RE UNDER *ATTACK!!*

CRASH!

IT'S THE MOLE MAN'S *SUBTERRANEANS!* THEY'VE REACHED THE SURFACE!!

TAKE COVER, RICK! *WE'LL* HANDLE THIS! IT'S ONLY A SMALL SQUAD OF THEM!

YOUR *TEEN BRIGADE* CAN ALERT THE ARMY IF THEIR NUMBERS INCREASE!

THEY'RE SMALL IN SIZE AND NUMBERS, BUT THEY HAVE *STRANGE, POWERFUL* WEAPONS!! TAKE NO UNNECESSARY CHANCES!

I'LL SAY THEIR WEAPONS ARE POWERFUL! THEY EFFORTLESSLY *MAGNETIZED* MY SHIELD RIGHT IN MID-AIR!

WELL, THERE'S MORE TO COMBAT THAN A SPINNING SHIELD!

THE SOONER WE *FINISH* THIS, THE SOONER WE'LL BE ABLE TO TACKLE YOUR *MASTER* DOWN BELOW!

IT'S LUCKY FOR YOU TWO THAT YOU ONLY TACKLED *ME!* I'D HATE TO THINK WHAT *THOR* OR *IRON MAN* WOULD HAVE DONE TO YOU!!

DON'T BE *GREEDY*, CAP! LEAVE SOME FOR *US!*

UH-OH! THIS CHARACTER IS TRYING TO ATTACK CAP FROM BEHIND! I'VE GOT TO *STOP* HIM!!

I'M *IN* FOR IT NOW!! HE *SEES* ME!

OHHH! YOU NEVER KNOW *WHAT* THEY'LL COME UP WITH NEXT!! HE SPRAYED SOME *GAS* AT ME!!

CAN'T *SEE!!* AND... IT'S CLOGGING MY NOSE!! CAN'T CATCH MY BREATH!! I'M *CHOKING!*

BUT, SUDDENLY... THE SOUND OF HEAVY, CLANKING FOOTSTEPS IS HEARD, AND THEN A MIGHTY GUST OF COMPRESSED AIR SHOOTS OUT....!

THIS'LL TAKE CARE OF THOSE GAS FUMES, LITTLE PARTNER!

WOOSH!

≥GULP≤ IF— IF I WASN'T AFRAID OF RUSTING YOUR ARMOR... I'D *KISS* YOU!!

10.

However, the sinister subterraneans do not share the Wasp's concern for Iron Man's armor, and, a second later...

I'M BEING SPRAYED WITH A FLAME-THROWER! IF IT HEATS MY IRON KIMONO MUCH MORE, I'LL *ROAST* IN HERE!

KEEP COOL, GOLDEN BOY! *I'LL* DOUSE THAT FLAME FOR YOU!

Darting around and around, using her "wasp's sting" with the same telling effectiveness as the winged creature for which she's named, the courageous flying *Wasp* causes her startled foe to drop his weapon...!

I'M LUCKY THEY FORGOT THE D.D.T.!

MEANWHILE...

RETURN FROM WHENCE YOU CAME! OUR FIGHT IS NOT WITH *YOU!*

YOU POSSESS NOT THE CAPACITY TO KNOW WHAT YOU DO! WE ARE CONTENT TO MERELY DESTROY YOUR WEAPONS!

Finally, the almost helpless subterraneans realize their attack has failed, as the fighting Avengers make short work of their remaining arms!

WHRRRR CLANG!

WOK!

THUP!

AND SO...

ENOUGH! THEY HAVE LOST THEIR WILL TO FIGHT!

NOW THAT WE'VE *GOT* THEM, WHAT'LL WE *DO* WITH THEM!?

LOOK! A SUDDEN *MIST* IS ENVELOPING THEM!

11.

33

IT'S SO THICK... SO BLINDING... I CAN HARDLY EVEN *FLY* THROUGH IT!

DO NOT TRY, WASP! STAY BACK! HOLD YOUR BREATH... *ALL* OF YOU! IT MAY BE POISONOUS!

SUPER POWERS ARE OKAY WHEN YOU *NEED* 'EM AVENGERS! BUT LITTLE OL' *RICK* KNOWS THE WAY TO TAKE CARE OF THAT SMOKE!

ALL I HAVETA DO IS SWITCH ON THE *EXHAUST FAN*... LIKE THIS!

GOOD THINKING, BOY... BUT...!

THE SUBTERRANEANS HAVE *VANISHED!*

WELL, GOOD RIDDANCE, *I* SAY!

THEY WILL TROUBLE US NO FURTHER! NOW WE MUST FIND A WAY TO REACH THE CORE OF EARTH!

CAP, YOU AND RICK RUSH TO STARK'S WEST SIDE WAREHOUSE AND BRING ME THREE MODEL X-75G TRANSISTOR TUBES! MEANTIME, WE'LL SET THINGS UP AT THE ARMS FACTORY!

YOU *HEARD* THE MAN, RICK! LET'S *GO!*

I'M RIGHT *WITH* YA, CAP!

BUT, UPON REACHING THE GLOOMY BUILDING, THEY FIND...

WE'RE JUST IN TIME, LAD! SOMEONE IS STEALING STARK'S SUPPLIES!

LOOKS LIKE *FOUR* OF 'EM, CAP... AND THEY'RE *ARMED!*

SO ARE *WE*, RICK! WE'VE GOT A SHIELD... COURAGE... AND SKILL! NO WEAPONS ARE GREATER!

LOOK OUT, YOU GUYS! THAT CRATE'S *VALUABLE!*

HEY! SOME- THING'S *ALIVE* UNDER OUR FEET!

IT'S *CAPTAIN AMERICA!* WE GOTTA STOP 'IM!

DON'T *SHOOT*, YOU FOOL! THE *COPS*'LL HEAR YA!

MONK WILL TAKE CARE OF 'IM!

ONE JUST RAN AWAY... SO I'VE ONLY *THREE* TO HANDLE! IT SHOULDN'T DELAY ME TOO LONG!

12.

LIKE A CRASHING, CHARGING, CAREENING BATTERING RAM, THE RED WHITE AND BLUE AVENGER HURTLES INTO HIS SLOWER-MOVING FOES BEFORE THEY CAN MAKE ANOTHER MOVE..!!

WHAM!

THUD..!

BUT THE ONE CALLED MONK, WHO HAD BEEN WAITING SILENTLY BEHIND THE CRATE, FLOORS CAP WITH A POWERHOUSE RIGHT WHICH THE UNWITTING CRUSADER HAD RACED SMACK DAB INTO!

WHUP!

UHHH...!

CAP!!

WITHOUT A MOMENT'S HESITATION, CAP'S SCRAPPY TEEN-AGE SIDEKICK HURLS HIMSELF INTO THE FRAY, DELIVERING A FAST DESPERATE KARATE BLOW...!

I DON'T CARE HOW BIG YOU ARE, YA CREEP!

BUT, WITH THE RASH EAGERNESS OF YOUTH, RICK JONES HAD BEEN TOO HASTY, AND THUS...

YA JUST GRAZED ME! AND I DON'T GIVE NOBODY A SECOND CHANCE!

THEN, WITH THE COLD, STEELY MENACE OF A RIPSAW, A CHALLENGING VOICE RINGS OUT...!

HOLD IT, MISTER! YOU HAVEN'T FINISHED WITH ME YET!

YOU DIDN'T THINK YOUR ONE BLOW COULD STOP A MAN WHO SPENT HIS LIFE LEARNING HOW TO ROLL WITH A PUNCH, DID YOU?

AND, BY THE WAY, YOU COULD USE A LITTLE OF THAT LEARNING, YOURSELF!

PAY ATTENTION WHEN SOMEONE TALKS TO YOU!!

OH WELL, MAYBE I'LL JUST WRITE YOU A LETTER!

I HATE TO LOSE MY TEMPER ...BUT WHEN I SEE SOMEONE THREATENING A KID..!

13.

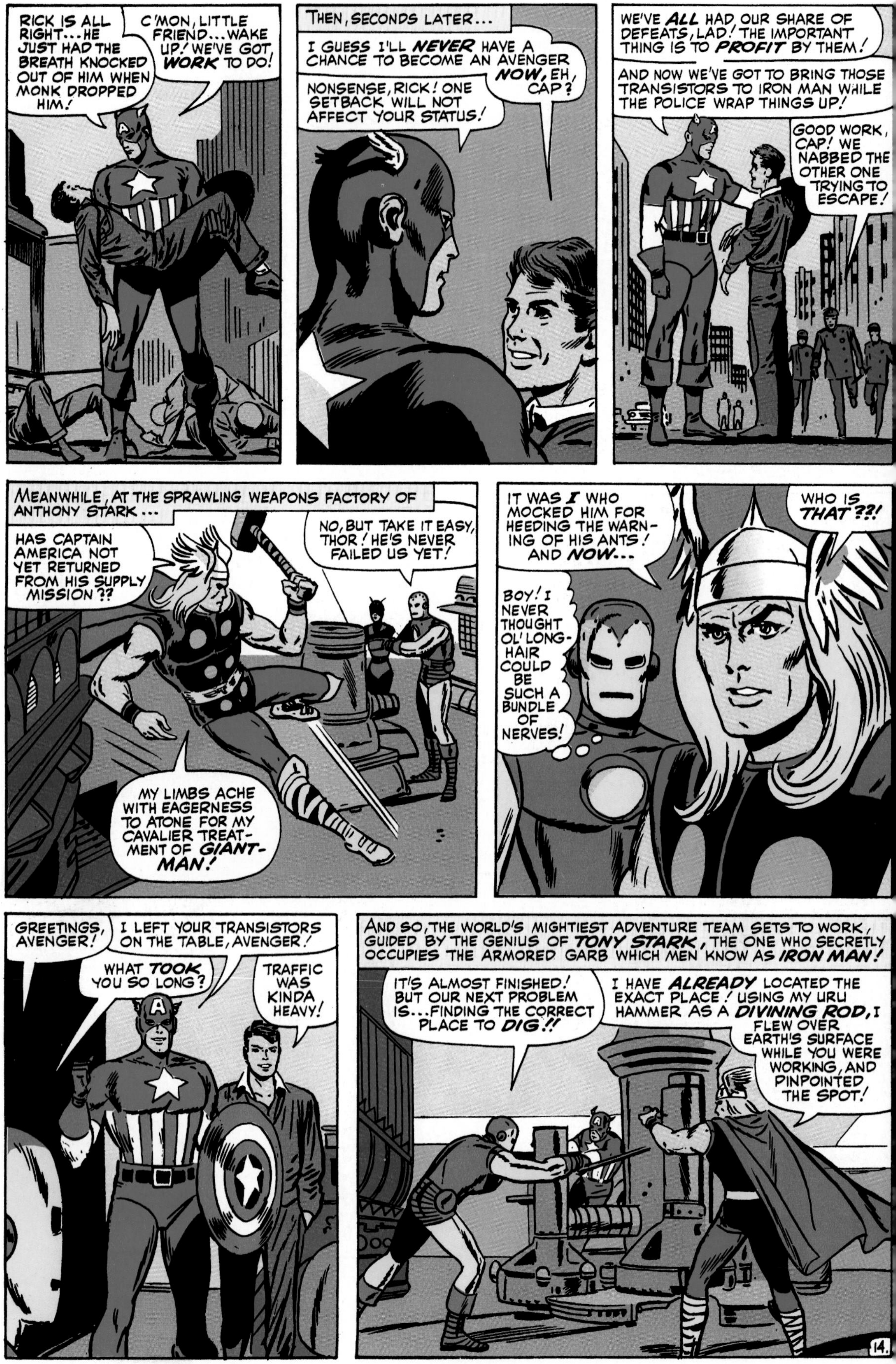
RICK IS ALL RIGHT...HE JUST HAD THE BREATH KNOCKED OUT OF HIM WHEN MONK DROPPED HIM!
C'MON, LITTLE FRIEND...WAKE UP! WE'VE GOT WORK TO DO!
THEN, SECONDS LATER...
I GUESS I'LL NEVER HAVE A CHANCE TO BECOME AN AVENGER NOW, EH, CAP?
NONSENSE, RICK! ONE SETBACK WILL NOT AFFECT YOUR STATUS!
WE'VE ALL HAD OUR SHARE OF DEFEATS, LAD! THE IMPORTANT THING IS TO PROFIT BY THEM!
AND NOW WE'VE GOT TO BRING THOSE TRANSISTORS TO IRON MAN WHILE THE POLICE WRAP THINGS UP!
GOOD WORK, CAP! WE NABBED THE OTHER ONE TRYING TO ESCAPE!
MEANWHILE, AT THE SPRAWLING WEAPONS FACTORY OF ANTHONY STARK...
HAS CAPTAIN AMERICA NOT YET RETURNED FROM HIS SUPPLY MISSION??
NO, BUT TAKE IT EASY, THOR! HE'S NEVER FAILED US YET!
MY LIMBS ACHE WITH EAGERNESS TO ATONE FOR MY CAVALIER TREATMENT OF GIANT-MAN!
IT WAS I WHO MOCKED HIM FOR HEEDING THE WARNING OF HIS ANTS! AND NOW...
BOY! I NEVER THOUGHT OL' LONG-HAIR COULD BE SUCH A BUNDLE OF NERVES!
WHO IS THAT??!
GREETINGS, AVENGER!
I LEFT YOUR TRANSISTORS ON THE TABLE, AVENGER!
WHAT TOOK YOU SO LONG?
TRAFFIC WAS KINDA HEAVY!
AND SO, THE WORLD'S MIGHTIEST ADVENTURE TEAM SETS TO WORK, GUIDED BY THE GENIUS OF TONY STARK, THE ONE WHO SECRETLY OCCUPIES THE ARMORED GARB WHICH MEN KNOW AS IRON MAN!
IT'S ALMOST FINISHED! BUT OUR NEXT PROBLEM IS...FINDING THE CORRECT PLACE TO DIG!!
I HAVE ALREADY LOCATED THE EXACT PLACE! USING MY URU HAMMER AS A DIVINING ROD, I FLEW OVER EARTH'S SURFACE WHILE YOU WERE WORKING, AND PINPOINTED THE SPOT!
14.

THUS, A FEW HOURS LATER...

ARE WE NEARLY *THERE*, THOR? I'M GETTING TIRED OF STOPPING SO OFTEN TO RECHARGE MY TRANSISTORS!

IT IS JUST A SHORT DISTANCE AHEAD, AVENGER!

WITHIN MINUTES, A SPEEDY, SPECIALLY-CHARTERED JET DELIVERS THE REMAINING TWO TEAM MEMBERS TO THE CHOSEN *SITE*...

SAY, CAP... WHO PAYS FOR THAT CHARTERED JET? *US*, OR THE AVENGERS PETTY CASH FUND?

WE CAN DISCUSS THAT AT OUR NEXT MEETING, LITTLE LADY!

RIGHT NOW, I HAVE A HUNCH WE'LL SOON BE FACING MORE PRESSING PROBLEMS!

AND, THE *CAUSE* OF THOSE "PROBLEMS" SPEAKS TO HIS RETURNED SUBTERRANEAN SQUAD, MANY MANY LEAGUES BENEATH THE FEET OF THE AVENGERS...

WHAT!? YOU *FAILED?!!*

YET YOU *DARED* RETURN HERE?? WHY DIDN'T YOU *REMAIN* ON THE SURFACE, TO ATTACK *AGAIN*??

I DIDN'T ORDER YOUR RETURN! HOW DID YOU GET *BACK*??

I BROUGHT THEM BACK, MOLE MAN!

A GUTTURAL VOICE! ONE I HAVE NEVER HEARD BEFORE! BUT...*WHO..?*

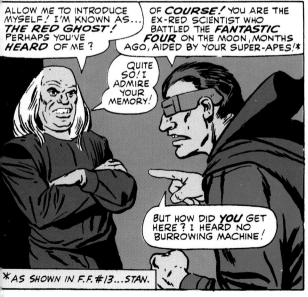

ALLOW ME TO INTRODUCE MYSELF! I'M KNOWN AS... THE *RED GHOST!* PERHAPS YOU'VE *HEARD* OF ME?

OF *COURSE!* YOU ARE THE EX-RED SCIENTIST WHO BATTLED THE *FANTASTIC FOUR* ON THE MOON, MONTHS AGO, AIDED BY YOUR SUPER-APES!*

QUITE SO! I ADMIRE YOUR MEMORY!

BUT HOW DID *YOU* GET HERE? I HEARD NO *BURROWING* MACHINE!

*AS SHOWN IN F.F. #13...STAN.

HAVE YOU FORGOTTEN? I POSSESS THE POWER TO MAKE MYSELF *UNSOLID!* I MERELY DRIFTED FROM THE SURFACE! BUT, I HAVE LEARNED TO *PROJECT* THAT POWER...TO MAKE *OTHERS* UNSOLID... *THAT* IS HOW I RETURNED YOUR SUBTERRANEANS!

AND YOUR SUPER-APES ...WHAT OF *THEM*?

THEY WERE TOO UN-PREDICTABLE! I NEED *NO ONE* NOW ...EXCEPT *YOU!!*

15.

I FEEL THAT A COMBINATION OF OUR RATHER UNUSUAL "TALENTS" WOULD MAKE US THE MOST UNBEATABLE TEAM THE WORLD HAS EVER KNOWN!

PERHAPS YOU ARE *RIGHT!* BUT WE HAVE A MORE URGENT PROBLEM RIGHT NOW!

HEAR THAT *ALARM?* IT SIGNALS THE APPROACH OF AN *ENEMY!* IF YOU WANT TO TEAM UP, LET ME SEE HOW MUCH *HELP* YOU CAN BE IN THE COMING BATTLE!

WHHHEEEEEEEEE

AND, LITTLE DREAMING THE *SECOND* MENACE THAT AWAITS THEM, THE MIGHTY AVENGERS BORE EVER DEEPER, AS THEY APPROACH THE VERY CORE OF EARTH....!

WHY HAVE YOU BECOME *WASP-SIZED* SO SOON, LITTLE LADY?

WE HAVEN'T HEARD FROM *GIANT-MAN* FOR SO LONG! IF HE'S IN DANGER, I WANT TO BE ABLE TO HELP HIM *IMMEDIATELY!*

A LAUDABLE SENTIMENT, *FEMALE!* AND NOW, WE ARE ABOUT TO *LEARN* HIS FATE! WE HAVE REACHED OUR DESTINATION!

LOOK SHARP, AVENGERS! THE MOLE MAN HAS WEAPONS TOTALLY DIFFERENT FROM ANYTHING ON THE SURFACE!

IT'S SO *QUIET!* NO SIGN OF *GIANT-MAN!*

IF HE *LIVES,* WE'LL SAVE HIM, WASP! AND IF HE DOES *NOT*...THEN VENGEANCE SHALL BE OURS!

I SEE SOMETHING AHEAD... LIKE A GIGANTIC FENCE OF LIVING LIGHTS! LET'S GO!

AVENGERS ATTACK!

CAREFUL, THOR! THOSE LIGHTS MAY ACTIVATE SOME STRANGE, DEADLY BOOBY TRAP!

STAND BACK! MY THUNDERING HAMMER SHALL CLEAR A PATH NO MATTER *WHAT* THE DANGER!

AND YET, THE RAYS FADE *TOO* EASILY! I LIKE IT NOT!

LOOK! ON THAT LEDGE ABOVE! A *FIGURE*... WITH A *RAY GUN* AIMED AT US!

SCATTER!! I'LL TRY TO DIVERT THE BEAM BY MAGNETIC REPULSION!

6

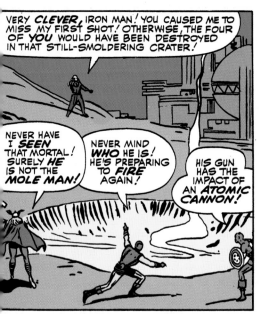

VERY *CLEVER*, IRON MAN! YOU CAUSED ME TO MISS MY FIRST SHOT! OTHERWISE, THE FOUR OF *YOU* WOULD HAVE BEEN DESTROYED IN THAT STILL-SMOLDERING CRATER!

NEVER HAVE I *SEEN* THAT MORTAL! SURELY *HE* IS NOT THE *MOLE MAN!*

NEVER MIND *WHO* HE IS! HE'S PREPARING TO *FIRE* AGAIN!

HIS GUN HAS THE IMPACT OF AN *ATOMIC CANNON!*

I 'AM THE *RED GHOST!* IT PLEASES ME THAT MY NAME SHALL BE THE *LAST* YOU WILL EVER *HEAR!*

THOUGH I AM GRIEVED THAT *YOU* WILL BE MY FIRST VICTIMS... RATHER THAN THE ACCURSED *FANTASTIC FOUR!* BUT, THEIR TURN WILL COME SOON!

MISTER, IF TALKING BIG PAID OFF AT THE BOX OFFICE, YOU'D BE A *STAR!* BUT IN *THIS* LEAGUE, IT'S WHAT YOU *DO* THAT COUNTS!

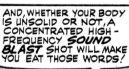

AND, WHETHER YOUR BODY IS UNSOLID OR NOT, A CONCENTRATED HIGH-FREQUENCY *SOUND BLAST* SHOT WILL MAKE YOU EAT THOSE WORDS!

BUT, SUDDENLY, ANOTHER UNEXPECTED DANGER LOOMS UP...

UH-OH! DIG THE KING-SIZED FLY SWATTER!

AND IT LOOKS LIKE *WE'RE* THE "FLIES"!

THIS IS RIGHT UP MY ALLEY! *I'LL* HOLD IT BACK WHILE YOU ALL HUNT FOR HIGH-POCKETS! NOW *SCAT!*

DO NOT DRAIN YOUR TRANSISTORS OF TOO MUCH ENERGY, AVENGER!

I FEEL WE SHALL HAVE *NEED* OF YOU BEFORE LONG!

MEANWHILE, THE EAGER *WASP* HAS ALREADY *FOUND* HER CAPTIVE PARTNER...!

OH, HANK... YOU'RE *ALIVE!*

LOOK OUT, HONEY! *BEHIND* YOU!

POWER DIVE, JAN... AS I'VE TAUGHT YOU... *NOW!*

PERFECT! NOW HEAD FOR THAT FORWARD SWITCH ON THE CONTROL PANEL BELOW YOU!

POW!

YES, SIR, BOSS!

BLAT!

PUSH IT! HARDER! *HARDER!* IT'S THE ONLY THING THAT WILL FREE ME! I'M BATHED IN AN ANTI-CYBERNETIC RAY IN HERE!

CAN'T *DO* IT... IT'S TOO HEAVY! IT... UHHH... *THERE!* IT'S OPEN!

CLICK!

17.

NO SOONER IS THE 12-FOOT TITAN RELEASED, THAN...

OUT OF THE WAY, LITTLE MEN! I'M AFTER YOUR *MASTER!*

FLY TO MY SHOULDER, JAN! WE'RE *MOVING* NOW!

MEANWHILE, THE MACABRE *MOLE MAN*, AS YET UNAWARE OF HIS PRISONER'S ESCAPE, PREPARES TO RENEW HIS ATTACK UPON THE AVENGERS...

THESE HYPER-IONIC ROCKETS CAN STOP ANYTHING THAT LIVES!

WHOOSH!

BUT THE ARCH-VILLAIN HAS NOT RECKONED WITH THE AWESOME HAMMER OF *THOR!*...

SPLATT!

...WHOSE WHIRLING FORCE HURLS THE ROCKETS BACK TO THEIR SOURCE!

NO! NO! WHA...?? THEY...THEY'RE PASSING RIGHT *THROUGH* ME!

OF COURSE, MY NEW-FOUND PARTNER! I HAVE MADE *YOU* AS UNSOLID AS I! I *VOWED* WE WOULD BE *INVINCIBLE!*

STAY *WITH* 'EM, AVENGERS! I'LL JUST MAKE SURE WE NEVER HAVE TO WORRY ABOUT THESE MISSILE LAUNCHERS *AGAIN!*

WHOP!

BUT, THEN...

UH OH! MORE ARMED SUBTERRANEANS UP AHEAD!

LET'S PULL THE RUG OUT FROM UNDER 'EM!

PWYKK!

Y'KNOW SOMETHING, AVENGER? YOU CATCH ON *QUICK!*

MY COMPLIMENTS TO YOU, TOO, AVENGER!

18

NOW YOU WAIT RIGHT THERE, LITTLE FRIENDS...UNTIL WE GET A SIGN READING, "DO NOT OPEN TILL XMAS!"

IRON MAN! QUICKLY! YOU ARE NEEDED HERE!

SECONDS LATER...

YOUR MIGHTY EFFORTS HAVE BEEN IN VAIN! IF I PUSH THIS SWITCH, I CAN DESTROY ALL LIFE ON THE SURFACE OF THE EARTH, BY INCREASING ITS AXIS SPEED!

IT IS THIS MACHINE WHICH HAS CAUSED THE UPHEAVALS WHICH AROUSED YOUR NOTICE ABOVE! AND IT IS THIS MACHINE WHICH GIVES ME MASTERY OVER ALL OF YOU!

HAH! SEE THE BEWILDERMENT ON THEIR FACES!...THE SHOCK...THE DISMAY! THEY KNOW THEY ARE DOOMED!

I SHALL SLAY ALL OF YOU... SAVE ONE! THAT ONE WILL RETURN TO THE SURFACE WITH MY DEMAND FOR UN-CONDITIONAL SURRENDER FROM THE HUMAN RACE!

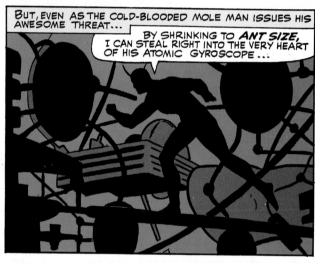

BUT, EVEN AS THE COLD-BLOODED MOLE MAN ISSUES HIS AWESOME THREAT...

BY SHRINKING TO ANT SIZE, I CAN STEAL RIGHT INTO THE VERY HEART OF HIS ATOMIC GYROSCOPE...

AND, WITH MY EXPERIENCE IN SUCH COMPLEX MECHANISMS, IT'S AN EASY MATTER FOR ME TO FIND THE EXACT CONNECTIONS WHICH, IF ALTERED, WILL CAUSE A PARALYZING SERIES OF SHORT CIRCUITS!

ZITT!
ZITT!
ZITT!
ZITT!

YOUR MACHINE! IT STOPPED!

BUT...THAT'S IMPOSSIBLE! AND, YET...!

THE HUMMING HAS STOPPED!

SOMETHING HAS DESTROYED ITS POWER CIRCUITS!

THEN WHAT ARE WE WAITING FOR??! THEY CAN'T STOP US NOW!

19.

41

BUT, AT THAT DRAMATIC MOMENT, THE ANT-SIZED AVENGER SUDDENLY ZOOMS UP TO HIS FULL TWELVE-FOOT FIGHTING SIZE, AND...

HOWDY, MEMBERS! WELCOME TO THE CLUB!

I'LL BE READY TO JOIN YOU AGAIN FOR FUN AND GAMES AS SOON AS I PUT THE KIBOSH ON THE MOLE MAN AND HIS NEW LITTLE PLAYMATE!

IT IS USELESS, TITANIC ONE! THEY HAVE THE POWER TO BECOME UNSOLID..!

... WE MUST FIRST DEVISE A METHOD OF HOLDING THEM!

THEY'VE STOPPED CHASING US! IN FACT, THEY'RE RUNNING THE OTHER WAY! WHY??

THAT IS THE DIRECTION THEY CAME FROM! THEY MUST BE PLANNING TO... LOOK! WHAT IS THOR DOING?

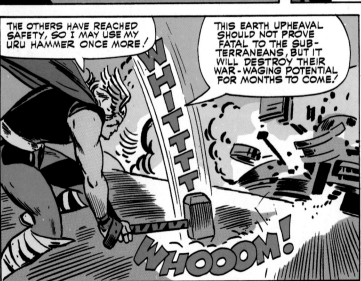

THE OTHERS HAVE REACHED SAFETY, SO I MAY USE MY URU HAMMER ONCE MORE!

THIS EARTH UPHEAVAL SHOULD NOT PROVE FATAL TO THE SUB-TERRANEANS, BUT IT WILL DESTROY THEIR WAR-WAGING POTENTIAL FOR MONTHS TO COME!

WHITTTT WHOOOM!

GOOD WORK, THOR! NOW, ALL OF YOU FOLLOW CAP BACK THROUGH OUR ESCAPE ROUTE WHILE I SEAL OFF THESE TUNNELS! IF WE'RE LUCKY, THIS WILL TRAP THEM ALL DOWN HERE FOREVER!

WE HATE TO LEAVE WITHOUT SAYING "GOODBYE", MOLE MAN, BUT...!

BAROOM!

THE NEXT DAY, BACK ON THE SURFACE AGAIN...

WHEN HIGH-POCKETS ARRIVES, WE'LL HAVE TO GIVE HIM A UNANIMOUS APOLOGY AND A VOTE OF THANKS! HMM, NOT A BAD PICTURE OF ME!

COME TO ORDER, WASP! WE ARE WAIT-ING!

AW, LET HER RELAX, PAL! THAT LITTLE GAL'S EARNED IT!!

DAILY STANDARD
AVE...RS STOP ...N PLOT ...ARTH

MEANWHILE, IN THE RUINS OF THE MOLE MAN'S ONCE PROUD SUB-TERRANEAN EMPIRE, WE FIND...

IF NOT FOR YOUR MACHINE FAILING, WE'D HAVE WON!

A LOT OF HELP YOU WERE TO ME! YOU'RE JUST DEAD WEIGHT!

SO YOU SEE, NOBODY'S PERFECT! BUT IF YOU'RE A TRUE MARVEL MADMAN, YOU KNEW THAT ALL THE TIME, DIDN'T YOU??!

The End

20.

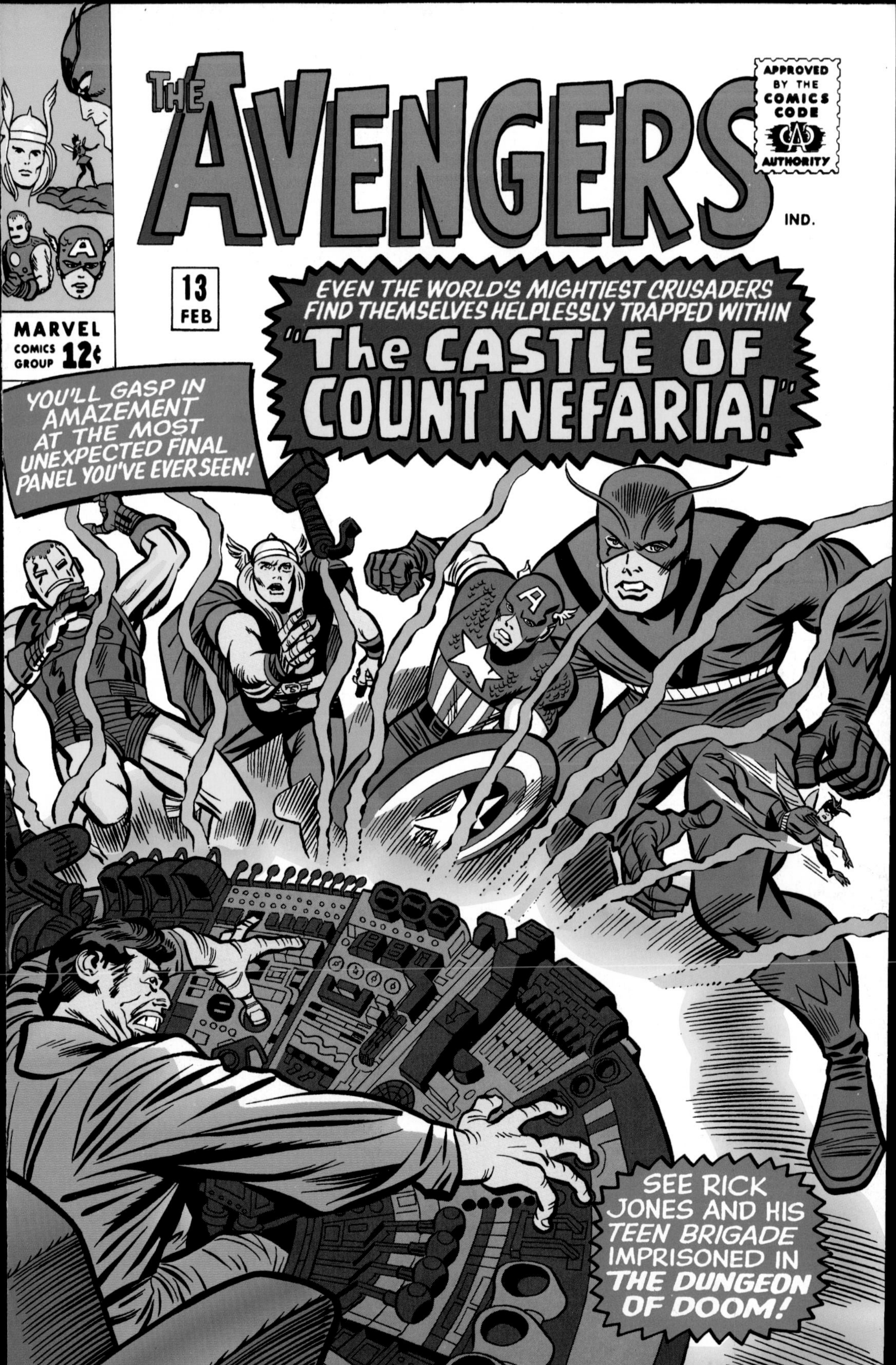

THE AVENGERS
APPROVED BY THE COMICS CODE AUTHORITY
IND.
13 FEB
MARVEL COMICS GROUP 12¢
EVEN THE WORLD'S MIGHTIEST CRUSADERS FIND THEMSELVES HELPLESSLY TRAPPED WITHIN
"The CASTLE OF COUNT NEFARIA!"
YOU'LL GASP IN AMAZEMENT AT THE MOST UNEXPECTED FINAL PANEL YOU'VE EVER SEEN!
SEE RICK JONES AND HIS TEEN BRIGADE IMPRISONED IN THE DUNGEON OF DOOM!

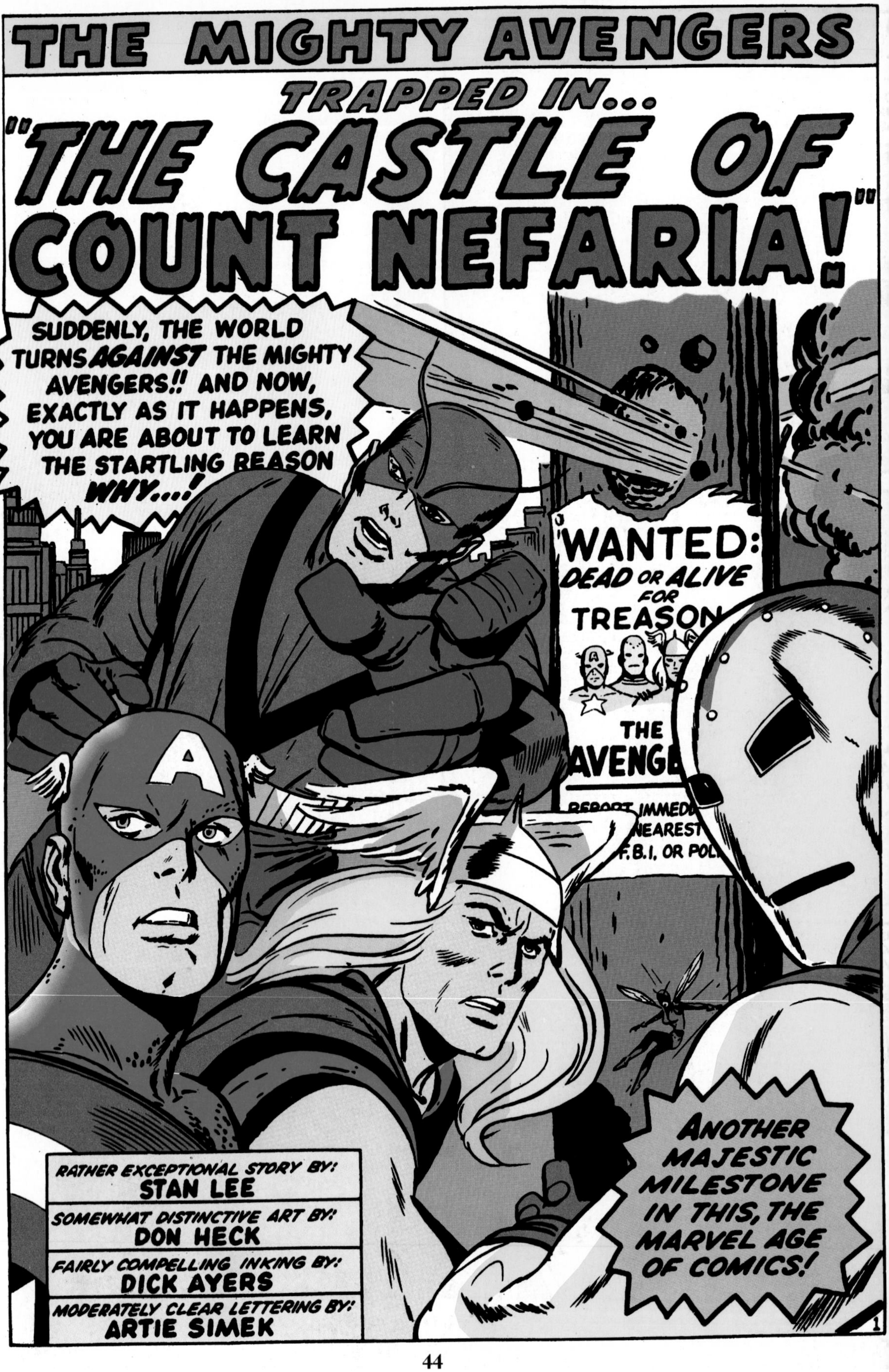
THE MIGHTY AVENGERS
TRAPPED IN...
"THE CASTLE OF COUNT NEFARIA!"
SUDDENLY, THE WORLD TURNS AGAINST THE MIGHTY AVENGERS!! AND NOW, EXACTLY AS IT HAPPENS, YOU ARE ABOUT TO LEARN THE STARTLING REASON WHY...!
WANTED: DEAD OR ALIVE FOR TREASON
THE AVENGE
REPORT IMMED
NEAREST
F.B.I. OR POL
RATHER EXCEPTIONAL STORY BY: STAN LEE
SOMEWHAT DISTINCTIVE ART BY: DON HECK
FAIRLY COMPELLING INKING BY: DICK AYERS
MODERATELY CLEAR LETTERING BY: ARTIE SIMEK
ANOTHER MAJESTIC MILESTONE IN THIS, THE MARVEL AGE OF COMICS!
1

GREAT CITY NEVER TRULY SLEEPS! IT IS ALWAYS PULSATING WITH LIFE, FILLED WITH DRAMA, AND THREATENED BY--*CRIME!*

STEP ON IT! LOAD 'EM UP AND WE'LL TAKE OFF!

THIS IS THE *LAST* OF 'EM! NOW LET'S GET *OUTA* HERE!

SO FAR, SO GOOD! THOSE FURS'LL BE WORTH A *FORTUNE* TO THE RIGHT BUYER!

DON'T COUNT YOUR TAKE TILL WE'RE IN THE *CLEAR!* HEY! WHAT'S THAT *ABOVE* US??

IT'S A *HAMMER!* IT--IT FELL FROM THE *SKY!*

FELL *NOTHIN'!!* IT WAS *THROWN* -- SMASHED RIGHT THRU OUR ENGINE BLOCK!

KA-POKK!

SKRAKK!

IRON MAN!

OKAY, BOYS! THE PARTY'S OVER!

HE RIPPED THAT STEEL DOOR LIKE IT WAS *PAPER!*

HEY! GO EASY WITH THAT *HAMMER*, MISTER! ALL WE DID WAS PASS A STOP SIGN!

SILENCE! YOU WILL FOLLOW US TO THE POLICE-- IN THE NAME OF --*THE AVENGERS!*

A SHORT TIME LATER, AT AN EMERGENCY MEETING OF THE WORLD-WIDE CRIME CARTEL COMMONLY KNOWN AS THE *MAGGIA*, WE FIND...

THE AVENGERS ARE PUTTIN' US OUT OF BUSINESS!

BETWEEN THEM AND THE COPS, WE'VE BEEN OPERATIN' AT A *LOSS* FOR THE WHOLE FISCAL YEAR!

WHAT'S GONNA HAPPEN WHEN *THE COUNT* HEARS ABOUT IT??

DAILY O GLOBE
AVENGERS APPREHEND FUR BANDITS!

THE AVENGERS ON THE RAMPAGE

2

THEN, AT THAT VERY MOMENT...

THE *ELECTRO-RAY* SIGNAL! IT'S *HIM*--IT'S THE *COUNT!* HE MUST HAVE LEARNED OF WHAT HAPPENED LAST NIGHT!

BUT--HE'S THOUSANDS OF MILES AWAY! HOW COULD HE HEAR OF IT SO *SOON??*

YOU *FOOL!* HE'S THE MOST POWERFUL CRIME LORD ON *EARTH!* HE KNOWS *EVERYTHING!*

ANSWER HIM-- *QUICK!!* YOU KNOW THE PENALTY FOR KEEPING THE *COUNT* WAITING!

ALL RIGHT! STAND BACK, ALL OF YOU-- WHILE I TOUCH THE SENSITIZED ELECTRO-DISC!

I--I CAN FEEL IT BEGINNING TO *TINGLE!*

THE VERY SPLIT- SECOND THAT CONTACT IS MADE, A SIGNAL BEAM FLASHES HALF-WAY AROUND THE PLANET...

--TO THE REGAL CASTLE OF THE MAN WHOM THE WORLD KNOWS AS *COUNT NEFARIA!*

SO! HE IS TOUCHING THE ELECTRO-DISC!

NOW, ALL I NEED DO IS PRESS THIS BUTTON.

INSTANTANEOUSLY, A THREE-DIMENSIONAL IMAGE OF THE AMERICAN GANG LEADER APPEARS IN THE GREAT HALL OF COUNT NEFARIA'S CASTLE!

YOU--YOU BROUGHT MY IMAGE ALL THE WAY *HERE?!!* THAT MEANS I AM TO RECEIVE-- THE *PUNISHMENT!!* NO--*NO,* YOUR EXCELLENCY! I HAVE BEEN LOYAL TO YOU--!

SILENCE, YOU BUNGLER! IF THE *MAGGIA* CAN- NOT EVEN COMMIT A SIMPLE FUR ROBBERY SUCCESSFULLY, YOU ARE OF NO USE TO ME!

BUT, I AM *BLAMELESS!* *NO ONE* CAN STOP THE *AVENGERS!*

YOU DARE SAY THAT TO *ME??!* I CAN STOP *ANYONE!*

AND NOW, AT THE PRESS OF A BUTTON, I *ERASE* YOUR IMAGE! PREPARE FOR-- THE *PUNISHMENT!*

NO, EXCELLENCY! NOT *THAT!* NO! *NOOOO--!*

HE HAS BEEN BANISHED FROM THE MAGGIA! HE HAS NO PLACE TO GO-- NONE TO TURN TO! A FITTING PUNISHMENT FOR THOSE WHO FAIL COUNT NEFARIA!

BUT NOW, I MUST DEAL WITH THE MEDDLE-SOME AVENGERS!

ALREADY, A PLAN BEGINS TO FORM IN MY MIND!

NONE WILL SUSPECT! THE WORLD KNOWS ME ONLY AS EUROPE'S WEALTHIEST NOBLEMAN!

THUS, DAYS LATER... OH, LISTEN, HANK! "THE FAMOUS COUNT NEFARIA IS MOVING HIS ANCIENT CASTLE TO AMERICA, STONE BY STONE!"

WITH HIS MONEY, HE COULD SHIP IT TO THE MOON IF HE WANTED TO!

AND SO, THE FIRST PART OF THE COUNT'S FANTASTIC SCHEME IS PUT INTO EFFECT, AS HIS ENTIRE CASTLE IS DISMANTLED AND LOADED UPON A FLEET OF CARGO SHIPS...

THE COST OF THE PROJECT IS VIRTUALLY INCALCULABLE, BUT MONEY IS MEANINGLESS TO ONE OF THE WORLD'S RICHEST MEN...

THE VERY TRUCKS AND SHIPS WHICH DO THE INCREDIBLE HAULAGE TASK ARE OWNED BY COMPANIES WHICH HE HIMSELF CONTROLS!

FINALLY, IN A MATTER OF WEEKS, THE HERCULEAN JOB IS COMPLETED, AS THE CASTLE OF COUNT NEFARIA LOOKS DOWN UPON THE WINDING HUDSON RIVER FROM A COMMANDING SITE ATOP NEW JERSEY'S PALISADES...

EVERYTHING IS READY! NOW FOR PHASE TWO OF MY MASTER PLAN!

THE NEXT DAY... ACCORDING TO THE PAPER, NEFARIA IS OPENING HIS CASTLE TO THE PUBLIC-- AND ALL PROCEEDS WILL BE DONATED TO CHARITY!

I'D SURE LIKE TO SEE THAT STONE SHACK OF HIS!

YOU'LL GET YOUR CHANCE, RICK! HE'S INVITED THE AVENGERS THERE!

HE? HAS? WHY?

I'LL SHRINK DOWN SO I CAN HEAR BETTER!

COUNT NEFARIA WROTE A LETTER SAYING THAT IF WE ATTEND THE OPENING DAY CEREMONY, IT'S SURE TO BE A BIG SUCCESS! AND I, FOR ONE, COULDN'T AGREE MORE!

WE CAN'T SAY NO IF IT'S FOR CHARITY!

BESIDES, THEY SAY THE COUNT IS POSITIVELY FASCINATING!

4

47

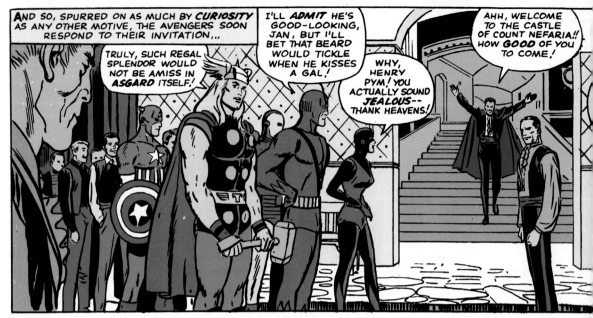

AND SO, SPURRED ON AS MUCH BY *CURIOSITY* AS ANY OTHER MOTIVE, THE AVENGERS SOON RESPOND TO THEIR INVITATION...

TRULY, SUCH REGAL SPLENDOR WOULD NOT BE AMISS IN *ASGARD* ITSELF!

I'LL *ADMIT* HE'S GOOD-LOOKING, JAN, BUT I'LL BET THAT BEARD WOULD TICKLE WHEN HE KISSES A GAL!

WHY, HENRY *PYM!* YOU ACTUALLY SOUND *JEALOUS*-- THANK HEAVENS!

AHH, WELCOME TO THE CASTLE OF COUNT NEFARIA!! HOW *GOOD* OF YOU TO COME!

RICK, YOU AND THE *TEEN BRIGADE* WAIT OUTSIDE TILL THE DOORS OPEN FOR THE PUBLIC!

SURE THING, CAP!

I WILL SHOW EACH OF YOU TO YOUR QUARTERS NOW!

QUARTERS? WHAT DO YOU *MEAN?*

TO SHOW MY *GRATITUDE* FOR YOUR VISIT, I HAVE ASSIGNED *EACH* OF YOU A CHAMBER WHERE YOU MAY FRESHEN UP AND REST A BIT BEFORE THE CEREMONY BEGINS!

THAT ONE IS *YOURS,* IRON MAN!

THANKS, COUNT! VERY THOUGHTFUL OF YOU!

THEN, AFTER EACH AVENGER HAS BEEN SHOWN TO THE PROPER CHAMBER...

THE *FOOLS!* THEY NEVER SUSPECTED A *THING!*

NOW, ALL THAT REMAINS IS TO SPRING THE TRAP!

IT SEEMS STRANGE TO HAVE SUCH MODERN-LOOKING BRIGHT LIGHTS IN SUCH AN ANCIENT CASTLE! I WONDER WHY NEFARIA HAD THEM INSTALLED?

THE CHAMBER IS BATHED IN A SHIMMERING LIGHT! BUT, FOR WHAT PURPOSE??

THEN, SLOWLY, THE LIGHTS BEGIN TO INCREASE IN INTENSITY, FOCUSING SHARPLY ON THE OCCUPANT OF EACH ROOM, UNTIL...

MY BRAIN SEEMS NUMB! MY THOUGHTS ARE BECOMING DULLED-- SLUGGISH--

IT'S ALMOST AS THOUGH THE VERY FABRIC OF *TIME* IS SLOWING DOWN--!

48

I'VE **DONE** IT! I'VE MANAGED TO PUT **EACH** OF THEM UNDER THE RAYS OF THE **TIME TRANSCENDER BEAMS!**

FOR THEM, TIME WILL APPEAR TO BE **STANDING STILL,** UNTIL THE LIGHTS ARE AGAIN SHUT OFF!

AND NOW, FOR THE **FINAL** PART OF MY INFALLIBLE PLAN!

WHILE THEY SIT, TRANCE-LIKE, IN THEIR CHAMBERS, I SHALL CREATE NEW THREE-DIMENSIONAL IMAGES OF THEM-- IMAGES WHICH I ALONE CAN CONTROL!

THERE! MY FIRST AVENGER IMAGE IS COMPLETED! THE OTHERS SHALL TAKE BUT A FEW SECONDS LONGER!

I HAVE NEVER BELIEVED IN HARMING MY VICTIMS **PHYSICALLY!** NO, MY METHODS ARE FAR MORE INGENIOUS --FAR MORE DEVASTATING!

I LET **OTHERS** PERFORM THE UNPLEASANT TASKS FOR ME! I MERELY PULL THE STRINGS!

THUS, SHOULD MY EMPIRE OF CRIME EVER TOPPLE, THE HANDS OF COUNT NEFARIA WILL ALWAYS BE CLEAN!

AND NOW, I AM **READY!** THE IMAGES ARE COMPLETED, AND EACH IS UNDER MY CONTROL!

SO, BY USING **THEM,** I SHALL **DESTROY** THE AVENGERS!

SECONDS LATER, FIVE DRAMATIC FIGURES APPEAR AT A HIGH-LEVEL PENTAGON MEETING...

THE AVENGERS ORDER YOU TO END THIS CONFERENCE IMMEDIATELY! WE ARE TAKING COMMAND!

ONLY THE MOST **POWERFUL** ARE FIT TO GOVERN! AND NONE ARE STRONGER THAN **WE!**

YOU ARE ALL **DISMISSED**-- IN THE NAME OF THE **AVENGERS!**

WITHIN ONE HOUR WE SHALL CANCEL ALL EXISTING LAWS AND ISSUE OUR **OWN!** FROM NOW ON, ONLY THE **AVENGERS** WILL MAKE AND ENFORCE THE LAW!

AND THOSE WHO DEFY US SHALL BE DESTROYED!

THIS IS **MADNESS!** IT CANNOT BE **TRUE!**

IT'S TRUE, ALL RIGHT! LOOK AT THEIR **FACES!** THEY **MEAN** IT!

WITHIN SECONDS, THE ONLY POSSIBLE ANSWER IS GIVEN!

ORDER COMPLETE MOBILIZATION! CANCEL ALL MILITARY LEAVES! THIS NATION WILL NEVER BOW TO ANY SHOW OF FORCE!

AND SO...

IT IS WE WHO WARN YOU! SURRENDER IMMEDIATELY, OR FACE THE ARMED MIGHT OF THE UNITED STATES! THERE IS NO OTHER CHOICE!

SO BE IT! YOU ARE AT WAR-- WITH THE AVENGERS!

WITHOUT ANOTHER WORD, THE FIVE FIGURES TURN AND DEPART-- FIVE FIGURES WHO ARE MERELY ELECTRO-IMAGES, SKILLFULLY MANIPULATED BY THE EVIL HANDS OF COUNT NEFARIA!!

I-I STILL CAN'T BELIEVE IT!

WHAT MADE THEM DO IT? HAVE THEY GONE MAD??

MINUTES LATER, AT AN EMERGENCY NEWS CONFERENCE...

THE PUBLIC IS URGED TO REMAIN CALM! A STATE OF NATIONAL EMERGENCY HAS BEEN DECLARED!

THEN, BEFORE THE DAY IS DONE, THE ENTIRE NATION LEARNS THE STAGGERING NEWS...

AND THEY CALLED THEMSELVES AMERICA'S DEFENDERS!! THE TRAITORS!

EXTRA!! WAR DECLARED! EXTRA!

SPECIAL WAR EXTRA!

AVENGERS CHALLENGE UNITED STA...

AVENGERS DECLARE WAR ON U.S.!

"SHOOT ON SIGHT" ORDERS ARMY!

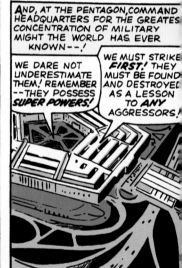

AND, AT THE PENTAGON, COMMAND HEADQUARTERS FOR THE GREATEST CONCENTRATION OF MILITARY MIGHT THE WORLD HAS EVER KNOWN--!

WE DARE NOT UNDERESTIMATE THEM! REMEMBER --THEY POSSESS SUPER POWERS!

WE MUST STRIKE FIRST! THEY MUST BE FOUND AND DESTROYED AS A LESSON TO ANY AGGRESSORS!

YET, I FIND IT HARD TO ISSUE THE ORDER! THEY HAVE DONE SO MUCH FOR OUR COUNTRY IN THE PAST! WE HAVE FOUGHT SIDE-BY-SIDE--- AGAINST OVERWHELMING ODDS!

UNTIL THIS VERY DAY, I'D HAVE GIVEN MY LIFE IN DEFENSE OF ANY ONE OF THEM!!

BUT NOW, THE DIE IS CAST! THERE'S NO TURNING BACK--!

PUT OPERATION SEEK AND DESTROY INTO EFFECT AT ONCE! HAVE EVERY SECTOR COMMANDER REPORT TO ME HOURLY! DIS-MISSED!

BY NIGHTFALL, WANTED POSTERS APPEAR THRUOUT THE NATION! INDEED, THE GENERAL WAS RIGHT--THERE IS NO TURNING BACK!

NEVER THOUGHT I'D SEE THE DAY I'D BE READING SOMETHING LIKE THIS!

WANTED! DEAD OR ALIVE THE AVENGERS!

WARNING: THEY ARE ARMED WITH THE MOST AWESOME POWERS KNOWN TO MAN!

7

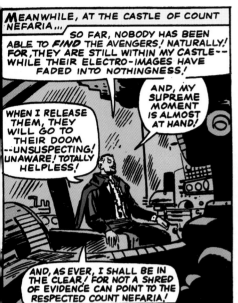

MEANWHILE, AT THE CASTLE OF COUNT NEFARIA...

SO FAR, NOBODY HAS BEEN ABLE TO *FIND* THE AVENGERS! NATURALLY! FOR, THEY ARE STILL WITHIN MY CASTLE-- WHILE THEIR ELECTRO-IMAGES HAVE FADED INTO NOTHINGNESS!

AND, MY SUPREME MOMENT IS ALMOST AT HAND!

WHEN I RELEASE THEM, THEY WILL GO TO THEIR DOOM --UNSUSPECTING! UNAWARE! TOTALLY HELPLESS!

AND, AS EVER, I SHALL BE IN THE CLEAR! FOR NOT A SHRED OF EVIDENCE CAN POINT TO THE RESPECTED COUNT NEFARIA!

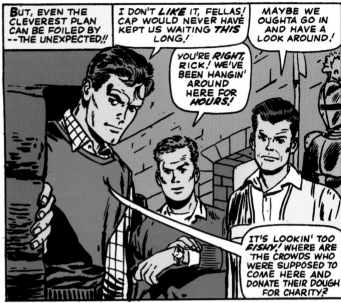

BUT, EVEN THE CLEVEREST PLAN CAN BE FOILED BY --THE UNEXPECTED!!

I DON'T *LIKE* IT, FELLAS! CAP WOULD NEVER HAVE KEPT US WAITING *THIS* LONG!

MAYBE WE OUGHTA GO IN AND HAVE A LOOK AROUND!

YOU'RE *RIGHT*, RICK! WE'VE BEEN HANGIN' AROUND HERE FOR *HOURS!*

IT'S LOOKIN' TOO *EISHY!* WHERE ARE THE CROWDS WHO WERE SUPPOSED TO COME HERE AND DONATE THEIR DOUGH FOR CHARITY?

AND SO, RICK JONES AND HIS TEEN BRIGADE BEGIN THEIR OWN "TOUR" OF THE STRANGE CASTLE...!

LOOK! UP AHEAD! SOME KINDA GIANT CONTROL ROOM!

BUT, THE EYES OF COUNT NEFARIA ARE EVERYWHERE, AND, AT THE TOUCH OF A BUTTON...

MY *MAGGIA* AGENTS WILL KNOW HOW TO HANDLE THIS MATTER!

THUS, WITHIN SECONDS, THE OUT-NUMBERED BAND OF TEEN-AGERS IS SEIZED...

...AND, UNCEREMONIOUSLY TOSSED INTO ONE OF THE CASTLE'S MANY PADLOCKED DUNGEON CELLS!

KNOW SOMETHIN', RICK? I'M BEGINNIN' TO THINK COUNT NEFARIA AINT EXACTLY THE BEST FRIEND US FUN-LOVIN' KIDS EVER HAD!

WHAT'S GOIN' ON, HERE? HOW COME THE *AVENGERS* LET HIM GET *AWAY* WITH IT??

THERE'S ONLY *ONE* ANSWER-- AND I DON'T *LIKE* IT! IT MUST BE THAT THE AVENGERS *CAN'T* HELP US--'CAUSE *THEY'RE* IN TROUBLE, TOO!

OH, *NO!* IF THAT NEFARIA CHARACTER COULD STAND UP TO THE *AVENGERS*, THEN *WE* HAVEN'T GOT A *CHANCE!*

8

NEXT, THE EVIL COUNT SHUTS OFF HIS MYSTIC CHAMBER LIGHTS -- THE LIGHTS WHICH CAUSED THE AVENGERS TO THINK THEY HAVE ONLY SPENT A FEW MINUTES WITHIN THE CASTLE...

THE CHARITY DIRECTOR JUST CALLED AND POST-PONED THE OPENING CEREMONY TILL *TOMORROW!* SO, IF YOU CAN RETURN THEN,...

SOUNDS LIKE A SLOPPY WAY TO RUN A CHARITY AFFAIR, MISTER! BUT, OKAY-- IF WE CAN MAKE IT, WE'LL BE HERE!

WHERE ARE RICK AND THE TEEN BRIGADE? I TOLD THEM TO WAIT HERE!

OH, EH-- THEY DECIDED TO EXPLORE THE AREA! THEY SAID THEY'D JOIN YOU LATER!

STRANGE! IT'S NOT LIKE THEM TO IGNORE AN ORDER!

HAH! ONCE YOU ARE DISCOVERED, YOU WILL NOT HAVE *TIME* TO WORRY ABOUT THOSE FOOL TEEN AGERS!

THAT *CALL* I MADE SHOULD HAVE THE ARMY HERE ANY MINUTE!

AND, ALMOST BEFORE THE AVENGERS ARE OUT OF EARSHOT, NEFARIA'S PREDICTION COMES TRUE!

PNEEEEEE!

WHO WOULD BE SO FOOL-HARDY AS TO ATTACK THE *AVENGERS??*

ARTILLERY FIRE! WHAT CAN IT MEAN?!!

WE CAN WORRY ABOUT *WHO* IT IS *LATER!* RIGHT *NOW*, WE'D BETTER *DEFEND* OURSELVES!

WASP! FLY TO MY SHOULDER --QUICKLY!

YES SIR, BIG MAN!

RIKKA RAKKA RAK

FIRE AT WILL! WE'VE GOT TO KEEP THEM REELING UNTIL THE PLANES AND THE TANKS CAN GET HERE!

RIKKA RAK

I MUST BE *SEEING* THINGS! THOSE LOOK LIKE *AMERICAN TROOPS* FIRING AT US!!

IT *CANNOT BE!* THEY MUST BE A FORCE OF EVIL FOES, DISGUISED AS INFANTRYMEN FOR THEIR OWN NEFARIOUS PURPOSES!

NO MATTER *WHO* THEY ARE THEY'RE OUT TO *FINISH* US!

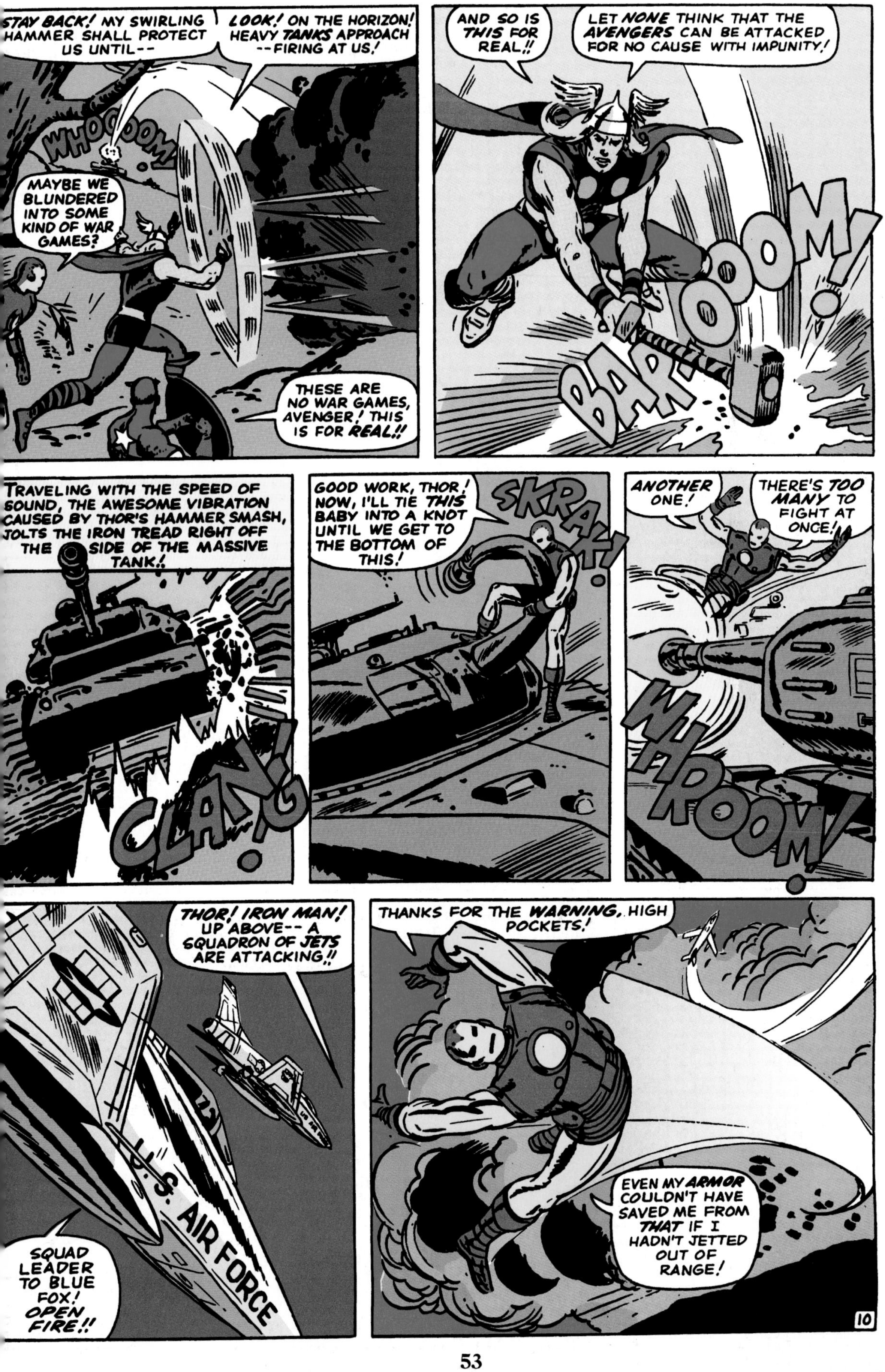
STAY BACK! MY SWIRLING HAMMER SHALL PROTECT US UNTIL--
LOOK! ON THE HORIZON! HEAVY TANKS APPROACH --FIRING AT US!
WHOOOOM
MAYBE WE BLUNDERED INTO SOME KIND OF WAR GAMES?
THESE ARE NO WAR GAMES, AVENGER! THIS IS FOR REAL!!
AND SO IS THIS FOR REAL!!
LET NONE THINK THAT THE AVENGERS CAN BE ATTACKED FOR NO CAUSE WITH IMPUNITY!
BAROOOOM!
TRAVELING WITH THE SPEED OF SOUND, THE AWESOME VIBRATION CAUSED BY THOR'S HAMMER SMASH, JOLTS THE IRON TREAD RIGHT OFF THE SIDE OF THE MASSIVE TANK!
CLANG!
GOOD WORK, THOR! NOW, I'LL TIE THIS BABY INTO A KNOT UNTIL WE GET TO THE BOTTOM OF THIS!
SKRAK!
ANOTHER ONE!
THERE'S TOO MANY TO FIGHT AT ONCE!
WHROOOM!
THOR! IRON MAN! UP ABOVE-- A SQUADRON OF JETS ARE ATTACKING!!
U.S. AIR FORCE
SQUAD LEADER TO BLUE FOX! OPEN FIRE!!
THANKS FOR THE WARNING, HIGH POCKETS!
EVEN MY ARMOR COULDN'T HAVE SAVED ME FROM THAT IF I HADN'T JETTED OUT OF RANGE!
10

THEY GIVE US NO TIME TO THINK--TO QUESTION THEIR PURPOSE--WE CAN ONLY *STRIKE!*

SQUAD LEADER TO BLUE FOX! I'M *HIT!* MUST *BAIL OUT!* *CONTINUE ATTACK* AS ORDERED!

SPYONG!

THOR'S HAMMER IS ENCHANTED! IT NEVER MISSES!

HE COULD HAVE SHATTERED MY ESCAPE MECHANISM--BUT DIDN'T *WHY??*

MEANTIME, THE COMBINED LAND-AIR ATTACK CONTINUES--!

AVENGERS!! WE MUST NOT BATTLE AN AMERICAN TASK FORCE! WE MUST *RETREAT!*

TO OUR EMERGENCY HEADQUARTERS THEN! WITH ALL DELIBERATE SPEED!!

BE WITH YOU IN A MINUTE, FELLAS!

CLANG!

IT'S PRETTY NEAT THE WAY YOUR SHIELD CAN KEEP SO MANY MEN AT BAY WITHOUT INJURING THEM, CAP!

YES, BUT I'M GLAD WE'RE TAKING OFF! I COULDN'T KEEP IT UP MUCH LONGER!

SAY! WHERE'S GIANT-MAN?

RIGHT HERE, GENTS! I'VE GOT SOME UNEXPECTED CALLERS--!

HERE! *THIS'LL* HOLD YOU FOR A WHILE AND YOU'LL BE NONE THE WORSE FOR WEAR!

HURRY, BIG FELLA!

SUDDENLY, REINFORCEMENTS ARRIVE ON THE SCENE, BUT THEN...

THIS'LL STOP THAT TWELVE-FOOT HIGH TRAITOR!!

HEY! WHERE'D HE GO??

H-HE JUST VANISHED!!

I THOUGHT YOU'D NEVER SHRINK IN TIME, HANK!

C'MON, JAN HONEY! WE'VE GOT THINGS TO DO!

A SHORT TIME LATER...

OUR FIRST JOB IS TO LEARN WHY WE'RE ALL UNDER ATTACK!

OH! THAT'S WHY YOU WANTED TO GET TO A NEWSSTAND AS SOON AS POSSIBLE!

RIGHT, JAN! BUT WHILE I'M ANT-SIZE, IT'S TOO HARD TO READ THE HEADLINES! THE PRINT IS TOO LARGE!

AND WE DON'T DARE GROW TO NORMAL SIZE TILL WE MAKE SURE WE'LL BE SAFE!

OHHH! WHAT'S HAPPENING?

SOMEONE'S TAKING A PAPER!

AH, THIS IS BETTER! I CAN READ IT FROM UP HERE!

OH, NO! IT--IT SAYS THAT WE'RE ALL WANTED-- FOR TREASON!! AND, LOOK AT THE REST!!

AVENG WANTED
NATI SEAR
FOR TREAS
NATION SEA
WOULD
DICTA

ALMOST NUMB WITH SHOCK, THE INSECT-SIZED AVENGERS READ THE WHOLE STORY, AND THEN RACE TO THEIR EMERGENCY HEADQUARTERS WITH HEAVY HEARTS--

IT'S LIKE SOME FANTASTIC NIGHTMARE! AND YET, IT'S TOO FRIGHTEN-INGLY REAL!

BUT THERE'S NO TRUTH TO ANY OF IT! HOW COULD IT HAVE HAPPENED??

I DON'T KNOW, JAN! BUT, ONE THING IS SURE --WE'LL LEARN THE ANSWER IF IT COSTS US OUR LIVES!

HALT! IDENTIFY YOURSELVES IN THE NAME OF THE AVENGERS!

GIANT-MAN AND WASP! AND I'M AFRAID THE NAME OF THE AVENGERS DOESN'T COUNT FOR MUCH THESE DAYS, PARTNER!

HOW RIGHT YOU BOTH ARE! WE JUST LEARNED OVER THE RADIO WHAT IT IS WE'RE ACCUSED OF!

WE'VE BEEN TRYING TO FIGURE IT OUT, AND THERE'S ONLY ONE ANSWER WE CAN COME UP WITH--!

SOME EVIL GROUP HAS IMPERSONATED US! BUT WE KNOW NOT WHO-- NOR HOW!!

IT ALL HAPPENED AFTER WE LEFT THE CASTLE OF COUNT NEFARIA! I CAN'T HELP FEELING THERE'S A *TIE-IN* SOMEWHERE!

CALL IT WOMAN'S INTUITION IF YOU WANT, BUT *I* FEEL THE SAME WAY!

SOMEHOW, I CAN'T REMEMBER OUR VISIT THERE TOO CLEARLY!

THAT'S STRANGE, CAP! NEITHER CAN *I*!

THOUGH I DID NOT MENTION IT BEFORE, *MY* MEMORY OF OUR VISIT IS HAZY, TOO!

IT *CAN'T* BE MERE COINCIDENCE! IT CAN ONLY MEAN *ONE THING*--!

RIGHT! THE ANSWERS WE SEEK *MUST* LIE BACK AT NEFARIA'S CASTLE!!

PERHAPS THE TEEN BRIGADE STUMBLED ONTO SOMETHING-- AND *THAT'S* WHY WE DIDN'T FIND THEM WHEN WE LEFT!

WELL?? WHAT ARE WE *WAITING* FOR? WE'VE GOT US A *CASTLE* TO VISIT!

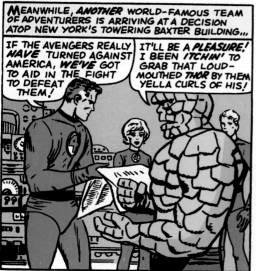

MEANWHILE, *ANOTHER* WORLD-FAMOUS TEAM OF ADVENTURERS IS ARRIVING AT A DECISION ATOP NEW YORK'S TOWERING BAXTER BUILDING...

IF THE AVENGERS REALLY *HAVE* TURNED AGAINST AMERICA, *WE'VE* GOT TO AID IN THE FIGHT TO DEFEAT THEM!

IT'LL BE A *PLEASURE!* I BEEN *ITCHIN'* TO GRAB THAT LOUD-MOUTHED *THOR* BY THEM YELLA CURLS OF HIS!

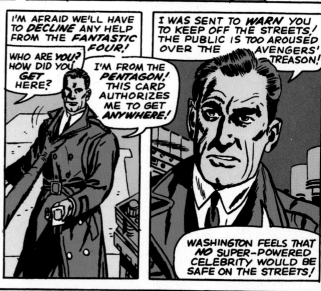

I'M AFRAID WE'LL HAVE TO *DECLINE* ANY HELP FROM THE *FANTASTIC FOUR!*

WHO ARE *YOU?* HOW DID YOU *GET* HERE?

I'M FROM THE *PENTAGON!* THIS CARD AUTHORIZES ME TO GET *ANYWHERE!*

I WAS SENT TO *WARN* YOU TO KEEP OFF THE STREETS! THE PUBLIC IS TOO AROUSED OVER THE *AVENGERS'* TREASON!

WASHINGTON FEELS THAT *NO* SUPER-POWERED CELEBRITY WOULD BE SAFE ON THE STREETS!

WITH TROOPS PATROLLING THE STREETS-- MARTIAL LAW PROCLAIMED THRUOUT THE NATION --YOU CAN UNDER-STAND THAT THE PUBLIC IS IN AN UGLY MOOD!

THE AVENGERS ARE SO *HATED* TODAY, THAT *ALL* SUPER-POWERED GROUPS HAVE BEEN DECLARED UNDER EMERGENCY *QUARANTINE!*

THUS, AS THE SITUATION GROWS INCREASINGLY GRIMMER, WE RETURN TO THE DANK DUNGEON PRISON WHICH HOUSES RICK JONES AND THE TEEN BRIGADE...

SO FAR, SO GOOD! IT'S A GOOD THING NEFARIA DIDN'T BOTHER *SEARCHING* US! I'LL HAVE THIS TRANS-MITTER PUT TOGETHER IN A FEW MORE MINUTES!

GOSH! ONLY *IRON MAN* COULD HAVE RIGGED UP A PORTABLE SENDING SET AS TINY AS *THAT* ONE!

IT'S LUCKY NO ONE TOLD THE COUNT THAT WE'RE ALL HAM RADIO BUFFS!

13

OKAY! SHE'S ALL SET NOW! KEEP IT QUIET, YOU GUYS! 'TEEN BRIGADE' CALLING AVENGERS! AVENGERS! COME IN--!

NOT A PEEP! BUT, IRON MAN ALWAYS HAS HIS MINIATURE RECEIVING SET ON! I DON'T GET IT!!

WHAT CAN WE DO NOW??

THUS, AS RICK JONES VAINLY TRANSMITS AN URGENT S.O.S., HE HAS NO WAY OF KNOWING THAT IRON MAN'S BUILT-IN RECEIVER HAS BEEN DAMAGED DURING HIS RECENT BATTLE WITH THE MILITARY TASK FORCE!

ALMOST AT NEFARIA'S CASTLE NOW! WONDER WHY WE'VE HEARD NOTHING FROM THE TEEN BRIGADE?

WELL, WE SHOULD BE LEARNING A LOT OF ANSWERS PRETTY SOON!

BUT, THOUGH THE AVENGERS CANNOT RECEIVE RICK'S SIGNAL-- THE SINISTER COUNT NEFARIA CAN!

MY MONITORS ARE PICKING UP A RADIO BEAM FROM DUNGEON B! THOSE BRATS ARE TRYING TO RADIO FOR HELP!

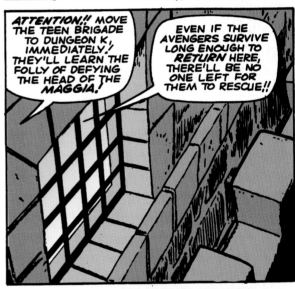

ATTENTION!! MOVE THE TEEN BRIGADE TO DUNGEON K, IMMEDIATELY! THEY'LL LEARN THE FOLLY OF DEFYING THE HEAD OF THE MAGGIA.

EVEN IF THE AVENGERS SURVIVE LONG ENOUGH TO RETURN HERE, THERE'LL BE NO ONE LEFT FOR THEM TO RESCUE!!

MINUTES LATER...

HEY! WHAT KIND OF A NUTTY PLACE IS THIS THEY TOSSED US INTO??

I DON'T LIKE IT, TED! THOSE SUCTION CUPS EACH CONTAIN A PASTY SUBSTANCE-- THEY MUST HAVE A PURPOSE --AND IT CAN'T BE ANYTHING GOOD!

HOW RIGHT YOU ARE, YOU YOUNG INTERLOPER!

ONE TOUCH OF THAT SUBSTANCE WILL PUT YOU IN A STATE OF PERPETUAL SUSPENDED ANIMATION!

GLAD YOU TOLD US! NOW WE WON'T TOUCH 'EM!

YOU THINK NOT? HAH! JUST WAIT AND SEE--!

14

NOTICE ANYTHING ABOUT THE WALLS ON EITHER SIDE OF YOU? NO, IT ISN'T YOUR IMAGINATION! THEY TRULY *ARE* COMING CLOSER TO YOU -- AND CLOSER -- AND *CLOSER!!*

RICK! HE'S *RIGHT!* IF THEY KEEP COMIN' CLOSER, THEY'LL -- THEY'LL *TOUCH* US!

SO THEY'LL *TOUCH* US! REMEMBER WHAT THE *AVENGERS* ALWAYS SAY! EVERYBODY'S GOTTA GO *SOME* TIME! IT'S HOW *BRAVELY* YOU DO IT THAT COUNTS!

IT LOOKS LIKE YOU'VE *GOT US,* NEFARIA -- BUT WE'RE NOT GONNA WHIMPER -- *NONE* OF US!

I'M JUST KINDA SORRY I WON'T BE HERE TO WATCH WHAT *YOU* DO WHEN THE *AVENGERS* CATCH UP WITH YA!

BUT *I* HAVE NO REASON TO FEAR THEM -- FOR I HAVE DONE *NOTHING!* SEE? I STOP THE MOVING WALLS NOW! THEY HAVE NOT TOUCHED YOU! YOU ARE COMPLETELY UNHARMED!

IT IS MY RULE *NEVER* TO DIRECTLY INJURE ANYONE! I AM TOO SMART FOR THAT!

IF ANYTHING HAPPENS TO YO NOW, IT WILL B YOUR *OWN* FAULT! FOR, YO ARE *PERFECTL* SAFE -- AND YO WILL *REMAIN* SAFE --

-- AS LONG AS YOU ARE ABLE TO STAND *WITHOUT MOVING!!*

HE'S *RIGHT!* IF WE MAKE TH SLIGHTEST MOVE, WE'LL TOUCH THAT SUBSTANCE! BUT -- HOW LONG CAN WE STAND *MOTIONLESS??!*

AS FOR THE *AVENGERS,* IF THEY *DO* RETURN HERE, THEY WILL FIND I HAVE ARRANGED AN UNEXPECTED WELCOME FOR *THEM,* ALSO!

I NEVER NOTICED THOSE STRANGE *DISCS* ON THE GROUND BEFORE! BUT, TIME ENOUGH FOR *THEM* LATER --!

BUT, THE THUNDER GOD IS *MISTAKEN!* NO SOONER DOES HIS FOOT TOUCH ONE OF TH DISCS, THAN A STRANGE MIST IS SUDDENLY RELEASED, AND...

I CANNOT *MOVE!* I AM COMPLETELY *PARALYZED!*

WHOOOOSH!

THOR'S IN TROUBLE! GOT TO HELP HIM! I'LL-- OHHH!

CAN'T *MOVE!* CAN'T EVEN SPEAK -- OR CRY OUT! THE MINUTE I *TOUCHED* HIM, THE SAME THING THAT HAPPENED TO *HIM* HAPPENED TO *ME!*

NO, WASP! DON'T! DON'T COME NEAR ME-- DON'T *TOUCH* ME! NO USE! CAN'T WARN HER!

WHAT IS IT?? HANK, WHAT *HAPPENED* TO YOU??

WE ARE UNDER THE POWER OF SOME POTENT CHEMICAL-- STRONG ENOUGH TO AFFECT MY MIGHTY BODY, WHICH NO MERE *PHYSICAL* FORCE CAN OVERCOME!

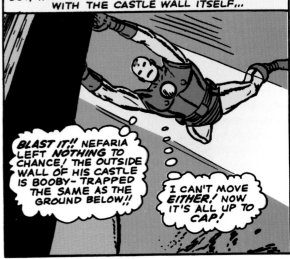

SEEING WHAT HAS HAPPENED TO HIS PARTNERS, THE QUICK-THINKING *IRON MAN* FLIES *OVER* THEM, HEADING FOR AN OPEN CASTLE WINDOW! BUT, THE INSTANT HIS ARMOR COMES IN CONTACT WITH THE CASTLE WALL ITSELF...

BLAST IT!! NEFARIA LEFT *NOTHING* TO CHANCE! THE OUTSIDE WALL OF HIS CASTLE IS BOOBY-TRAPPED THE SAME AS THE GROUND BELOW!!

I CAN'T MOVE *EITHER!* NOW IT'S ALL UP TO *CAP!*

THEY'RE LIKE INSECTS CAUGHT ON *FLY PAPER!* FIRST *THOR* WAS TRAPPED, THEN *GIANT-MAN* AND THE *WASP,* BY TOUCHING EACH OTHER!

BUT I'VE *GOT* TO MAKE IT! THERE'S SO MUCH AT *STAKE!*

ONLY *ONE* WAY TO GET IN WITHOUT TOUCHING A THING! I'LL TIE A THIN STRAND OF NYLON EMERGENCY CORD ONTO MY SHIELD, AND WHIRL IT LIKE A BOOMERANG--!

NOW-- EVERYTHING DEPENDS ON SWINGING IN THRU THAT WINDOW WITHOUT TOUCHING THE CASTLE WALL!!

HERE GOES--!

16

WITH THE DAZZLING SKILL OF A TRAINED ATHLETE -- AND THE UNSWERVING COURAGE OF A BORN AVENGER, THE RED-WHITE-AND-BLUE CRUSADER HURTLES THRU THE FATEFUL OPENING IN THE WALL OF THE SINISTER CASTLE!

MADE IT!!

THEN, FULLY ARMED AND READY FOR BATTLE ONCE MORE, *CAPTAIN AMERICA* SPRINGS INTO ACTION!

RUNNING FEET-- RACING DOWN THE HALL TOWARDS ME!!

IT'S CAPTAIN AMERICA!! GET 'IM!!

NOW TO PULL THE NYLON CORD BACK THRU THE WINDOW, TO RETRIEVE MY SHIELD!

I HAVE A FEELING I'LL BE NEEDING IT!

THE COSTUMED FOOL-- COMING HERE ALONE!

I'VE BEEN WAITIN' FOR A CHANCE TO TEAR INTO THAT OVER-RATED CLOWN!

LET'S SHOW 'IM HOW THE MAGGIA TREAT MASKED MEDDLERS!

THE MAGGIA, EH? NOW IT'S BEGINNING TO ADD UP!!

SORRY, BOYS! I'D LIKE TO STAY AND FINISH YOUR EDUCATION, BUT I'VE GOT OTHER MATTERS TO ATTEND TO FIRST!

YIIIIIIII!

UNGHHH!

WHAM!

OOOOOOF!

MORE OF THEM! COMING UP THAT LADDER!

NICE TRY, BOYS-- BUT NEXT TIME TAKE AN ELEVATOR!

EEEII

THUNK

NOOOOO!

LOOK-- IT'S **CAP**!! QUICK, CAP-- OVER **HERE**!
...T, BE CAREFUL!! DON'T TOUCH THOSE BARS!
...E--WE CAN'T **MOVE**--NOT EVEN A **MUSCLE**!!

...CK-- AND THE
...BRIGADIERS!!
...WHAT THE
...CKENS HAVE YOU
ALL GOTTEN
YOURSELVES
INTO??!

THIPPP!

IT'S OUR OWN **FAULT**--FOR DISOBEYING YOU!

COUNT NEFARIA **CAUGHT** US--AND TRAPPED US IN HERE!

W-WE CAN'T STAND SO **STILL** MUCH LONGER!!

HURRY, CAP! IF ONE OF US EVEN **SNEEZES**, WE'LL BE DONE FOR!

JUST ANOTHER FEW SECONDS, LAD! *UHNHHH!* I WISH I HAD **IRON MAN** HERE AT A TIME LIKE THIS!! *THERE--* I'M **GETTING** IT!!

WE **KNEW** THE AVENGERS WOULDN'T LET US DOWN! WE **KNEW** IT!

...HIS IS THE **ANTIDOTE** TO FREE THE OTHERS!
...EFARIA KEPT **TAUNTING** US WITH IT--HE KEPT IT JUST OUT OF OUR REACH!

YOU TAKE IT, RICK--YOU'LL KNOW WHAT TO **DO** WITH IT! NOW ALL OF US MUST **SEPARATE**, TO MAKE IT DIFFICULT FOR NEFARIA TO KEEP TRACK OF US THRU HIS SPY DEVICES! **MOVE!**

DON'T WORRY, CAP! WE WON'T LET YOU DOWN!

I'LL GO **THIS** WAY!

18

THERE'S A **DESTROYER** STEAMING UP THE HUDSON! JUST WHAT I **HOPED** FOR!

IF I CATCH THE SUN'S RAYS JUST RIGHT, THEY'RE **SURE** TO SEE MY SIGNALS!

THERE! I'VE DONE ALL I CAN! FROM NOW ON, THERE'S NOTHING TO DO BUT **HOPE!**

MEANWHILE, NEFARIA LOCATES CAP ON HIS COMPLEX SPY-MASTER MONITOR...

I'VE TRAPPED ALL THE **OTHERS!** HE IS THE WEAKEST! THIS SHOULD BE **EASY!**

I THOUGHT I **HEARD** SOMETHING--BEHIND ME--LIKE THE SOUND OF A PANEL SOFTLY SLIDING OPEN--

BUT, BEFORE THE GALLANT AVENGER CAN TURN AROUND...!

SOMETHING **TOUCHED** ME!! LIKE A RAY OF COLD LIGHT! IT'S CHILLING MY LIMBS! I-I CAN'T **MOVE!!**

WELL DONE! HE IS THE **LAST** OF THEM! TAKE HIM TO **DUNGEON G!**

YES, EXCELLENCY!

AND SO...

IT IS A PITY THE WORLD CAN NEVER KNOW HOW I HAVE COMPLETELY OUTSMARTED AND DEFEATED THE MIGHTY AVENGERS!

BUT NOW, I MUST SUMMON THE POLICE! I SHALL BE A **HERO** FOR CAPTURING YOU!

DON'T **BET** ON IT, YOU POMPOUS PIPSQUEAK!

BRAKK

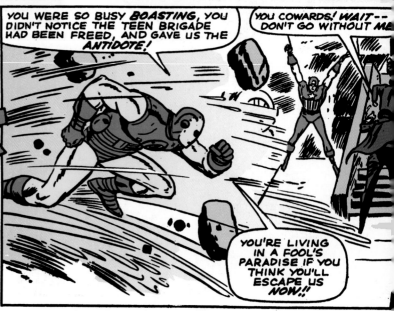

YOU WERE SO BUSY **BOASTING,** YOU DIDN'T NOTICE THE TEEN BRIGADE HAD BEEN FREED, AND GAVE US THE **ANTIDOTE!**

YOU COWARDS! WAIT-- DON'T GO WITHOUT ME!

YOU'RE LIVING IN A FOOL'S PARADISE IF YOU THINK YOU'LL ESCAPE US **NOW!!**

SCATTER! EVEN *IRON MAN* CAN'T CHASE US *ALL!*

IF WE CAN REACH OUR GUN CLOSET, WE'LL COME BACK AND POLISH HIM OFF!

THE ONLY POLISHING *YOU'LL* BE DOING IS IN THE PRISON WORKSHOP! I HOPE THIS WON'T MAKE YOU BOYS *AIRSICK!*

SOMETHING *GOT* US!! IT'S *LIFTING* US ALL OFF THE FLOOR!

I'M NOT AN *"IT"*, BOYS! I'M A *"HIM"*; THOSE IN THE KNOW CALL ME *GIANT-MAN!*

AHHH! THE COUNT IS TRYING TO FLEE!!

BUT THE HAMMER OF *THOR* SHALL CHANGE HIS PLANS!

PWAMM!

STAY BACK! DON'T *HURT* ME! I'VE HARMED NO ONE! ALL I DID WAS SEND ELECTRO-IMAGES OF YOU TO THE PENTAGON!

IT WAS A *JOKE!!* A PRANK! NOTHING MORE! S-STAY BACK!

IF YOU SPARE ME, I'LL GIVE YOU HALF OF MY *MAGGIA* EMPIRE! YOU'LL BE *RICH* BEYOND YOUR DREAMS!

HAVE YOU HEARD *ENOUGH,* GENERAL?

YES, CAPTAIN AMERICA! I BELIEVE I HAVE!

I SHOULD HAVE *KNOWN* THE AVENGERS COULD NEVER BE GUILTY OF TREASON! AND, AS FOR *YOU,* NEFARIA,...!

THERE'S NO PLACE FOR *YOU* HERE! YOU'LL BE *DEPORTED* AT ONCE!

NO! YOU CAN'T SEND ME BACK! THE MAGGIA *PUNISHES* FAILURE!! *NO!!*

THAT IS *YOUR* PROBLEM, EXCELLENCY-- NOT OURS!! TAKE HIM AWAY!

I WONDER WHERE THE *WASP* IS? I HAVEN'T SEEN HER SINCE--

RICK!! WHAT *IS* IT? WHA-WHAT *HAPPENED??* SPEAK UP, BOY-- *TELL ME!*

DURING THE FIGHTING --A STRAY BULLET HIT HER! JUST A ONE-IN-A-MILLION CHANCE! SHE-- SHE WAS TRYING TO PROTECT *US!* IT ALL HAPPENED SO FAST--!

NO!! SHE'S SO *STILL*-- SO *LIFE*-*LESS*--!!

AND SO, AS ONE ADVENTURE COMES TO AN END, *ANOTHER* BEGINS! AN ADVENTURE IN LIFE AND DEATH-- ONE WHICH IS DESTINED TO TAKE THE MIGHTY AVENGERS TO THE FARTHEST REACHES OF EARTH, AND BEYOND, IN SEARCH OF-- THE *UNKNOWN!*

20

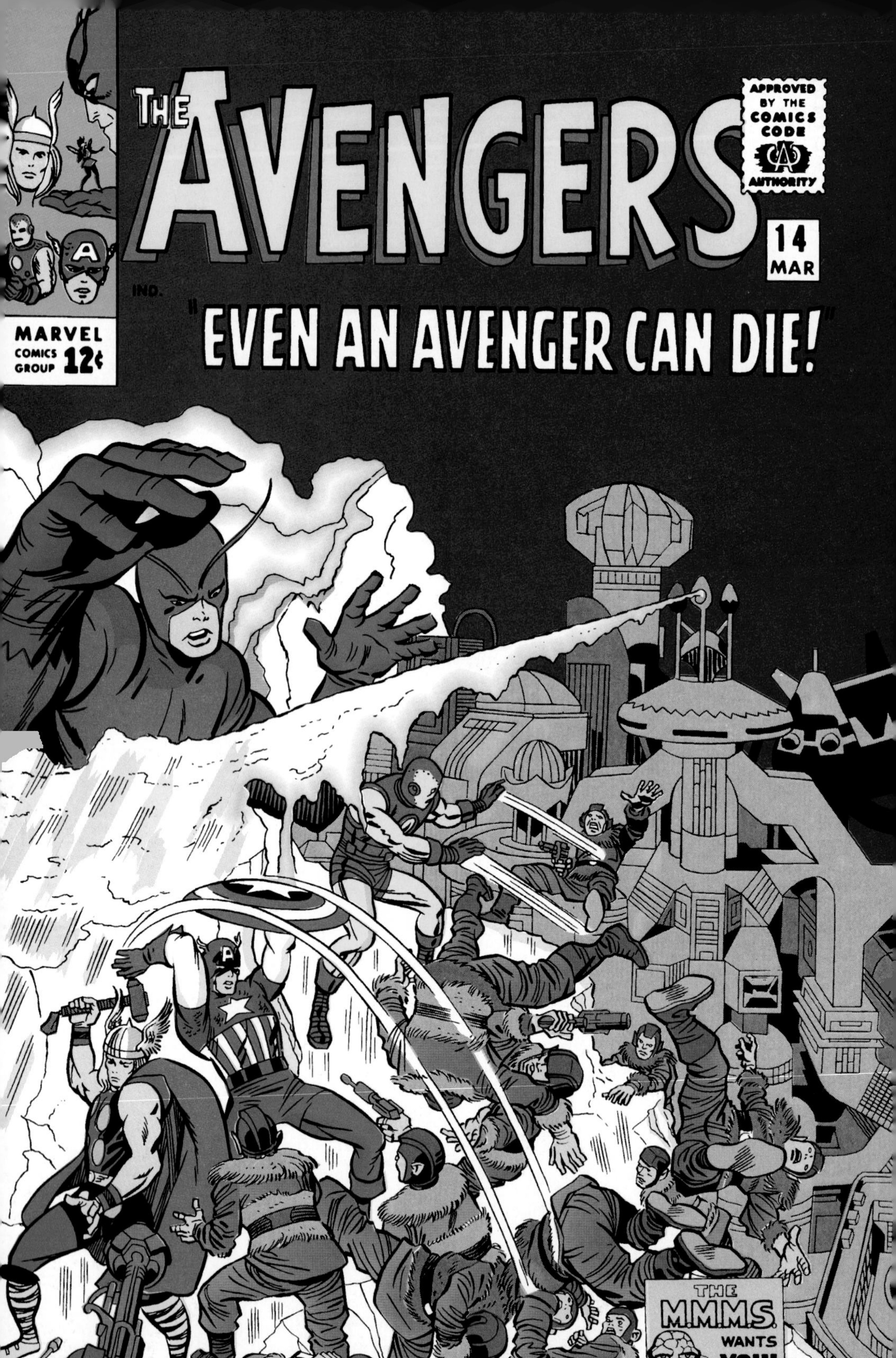
THE AVENGERS
APPROVED BY THE COMICS CODE AUTHORITY
14 MAR
IND.
MARVEL COMICS GROUP 12¢
"EVEN AN AVENGER CAN DIE!"
THE M.M.M.S. WANTS YOU!

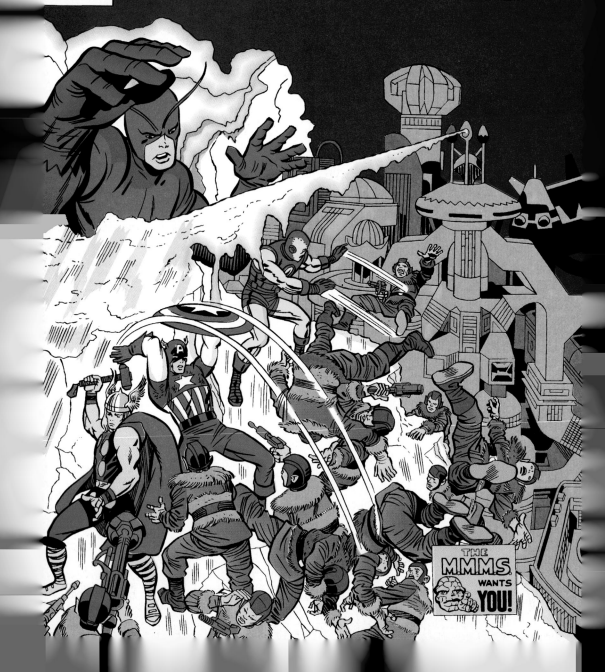

The MIGHTY AVENGERS

"EVEN AVENGERS CAN DIE!"

YES, EVEN TO THOSE WHO HAVE BECOME A *LEGEND* IN THEIR TIME, *DEATH* IS POSSIBLE! THE WASP NOW LIES CRITICALLY *WOUNDED!** DOES THIS MEAN THE *END* OF THE AVENGERS AS A GROUP? RACING ALONG THE CITY STREETS, OUR DESPERATE TEAM NOW FACES THE *GREATEST CRISIS* OF THEIR LIVES... ONE THAT WILL LEAD THEM ON A *LIFE AND DEATH MISSION* TO THE *FARTHEST CORNERS* OF THE GLOBE!

GIANT-MAN! GIVE HER TO ME! LET ME FLY WITH HER, AVENGER!

NO! NOBODY ELSE TOUCHES HER! FOLLOW ME, ALL OF YOU! I'LL GET HER TO THE HOSPITAL! I MUST!!

I KNOW HOW HE FEELS! HIS LOVE FOR HER IS SO GREAT THAT HE COULDN'T BEAR TO SEE ANYONE ELSE HOLD HER NOW BUT HIM!

WE'RE ALMOST THERE! I SEE THE HOSPITAL NOW!

PLOT AND EDITING BY:
STAN LEE
SCRIPT BY:
PAUL LAIKEN AND *LARRY LIEBER*
LAYOUTS BY:
JACK KIRBY
PENCILS BY:
DON HECK
INKING BY:
CHIC STONE
LETTERING BY:
S. ROSEN

NEVER IN COMICS MAGAZINE HISTORY HAS THERE BEEN A COLLABORATION TO EQUAL THIS ONE! ONLY THE MIGHTY MARVEL BULLPEN WOULD DARE ATTEMPT IT! AND NOW, FOR BETTER OR WORSE, HERE ARE THE NAMES OF THE TALENTED TEAM WHO PRODUCED THIS EPIC ---

*AS SEEN IN *AVENGERS #13*.. STAN.

MOMENTS LATER, THE FRANTIC AVENGERS BURST THROUGH A HOSPITAL CORRIDOR... THEIR PRECIOUS CARGO HANGING LIMP IN A *STRANGE LIFELESS TRANCE*...

CLEAR THE HALL!! EMERGENCY PATIENT COMING THROUGH! WHERE'S THE DOCTOR IN CHARGE??

THIS IS ONE TIME DR. BLAKE CANNOT HELP! HER INJURY REQUIRES A SURGEON OF FAR GREATER SKILL!

WE'VE GOT TO BE IN TIME! WE'VE JUST GOT TO!

QUICKLY, NURSE! WHERE CAN WE TAKE OUR WOUNDED FELLOW AVENGER?

CAPTAIN AMERICA! OH, SOMETHING TERRIBLE MUST HAVE HAPPENED! ...THE EMERGENCY ROOM IS AT THE END OF THE CORRIDOR!

INSIDE THE EMERGENCY ROOM, A GRIM-FACED PHYSICIAN EXAMINES THE MOTIONLESS PATIENT ON THE TABLE...

ALL MY STRENGTH... ALL MY POWER... USELESS TO ME NOW!! ONLY A STRANGER'S SKILL CAN SAVE THE ONE I LOVE!

SHE APPEARS TO HAVE DIFFICULTY BREATHING! ...I SUSPECT HER LUNG HAS BEEN INJURED!

WILL SHE MAKE IT, DOC? CAN YOU PULL HER THROUGH?!

THE BULLET HAS PUNCTURED HER LEFT LUNG! ...YOUR SUSPICION WAS QUITE CORRECT! TELL ME, HAVE YOU EVER HAD MEDICAL TRAINING??

NO TIME FOR THAT NOW! WE HAVE TO KNOW... WHAT CAN BE DONE TO SAVE THE GIRL??

I ALMOST GAVE MY MORTAL IDENTITY AWAY! I MUST BE MORE CAREFUL IN THE FUTURE!

WE CANNOT BE CERTAIN UNTIL WE TAKE X-RAYS! THE PICTURES WILL TELL US TO WHAT EXTENT THE LUNG HAS BEEN DAMAGED!

THEN WE STILL CAN'T KNOW... WE STILL MUST WAIT... UNABLE TO AID HER! ALL OF US... HELP-LESS!

WHY DON'T YOU ALL RETIRE TO THE WAITING ROOM? IT WILL BE A HALF HOUR BEFORE WE KNOW!

THERE'S NOTHING LEFT FOR US NOW, EXCEPT PRAYER!

AS THE DESPONDENT GROUP BEGINS THE LONG VIGIL IN THE WAITING ROOM, EACH PASSING SECOND SEEMS LIKE AN ETERNITY... AND THE STRAIN IS GREATEST ON THE ONE WHOSE LOVE LIES HOVERING BETWEEN LIFE AND DEATH!

EASY, BIG FELLOW! THEY'RE DOING ALL THEY CAN!

REMEMBER, MEDICAL SCIENCE CAN PERFORM MIRACLES TODAY!

I KNOW... I KNOW! BUT THIS WAITING IS TOO MUCH FOR ME! I'VE NEVER FELT SO HELPLESS BEFORE!

THEY'LL DO THEIR BEST FOR HER... JUST SIT TIGHT!

2

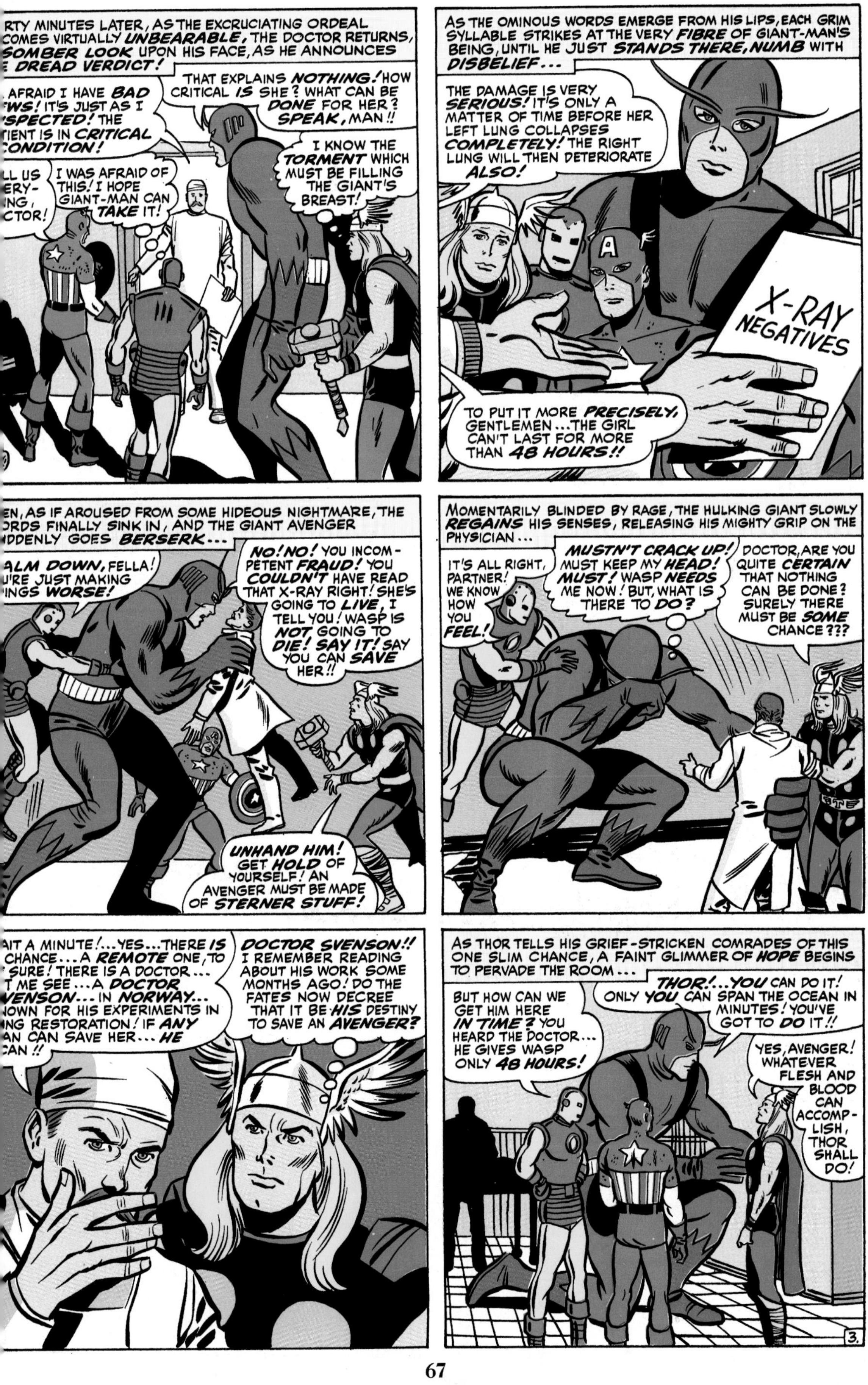

RTY MINUTES LATER, AS THE EXCRUCIATING ORDEAL COMES VIRTUALLY UNBEARABLE, THE DOCTOR RETURNS, SOMBER LOOK UPON HIS FACE, AS HE ANNOUNCES DREAD VERDICT!
AFRAID I HAVE BAD WS! IT'S JUST AS I SPECTED! THE TIENT IS IN CRITICAL CONDITION!
THAT EXPLAINS NOTHING! HOW CRITICAL IS SHE? WHAT CAN BE DONE FOR HER? SPEAK, MAN!!
LL US ERY- ING, CTOR!
I WAS AFRAID OF THIS! I HOPE GIANT-MAN CAN TAKE IT!
I KNOW THE TORMENT WHICH MUST BE FILLING THE GIANT'S BREAST!
AS THE OMINOUS WORDS EMERGE FROM HIS LIPS, EACH GRIM SYLLABLE STRIKES AT THE VERY FIBRE OF GIANT-MAN'S BEING, UNTIL HE JUST STANDS THERE, NUMB WITH DISBELIEF...
THE DAMAGE IS VERY SERIOUS! IT'S ONLY A MATTER OF TIME BEFORE HER LEFT LUNG COLLAPSES COMPLETELY! THE RIGHT LUNG WILL THEN DETERIORATE ALSO!
X-RAY NEGATIVES
TO PUT IT MORE PRECISELY, GENTLEMEN... THE GIRL CAN'T LAST FOR MORE THAN 48 HOURS!!
EN, AS IF AROUSED FROM SOME HIDEOUS NIGHTMARE, THE ORDS FINALLY SINK IN, AND THE GIANT AVENGER DDENLY GOES BERSERK...
ALM DOWN, FELLA! U'RE JUST MAKING INGS WORSE!
NO! NO! YOU INCOMPETENT FRAUD! YOU COULDN'T HAVE READ THAT X-RAY RIGHT! SHE'S GOING TO LIVE, I TELL YOU! WASP IS NOT GOING TO DIE! SAY IT! SAY YOU CAN SAVE HER!!
UNHAND HIM! GET HOLD OF YOURSELF! AN AVENGER MUST BE MADE OF STERNER STUFF!
MOMENTARILY BLINDED BY RAGE, THE HULKING GIANT SLOWLY REGAINS HIS SENSES, RELEASING HIS MIGHTY GRIP ON THE PHYSICIAN...
IT'S ALL RIGHT, PARTNER! WE KNOW HOW YOU FEEL!
MUSTN'T CRACK UP! MUST KEEP MY HEAD! MUST! WASP NEEDS ME NOW! BUT, WHAT IS THERE TO DO?
DOCTOR, ARE YOU QUITE CERTAIN THAT NOTHING CAN BE DONE? SURELY THERE MUST BE SOME CHANCE???
AIT A MINUTE!... YES... THERE IS CHANCE... A REMOTE ONE, TO SURE! THERE IS A DOCTOR... T ME SEE... A DOCTOR VENSON... IN NORWAY... NOWN FOR HIS EXPERIMENTS IN NG RESTORATION! IF ANY AN CAN SAVE HER... HE CAN!!
DOCTOR SVENSON!! I REMEMBER READING ABOUT HIS WORK SOME MONTHS AGO! DO THE FATES NOW DECREE THAT IT BE HIS DESTINY TO SAVE AN AVENGER?
AS THOR TELLS HIS GRIEF-STRICKEN COMRADES OF THIS ONE SLIM CHANCE, A FAINT GLIMMER OF HOPE BEGINS TO PERVADE THE ROOM...
BUT HOW CAN WE GET HIM HERE IN TIME? YOU HEARD THE DOCTOR... HE GIVES WASP ONLY 48 HOURS!
THOR!... YOU CAN DO IT! ONLY YOU CAN SPAN THE OCEAN IN MINUTES! YOU'VE GOT TO DO IT!!
YES, AVENGER! WHATEVER FLESH AND BLOOD CAN ACCOMPLISH, THOR SHALL DO!
3.

THUS, SHORTLY AFTERWARDS, A FAMILIAR COSTUMED FIGURE IS SEEN HURTLING OUT INTO SPACE...UNFLINCHING DETERMINATION ETCHED ON EVERY LINE OF HIS NOBLE FEATURES!

I SHALL NOT FAIL MY FELLOW AVENGERS! SOME-HOW...SOME WAY...I WILL *DO* IT! YET, EVEN AFTER I *FIND* DOCTOR SVENSON, HOW CAN I BE CERTAIN HE WILL *SAVE* THE WASP??

YOU'RE *IMAGINING* THINGS, HENRY! NOW GET AWAY FROM THAT *WINDOW!*

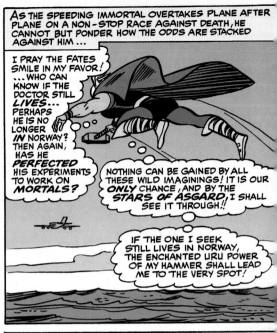

AS THE SPEEDING IMMORTAL OVERTAKES PLANE AFTER PLANE ON A NON-STOP RACE AGAINST DEATH, HE CANNOT BUT PONDER HOW THE ODDS ARE STACKED AGAINST HIM...

I PRAY THE FATES SMILE IN MY FAVOR! ...WHO CAN KNOW IF THE DOCTOR STILL *LIVES*... PERHAPS HE IS NO LONGER *IN* NORWAY? THEN AGAIN, HAS HE *PERFECTED* HIS EXPERIMENTS TO WORK ON *MORTALS?*

NOTHING CAN BE GAINED BY ALL THESE WILD IMAGININGS! IT IS OUR *ONLY* CHANCE, AND BY THE *STARS OF ASGARD*, I SHALL SEE IT THROUGH!!

IF THE ONE I SEEK STILL LIVES IN NORWAY, THE ENCHANTED URU POWER OF MY HAMMER SHALL LEAD ME TO THE VERY SPOT!

FINALLY, IN A MAJESTIC SWEEP FROM THE SKY, THOR LANDS UPON AN OBSCURE NORSE ROOFTOP...AND FOLLOWS THE SUBTLE, TINGLING PULL OF HIS MIGHTY MALLET, UNTIL...

THAT MUST BE THE ONE I SEEK! BUT, WHY DOES MY HAMMER *STILL* TINGLE? I MUST SUMMON HIM QUICKLY!

DOCTOR SVENSON!

GO AWAY, WHOEVER YOU ARE! CAN'T YOU SEE I'M IN THE MIDDLE OF AN *INTRICATE EXPERIMENT?* YOU ALMOST MADE ME SPILL THIS *FORMULA!*

THERE IS NO MASQUERADE PARTY IN THIS HOUSE! *OUT!*...OUT THIS *INSTANT,* DO YOU *HEAR?* WHATEVER YOU WANT, I CANNOT *HELP* YOU! LEAVE, OR I'LL HAVE YOU *THROWN OUT!*

YOU DO NOT *UNDERSTAND,* IMPATIENT ONE! I COME TO SEEK YOUR *PROFESSIONAL* HELP! IN AMERICA, A YOUNG FEMALE LIES DYING OF LUNG DAMAGE...YOU PERFORM OPERATIONS OF THIS NATURE... ONLY YOU CAN MAKE HER WELL AGAIN! YOU *MUST,* COME!

THEN, WITHOUT GIVING THE BEARDED SURGEON A CHANCE TO REPLY, ONE OF THE MOST POWERFUL ARMS IN THE UNIVERSE SEIZES HIM AS THOUGH HE'S WEIGHTLESS, AND...

THERE IS NO TIME FOR *DISCOURSE,* OBSTINATE ONE! LET US CONTINUE THE MATTER *EN ROUTE!* RIGHT NOW YOU ARE FLYING WITH *THOR!*

WHA-AT?? WHAT NONSENSE IS *THIS?* PUT ME *DOWN,* YOU LUNATIC!

YOU DON'T KNOW WHAT YOU'RE *DOING!* I'M NOT THE MAN YOU *THINK!* YOU'RE MAKING A MISTAKE!

RETRACING HIS BREATH-TAKING FLIGHT BACK TO AMERICA, THOR RETURNS TO HIS HIS DESTINATION IN LESS THAN ONE HOUR!

DOCTOR SVENSON! BUT *HOW?*..SO *QUICKLY?*

NEVER MIND THAT!...HERE IS YOUR *PATIENT,* DOCTOR!

NO! NO! I CAN'T HELP HER! I *CAN'T!*

THOR, I'LL NEVER *FORGET* YOU FOR THIS...*NEVER!* IT LOOKS LIKE THE BREAK WE'VE BEEN *WAITING FOR!*

BUT, WHY DOES SVENSON REFUSE?

4.

AS THE NORSE DOCTOR REFUSES TO EVEN *EXAMINE* THE PATIENT, GIANT-MAN CAN CONTROL HIMSELF NO LONGER... AND, IN ANOTHER FIT OF UNRESTRAINED FURY, *ATTACKS HIM...*

YOU *WILL* DO IT! I'LL MAKE YOU SURE *HER!*

WHA-A---?? WHAT'S *THIS*? HIS *FACE* CAME OFF IN MY *HANDS!* IT'S A *PLASTIC MASK!!*

I TOLD YOU TO LEAVE ME ALONE, YOU *FOOLS!* I'M NOT THE *REAL* DOCTOR! I'M NOT EVEN FROM YOUR *PLANET!* I'M FROM *ANOTHER GALAXY!!*

IT'S IN-CREDIBLE! I JUST CAN'T *BELIEVE* IT!

THE *REAL* DOCTOR IS BEING HELD BY MY PEOPLE, HIDDEN HERE ON *EARTH!*

ARG-GH! MY *THROAT!* I CAN'T *BREATHE!* I'M... I'M *DYING!!*

NO! YOU *CAN'T!* NOT BEFORE YOU TELL US WHERE YOUR PEOPLE ARE! THOR *COMMANDS* YOU!!

BUT, BEFORE THE FANTASTIC IMPOSTOR CAN FINISH HIS STORY...

TOO *LATE!* HE IS *DEAD!* NEVER BEFORE HAVE I WITNESSED SO *STRANGE* AN EVENT!

MY URU HAMMER *TOLD* ME SOMETHING WAS *AMISS!* BUT I DID NOT *HEED* IT!

YOU BRING BACK A *SURGEON* WHO TURNS OUT TO BE AN *ALIEN*... THEN SUDDENLY *DIES* FOR NO APPARENT REASON! WHAT DOES IT ALL ADD UP TO?

DON'T TAKE IT SO *HARD,* BIG FELLOW! WE'LL *STILL* SEARCH FOR THE *REAL* DOCTOR SVENSON! THE AVENGERS AREN'T *BEATEN* YET!

IT *DOES* LOOK BAD! ...BUT HOW CAN I BRING MYSELF TO *TELL* HIM?

OUR LAST HOPE... *GONE!* NOTHING MORE WE CAN DO! SOMEHOW I FEEL IT WAS *MY* FAULT... *WHY* DID I HAVE TO TAKE WASP WITH ME ON THAT LAST ASSIGNMENT? ...WHY COULDN'T THAT BULLET HAVE HIT *ME* INSTEAD OF HER?

BUT, HIS ANGUISH SPENT, THE GIANT FIGURE AGAIN COMPOSES HIMSELF AS HIS FELLOW AVENGERS STAND BY, UNDERSTANDINGLY, AND THEN...

WE'VE GOT TO USE *EVERY POWER* AT OUR *COMMAND* TO FIND THOSE *ALIENS!* IF THEY'RE ANYWHERE ON *EARTH* WE'LL *TRACK THEM DOWN!*

YOU'RE *RIGHT!* THERE'S NOTHING ELSE WE *CAN* DO! IT'S A *LONG SHOT,* BUT WE'VE GOT TO TAKE IT!

A WHOLE PLANET TO SEARCH AND ONLY SCANT HOURS REMAINING TO FIND SOME HIDDEN ALIENS! BUT FIND THEM WE *MUST!*

THE DECISION UNANIMOUSLY AGREED UPON, THE MIGHTY AVENGERS PREPARE TO EMBARK ON THE MOST INTENSIVE SEARCH EVER CONDUCTED...

LET US MEET AGAIN IN *EIGHT HOURS* TO EXCHANGE OUR INFORMATION!

IT PRETTY *CLOSE!* BUT WE'VE NO OTHER CHOICE! GOOD LUCK TO US ALL!

THAT'S CUTTING

IT'S A *RACE AGAINST TIME!* BUT WE'LL *MAKE IT!!*

WE'VE *GOT* TO FIND THEM! ...NOTHING ELSE *MATTERS!!*

5.

AND SO, IN A DESPERATE RACE AGAINST TIME...

GIANT-MAN'S SIZE AND STRENGTH CAN'T HELP JAN NOW!

I ONLY PRAY THAT HANK PYM'S SCIENTIFIC SKILL CAN SAVE HER!

SOON, IN THE SECRET NERVE CENTER OF AN INCREDIBLE COMMUNICATIONS NETWORK...

MY MASTER HELMET IS HOOKED IN TO ANT-HILLS THROUGH-OUT EVERY CONTINENT ON EARTH!

AT THIS MOMENT, BILLIONS OF ANTS ARE OBEYING MY COMMAND TO LOCATE ANY NON-HUMANS IN THEIR VICINITY!

THE INSECTS ARE ALL SENDING BACK NEGATIVE IMPULSES! NONE OF MY TINY SCOUTS HAS STRUCK PAY DIRT!

THE ALIENS MUST BE IN AN AREA UNINHABITED BY ANTS! BUT, WHERE IS THERE SUCH A PLACE ON THIS PLANET OF OURS?

AND, AT THAT INSTANT, ATOP A NEARBY MOUNTAIN...

ANY STRANGE SIGNALS YET?

NOT ONE THAT'S OUT OF THE ORDINARY, CAP! LOOKS LIKE WE SET UP OUR GIANT ANTENNA FOR NOTHING!

YEAH, ALL OUR TEEN BRIGADE'S GOT TO SHOW FOR ITS WORK ARE BLISTERS!

MORE THAN BLISTERS! OUR AERIAL IS INTER-CEPTING SIGNALS FROM ALL THE CIVILIZED CORNERS OF EARTH! NOW, AT ANY RATE, WE KNOW WHERE THE ALIENS AREN'T HIDING!

C'MON, RICK... TIME FOR US TO JOIN THE OTHER AVENGERS!

MEANWHILE, IRON MAN HAS DOFFED HIS ARMOR AND BROUGHT HIS OWN SCIENTIFIC GENIUS INTO PLAY...

THE WASP'S LIFE MAY WELL DEPEND ON THE PERFORMANCE OF MY NEW GEIGER-COUNTER MISSILE!

THERE IT GOES!

THE INSTRUMENT IS SCANNING EVERY INHABITED AREA OF EARTH! IF IT ENCOUNTERS ANY ALIEN RADIOACTIVITY, IT WILL INSTANTLY RECORD IT!

BUT, ONE COMPLETE EARTH ROTATION LATER...

IT RETURNED WITHOUT DETECTING A THING! THAT MEANS OUR QUARRY MUST BE HOLED UP IN SOME REMOTE, UNINHABITED SECTION OF EARTH... BUT WHERE?

6.

THEN, AS PRECIOUS MINUTES DWINDLE AWAY FOR THE CRITICALLY ILL *WASP*, HER DESPERATE PARTNERS ASSEMBLE AGAIN OUTSIDE HER DOOR!

ANY LUCK, THOR?

ILL FORTUNE BESETS US, FOR EVEN IN *ASGARD*, I COULD LEARN *NOTHING* ABOUT THE INTRUDERS FROM OUTER SPACE!

THEN THERE GOES OUR *LAST* HOPE!

PERHAPS WE ALREADY KNOW *ENOUGH!*

WE'VE LEARNED, BY THE PROCESS OF ELIMINATION, THAT THOSE WE'RE AFTER ARE HIDING IN A *FAR DISTANT, UNINHABITED* REGION OF EARTH! AN AREA WHERE NOT EVEN ANTS ARE FOUND!

THAT SUGGESTS BUT TWO LOCALES... THE *NORTH* OR *SOUTH POLES!*

OF COURSE! THEY'RE TOO *COLD* AND *BARREN* FOR ANTS! BUT WE'RE RUNNING OUT OF TIME! WE'VE GOT TO *FIND* THEM IN THE NEXT FEW HOURS!

NONE CAN MOVE AS QUICKLY AS *THE AVENGERS!* NONE HAVE THE POWER, THE VAST RESOURCES AT THEIR COMMAND, WHICH THE MIGHTY *AVENGERS* POSSESS! AND SO, MINUTES LATER...

HOW QUIET *GIANT-MAN* IS! HE STARES AHEAD WITH UNSEEING EYES!

POOR GUY! HE'S STILL IN A STATE OF NEAR-SHOCK!

IF THE *WASP* SHOULD DIE, HE'D... BUT LET'S NOT EVEN *THINK* OF IT!

FINALLY, REACHING A PREDETERMINED HEIGHT IN SPACE, EXACTLY BETWEEN THE TWO POLES, THOR'S ENCHANTED HAMMER TELLS WHAT THEY NEED TO KNOW...

MY URU HAMMER-HEAD IS POINTING TO THE *NORTH!* IT IS *THERE* WE WILL FIND WHAT WE SEEK!

STRAP YOURSELVES IN! I'M HEADING NORTH AT *FULL VELOCITY!*

EXACTLY TWENTY-THREE MINUTES LATER...

THERE IS NO SIGN OF LIFE! BUT, MY ENCHANTED HAMMER NEVER ERRS! PERHAPS THEY ARE HIDDEN BENEATH OUR FEET!

IT'S THE ONLY ANSWER! WE'LL HAVE TO DIG, WITH EVERY MEANS AT OUR COMMAND--BEFORE THE *COLD* STOPS US!

I'LL DIG TO CHINA WITH MY BARE HANDS IF IT MEANS SAVING THE *WASP!*

STAND BACK! I CAN DO THE JOB FASTER WITH MY *TRANSISTORS* THAN *ALL* OF YOU COMBINED!

7.

NO! NO! YOU'RE MELTING THE ICE TOO FAST! IRON-MAN! STOP! THE GROUND IS GIVING WAY! UHH! TOO LATE!!

WE WERE OVER A DEEP PIT! WE'VE BROKEN THROUGH!

GIANT-MAN! GROW TO YOUR LARGEST SIZE AND WEDGE YOURSELF AGAINST THE WALLS! IRON-MAN! USE YOUR JETS AND CATCH CAPTAIN AMERICA AS HE FALLS PAST! I SHALL BREAK MY OWN FALL BY EMPLOYING THE POWER OF MY HAMMER!

MOVING LIKE THE WELL-TRAINED TEAM THEY ARE, THE MIGHTY QUARTET BREAK THEIR FALL WITHIN SECONDS!

THANKS TO MY LARGE SIZE, I WON'T BE MORE THAN A LITTLE SHAKEN UP! ARE THE REST OF YOU ALL RIGHT!?

SURE THING, AVENGER! HANG ON, CAP, FOR A SAFE, TRANSISTOR-POWERED DESCENT!

THEN, FINALLY...

WELL, WE'RE STILL ALIVE, EVEN IF WE DON'T KNOW WHERE! BUT THIS REFRIGERATED TRAP WILL SOON BECOME OUR ICY TOMB, UNLESS WE TAKE SOME OF TONY STARK'S ANTI-FREEZE PILLS!

YOUR FRIEND, STARK, THINKS OF EVERYTHING! I SOMETIMES WONDER WHY HE IS NOT AN AVENGER, TOO!

HE IS, PARTNER... IF YOU ONLY KNEW!

SWALLOW THEM QUICKLY! EVERY SECOND COUNTS! WE CAN'T LET THE WASP DIE... NOT NOW... NOT WHEN WE MAY BE SO CLOSE!

BUT SUDDENLY, A SECTION OF GLACIAL WALL SLIDES OPEN...

BEHOLD! EARTH-MEN!

THEY HAVE DISCOVERED US! IF THEY ESCAPE, THEY WILL ALERT OTHERS!

FEAR NOT! OUR ICE-GUNS WILL STOP THEM!

ICE... FORMING ALL AROUND ME!

DON'T WORRY, BIG FELLA! WE WON'T LET THEM STOP US! WE CAN'T!

FIGHT, AVENGERS!! TO THE DEATH!

I SCORED A DIRECT HIT!

8.

FOR A MOMENT, *GIANT-MAN* SEEMS DEFEATED! BUT, THE FURY IN HIS BREAST...THE ACHE IN HIS HEART...THE FEAR FOR HIS BELOVED, ARE TOO GREAT TO BE OVERCOME!

DID YOU THINK MERE ICE COULD STOP AN *AVENGER* WHOSE LOVED ONE LIES IN MORTAL DANGER?!

THE *WASP* MUST BE *SAVED!* NOTHING ELSE MATTERS! *NOTHING!*

ROUTING HIS CAPTORS, *GIANT-MAN* QUICKLY JOINS HIS COMRADES-IN-ARMS...

THE PATROL CAME OUT OF THIS TUNNEL!

HURRY...IT MAY LEAD TO THE MAIN ALIEN FORCE, WHERE I PRAY WE'LL FIND DR. SVENSON, THE ONE MAN ON EARTH WHO CAN RESTORE THE *WASP* TO HEALTH!

FEAR NOT, MY FRIEND! IF HE'S THERE, WE'LL *FIND* HIM! THOR *VOWS* IT!

BUT, EVEN THE MIGHTY *AVENGERS* ARE STARTLED BY THE SENSES-SHATTERING SIGHT THEY ENCOUNTER!

SUBTERRANEAN *BUILDINGS!* THEY COMPRISE AN *ENTIRE CITY!*

BY ASGARD! WHAT INCREDIBLE CIVILIZATION HAVE WE STUMBLED UPON??

IT'S SO *HUGE!* SO *COMPLEX!* HOW WILL WE EVER *LOCATE* DR. SVENSON??

THEN, BEFORE THAT FATEFUL QUESTION CAN BE ANSWERED, THE FOUR ADVENTURERS ARE SHOWERED IN A BURST OF UNEARTHLY ENERGY!

A STRANGE, SHIMMERING LIGHT! I CAN'T RESIST IT!

THE *BLINDING* RAYS ARE PERVADING MY ENTIRE BODY!

IT IS *DONE*, SIRE! I HAVE *FROZEN* THE VERY MOLECULES OF THE INTRUDERS...CAUSING *TOTAL PARALYSIS!!*

EXCELLENT! TAKE THE PRISONERS TO OUR SOVEREIGN, *AT ONCE!*

9.

AND, WHILE THE FRAIL LIFE OF A STRICKEN GIRL HANGS PRECARIOUSLY IN THE BALANCE, THOSE WHO WOULD SAVE HER FIND THEMSELVES REDUCED TO UTTER HELPLESSNESS...

WE RENDERED THE EARTHMEN IMMOBILE! BUT THEIR *HEARING* IS UNIMPAIRED, AS OGOR ORDERED!

SO! LISTEN WELL, EARTHLINGS! I, OGOR, AM RULER OF THE *KALLUSIANS!* FOR AGES, WE DWELT PEACEFULLY IN A FAR DISTANT GALAXY!

BUT THEN, IN THE EVER-CHANGING COURSE OF COSMIC EVENTS, AN *INTER-PLANETARY WAR* BROKE OUT!

"PLANETS BATTLED PLANETS! ALIEN ARMIES FOUGHT ON A SCALE BEYOND YOUR COMPREHENSION! FOR CENTURIES, OUR VERY HEAVENS SHOOK WITH THE NIGHTMARE OF UNENDING CONFLICT..."

"FINALLY, BATTLE-WEARY AND OUTNUMBERED, WE KALUSIANS FLED FROM THE GALAXY WITH OUR FOE IN PURSUIT! AFTER MONTHS OF DESPERATE SEARCHING, WE AT LAST FOUND A WORLD WHERE WE COULD HIDE TO REPAIR OUR WEAPONS AND REGROUP OUR FORCES!"

OF ALL THE PLANETS IN THIS SOLAR SYSTEM, ONLY YONDER ONE SUSTAINS ANIMAL AND VEGETABLE LIFE!

IT IS THE FIRST HABITABLE WORLD WE HAVE FOUND! PREPARE TO *LAND!!*

10.

"ONCE ON EARTH, HOWEVER, WE DISCOVERED WE COULD NOT *SURVIVE* IN YOUR ATMOSPHERE... AND OUR OWN TYPE OF OXYGEN WAS NOT ENOUGH TO SUSTAIN US INDEFINITELY! THE SUPPLY WAS SLOWLY *DWINDLING!* IT APPEARED WE WERE DESTINED TO *PERISH!*"

MASTER! I CANNOT *BREATHE!* I BEG OF YOU... MORE *OXYGEN!*

ALAS, OUR SUPPLY IS *RATIONED!* WE CANNOT GIVE HIM ANOTHER MAN'S SHARE! WE ARE ALL *DOOMED!*

WE WILL NEVER SURVIVE LONG ENOUGH TO REGROUP OUR FORCES AND RETURN TO *KALLU!*

"WHEN ALL LOOKED *HOPELESS*, A STROKE OF GOOD FORTUNE CAME UPON US! YOUR *DOCTOR SVENSON* WAS ON AN EXPEDITION IN THIS AREA AND ACCIDENTALLY STUMBLED INTO OUR MIDST..."

THE EARTH MAN CLAIMS TO BE A *SCIENTIST!* PERHAPS HE CAN *HELP* US!

I AM DOING RESEARCH ON RESPIRATION IN ARCTIC REGIONS! BUT *WHO ARE YOU?*

FATE HAS SENT YOU TO US! WE MUST INFORM *THE MASTER* OF THIS!

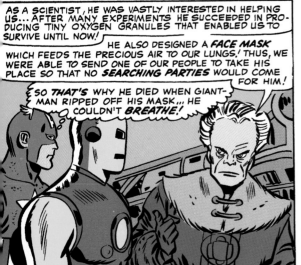

AS A SCIENTIST, HE WAS VASTLY INTERESTED IN HELPING US... AFTER MANY EXPERIMENTS HE SUCCEEDED IN PRODUCING TINY OXYGEN GRANULES THAT ENABLED US TO SURVIVE UNTIL NOW!

HE ALSO DESIGNED A *FACE MASK* WHICH FEEDS THE PRECIOUS AIR TO OUR LUNGS! THUS, WE WERE ABLE TO SEND ONE OF OUR PEOPLE TO TAKE HIS PLACE SO THAT NO *SEARCHING PARTIES* WOULD COME FOR HIM!

SO *THAT'S* WHY HE DIED WHEN GIANT-MAN RIPPED OFF HIS MASK... HE COULDN'T *BREATHE!*

WE MASTERED YOUR LANGUAGE OVER THE MANY YEARS BY PICKING UP YOUR RADIO AND TELEVISION SIGNALS WITH OUR *STELLAR-TRANSMITTOR!* YOU SEE, WE KNOW *EVERYTHING* ABOUT YOU! BUT ENOUGH *TALK!*... YOU WILL LEAVE HERE WHEN *WE* SAY! BUT *NOT* WITH DOCTOR SVENSON!

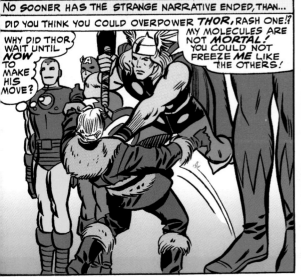

NO SOONER HAS THE STRANGE NARRATIVE ENDED, THAN...

DID YOU THINK YOU COULD OVERPOWER *THOR,* RASH ONE!? MY MOLECULES ARE NOT *MORTAL!* YOU COULD NOT FREEZE *ME* LIKE THE OTHERS!

WHY DID THOR WAIT UNTIL *NOW* TO MAKE HIS MOVE?

I ONLY *PRETENDED* TO BE FROZEN, HOPING HE WOULD REVEAL TO ME WHERE DOCTOR SVENSON IS BEING HELD! SINCE HE DID *NOT,* I MUST RESORT TO MORE AGGRESSIVE MEANS!

ORDER YOUR PEOPLE TO RELEASE MY FELLOW AVENGERS... OR FACE THE FULL WRATH OF THOR!

I MUST NEVER BE TOUCHED BY EARTHLY HANDS! WE SHALL DO AS HE SAYS... THEN DEAL WITH THE INSOLENT ONE *LATER!*

YOU SPEAK *WISELY,* MASTER!...HE DOES POSSESS A MOST AWESOME POWER!

THE KALLU CHIEFTAIN GIVES HIS SIGNAL, AND A BLINDING RAY OF LIGHT BURSTS FORTH...FREEING THE AVENGERS FROM THEIR PRISON OF ICE...

PHIZZZZT!

ZAWISST!

IT IS *DONE!* *NOW,* WILL YOU RELEASE YOUR GRASP ON ME, EARTH MAN?

NO!...I AM NOT FINISHED WITH YOU *YET!* TELL US WHERE YOU ARE HIDING DOCTOR SVENSON! WE MUST TAKE HIM BACK *AT ONCE!*

PHIZZZZT!

BUT, EVEN A THUNDER GOD CANNOT HAVE EYES IN THE BACK OF HIS HEAD...

THERE! NOW *I* HAVE THE MAGIC WEAPON! WITHOUT IT, YOU ARE *POWER-LESS!*

YOU MAY *TOUCH* THE ENCHANTED HAMMER, BUT NONE CAN LIFT IT, SAVE *THOR!*

SEIZE HIM!! WE CAN *NEVER* GIVE UP OUR *EARTH DOCTOR! DESTROY* THE INTRUDERS!!

ATTACK!!...IF WE LOSE THE CAPTIVE EARTHLING, WE SHALL SURELY PERISH!

THEY MUST NOT LEAVE HERE *ALIVE!* OUR PRESENCE MUST BE KEPT SECRET!

AND SO, THE INEVITABLE BATTLE BEGINS...

A THOUSAND OF *THEM* AGAINST FOUR OF *US!* YET, WE MUST TRIUMPH----AND WITHIN *MINUTES,* IF WE'RE TO SAVE THE WASP!

BEFORE WE CRUSH YOU ALL...*SPEAK!!* WHAT HAVE YOU DONE WITH THE DOCTOR?

LOOK OUT FOR THEIR *ICE RAYS!* REMEMBER HOW THEY STOPPED US *LAST* TIME!

EARTH *BRAGGART!* IT IS *YOU* WHO SHALL BE CRUSHED BY OUR SUPERIOR FORCE!

12.

As the wild scramble continues, massive giant arms reach out and scoop up aliens by the handful...

GOT TO MAKE *QUICK WORK* OF THEM! NO TIME TO *LOSE*! MUST BRING THAT DOCTOR BACK TO SAVE *JAN*!

With one powerful thrust, the Kallusians are tossed about like puppets on a string...

MUST TAKE MY MIND OFF WASP! WORRYING CAN'T HELP HER NOW! ONLY *FIGHTING* CAN!

WHISSH!

WHASSH!

THE GIANT ONE FIGHTS LIKE AN *ENTIRE ARMY*!

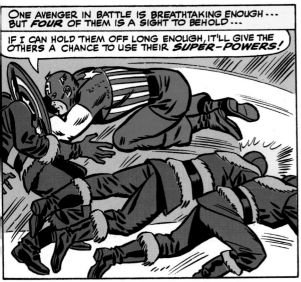

One Avenger in battle is breathtaking enough...

IF I CAN HOLD THEM OFF LONG ENOUGH, IT'LL GIVE THE OTHERS A CHANCE TO USE THEIR *SUPER-POWERS*!

WISH I KNEW HOW MUCH *TIME* HAS ELAPSED!...DID THE 48 HOURS GO BY WHILE WE WERE *FROZEN*?

I'D HATE TO THINK WE'RE FIGHTING A *LOSING* BATTLE AGAINST THE *CLOCK*!

THIS ONE IS A *MAGICIAN*!

Iron Man's whirling repulsors spin the attackers around until the whole area vibrates in a pulsating rhythm...

WHIRRR!

LET ME KNOW WHEN YOU'VE HAD *ENOUGH*! I COULD KEEP THIS UP *ALL DAY*!!

I WISH I WERE *REALLY* THAT CONFIDENT! BUT AN *AVENGER* MUST SHOW NO FEAR!

WHIRRR!

WHAT ELECTRONIC WIZARDRY IS *THIS*?

WHIRR!

HE IS *HERE*! NO!.. HE IS OVER *THERE*!

HE IS *EVERYWHERE*! HE HOPS ABOUT LIKE A *MECHANICAL MAN*!

YOU *FOOLS*! CAN'T YOU SEE THAT HE *IS*?!

MY TRANSISTORS CAN'T LAST MUCH LONGER! IT'LL BE UP TO THE *OTHERS* IN ANOTHER FEW SECONDS!

THERE HE GOES! AFTER HIM!!

13.

AND THOSE OTHERS ARE NOT FOUND WANTING!! ONE SMASH OF THOR'S THUNDEROUS MALLET UPON THE BARREN FLOOR SENDS SCORES OF KALLU SOLDIERS CAREENING ABOUT IN COMPLETE CHAOS...

TAKE NOTE, I SAY! DO NOT MAKE THOR MISUSE HIS WEAPON AND BLOW YOU ALL TO SMITHEREENS!

HE DID NOT TOUCH US...YET WE GO FLYING!

WE DO NOT WISH TO DO YOU HARM! GIVE US THE ONE WE SEEK AND YOU WILL BE SPARED!

WE CANNOT!! WITHOUT HIM, WE MUST LEAVE THIS ACCURSED PLANET AHEAD OF SCHEDULE!

BAVA-VOOM!

THEN, IN A FINAL FIT OF RAGE, THE NORSE GOD HURLS HIS URU HAMMER INTO THE AIR...

HERE IS BUT A SAMPLE OF THE VENGEANCE YOU FACE, WHEN YOU INCUR THE ANGER OF THOR!

EVEN OUR ADVANCED TECHNOLOGY HAS NOT COME UP WITH A WEAPON SUCH AS THAT!

ZOOOMMM!

BUT WE HAVE OTHER WEAPONS, AS THEY SHALL SOON LEARN!

AS BOTH SIDES PREPARE FOR A LAST DITCH FIGHT TO THE FINISH, A VOICE IS HEARD ABOVE THE DIN...

STOP!! CEASE THIS SENSELESS BATTLE IMMEDIATELY! THERE IS NO NEED TO CONTINUE THE CARNAGE!

I AM DOCTOR SVENSON!

I INSIST THAT YOU HALT YOUR ATTACK...OR I WILL NO LONGER SERVE YOU!

IT APPEARS THAT WE HAVE NO CHOICE! I WILL GIVE THE ORDER!

CEASE FIRING!!

14

RESTRAIN THE GIANT ONE! THERE IS THE LOOK OF A RAMPAGING *MADMAN* ABOUT HIM!

DOCTOR...*LISTEN!* THERE IS A GIRL IN AMERICA... SHE'S *DYING*...ONLY *YOU* CAN SAVE HER! EVERY SECOND COUNTS!

WE'VE TRAVELLED HALF-WAY ROUND THE WORLD TO FIND YOU! WE CAN'T FAIL NOW! YOU MUST COME BACK WITH US... *IMMEDIATELY!*

WE DON'T KNOW WHAT PRESSURE THEY'VE USED TO *KEEP* YOU HERE, DOCTOR, BUT THEY CAN'T HOLD YOU ANY LONGER... *WE'LL SEE TO THAT!*

YOU DON'T UNDERSTAND HOW *POWERFUL* THEY ARE! THEY HAVE WEAPONS WHICH CAN DESTROY ALL OF EARTH IN AN INSTANT!

BUT, THEY'RE NOT INTERESTED IN *US!* THEY SIMPLY WANT TO HIDE FROM THOSE WHO ARE *SEARCHING* FOR THEM!

WE PLEDGED TO CAUSE NO HARM TO EARTH IF HE WOULD GIVE US THE CARE WE NEED TO ALLOW US TO HIDE ON THIS PLANET UNTIL OUR ENEMIES HAVE GONE!

SO, I'VE STAYED OF MY OWN FREE WILL.. *NOT* AS A PRISONER!

AND, EVEN AS THE MONARCH OF THE ALIEN KALLU SPEAKS, A VAST FLEET OF STARSHIPS COMBS THE GALAXIES FOR THE ONES WHO HAVE TAKEN REFUGE ON EARTH!

HYPER-SENSITIVE ROBOT *DETECTORS* ARE ROCKETED TO EVERY PLANET WHICH THE SPEEDING FLEET PASSES, TO SEEK OUT THE ONES IN HIDING!

AND, BY THE MEREST WHIM OF CHANCE, ONE SUCH DETECTOR ENTERS OUR OWN *SOLAR SYSTEM*, PASSING OVER THE ICY MOUNTAINS OF PLUTO AND CONTINUING ON ITS FATEFUL COURSE...

15.

THEN, WHILE PASSING OVER THE BARREN MOON OF EARTH, ITS INCREDIBLY SENSITIVE DETECTION MECHANISM PICKS UP THE FIRST FAINT TRACE OF THE KALLU, AS IT SENDS A DELTANOID RAY HURTLING TOWARDS THE ARCTIC REGION...!

WITHOUT WARNING, THE POWERFUL RAY SHATTERS THE KALLU MONITORING STATION, PREVENTING IT FROM SOUNDING AN ALARM!

BUT, ONE ALIEN, OFF ON A MISSION OF EXPLORATION, IS ABLE TO SURVIVE THE BLAST AND CRY INTO A HIDDEN SPEAKER TUBE...

THEY'VE FOUND US... SOUND THE ALARM... THEY'VE FOUND US!!

THEN, THOUSANDS OF FEET BELOW THE SURFACE...

WE ARE DISCOVERED!! BEGIN OPERATION LAST RESORT IMMEDIATELY!!

WE HAD HOPED TO AVOID THIS... BUT NOW, WE HAVE NO CHOICE! WE MUST DO BATTLE, HERE AND NOW!

NO! YOU CAN'T! A WAR BETWEEN TWO SUCH POWERFUL FORCES COULD DESTROY THE EARTH! THE HUMAN RACE COULD NEVER SURVIVE!

YOU PROMISED IT WOULD NEVER HAPPEN IF I HELPED YOU!

WE KEPT OUR PROMISE... WHILE WE COULD! NOW THE DECISION IS NO LONGER OURS!

BESIDES, IN AN INTER-GALACTIC WAR SUCH AS THIS, ONE PLANET MEANS NOTHING!

I'VE HEARD ENOUGH!

SOUND THE BATTLE CRY...!

AVENGERS ASSEMBLE!

EARTH MUST BE SAVED! LEAVE AT ONCE, OR YOU FIGHT US, AS WELL!

16.

STOP!! WE CAN AFFORD NO OTHER DISTRACTIONS, NO MATTER HOW MINOR! YOU WIN! WE SHALL *LEAVE* YOUR PRIMITIVE WORLD AND ENGAGE OUR FOES IN OUTER SPACE!

IF YOUR TONGUE SPEAK FALSE... *BEWARE!*

SET YOUR MINDS AT EASE! I HAVE LEARNED THAT THE KALLU NEVER LIE!

ENTER THE *MATTER DISPLACER!* IT WILL TRANSPORT YOU TO YOUR PLACE OF ORIGIN INSTANTANEOUSLY!

KEEP YOUR EYE ON THE DOCTOR, IRON MAN! WE DON'T GO *WITHOUT* HIM!

I AM RIGHT BEHIND YOU! YOU HAVE *EARNED* MY SERVICES AVENGER!

THEN, SEEMINGLY IN THE SAME SPLIT-SECOND...

IT WAS LIKE STEPPING THROUGH A DOORWAY INTO ANOTHER WORLD!

INCREDIBLE! WE HAVE BEEN USHERED THROUGH SOME SORT OF FANTASTIC *SPACE WARP!*

NO TIME FOR IDLE TALK NOW! WE'VE GOT TO REACH THE *HOSPITAL!*

THE WASP'S 48 HOURS ARE ALMOST *UP!*

THUS, A FEW FRANTIC MOMENTS LATER...

SHE'S STILL *ALIVE!* WE HAVE *THAT* MUCH TO BE THANKFUL FOR!

BUT-- EVEN FROM *HERE* I CAN SEE HOW WEAK HER BREATHING IS... HOW FAINT HER PULSE!

DOCTOR, I *MUST* KNOW! ARE YOU IN TIME TO...TO *SAVE* HER??

I CANNOT ANSWER THAT FOR CERTAIN YET! SHE IS MOST *CRITICAL!*

WE MUST PREPARE FOR SURGERY AT *ONCE!*

I SHALL USE MY OWN OPERATIVE METHODS... AND THE REST WILL BE IN THE HANDS OF FATE!

17.

81

WE ARE **READY** FOR YOU, DOCTOR!

DOCTOR, LISTEN... YOU'VE **GOT** TO SAVE HER! DO YOU **HEAR** ME?? YOU CAN'T LET HER DIE!

I SHALL DO MY BEST! YOU MUST HAVE FAITH!

GET **HOLD** OF YOUR-SELF, AVENGER! IF **ANY-ONE** CAN SAVE HER... SVENSON CAN!

LET HIM **GO**, GIANT-MAN! THERE'S NOTHING MORE **WE** CAN DO!

EVEN THE POWER OF **THOR** CAN-NOT HELP AT THIS CRUCIAL MOMENT!

NEVER HAVE I SEEN **CAPTAIN AMERICA** LOOK SO GRIM HE, TOO, KNOWS WHAT IT MEANS TO LOSE SOMEONE NEAR AND DEAR!

I PRAY **GIANT-MAN** WILL NOT ALSO SUFFER SUCH A LOSS!

AND, AS THE MOTIONLESS WASP HOVERS BETWEEN LIFE AND DEATH, WE RETURN TO THE KALLU BASE, WHERE WE FIND...

OUR DEFENSIVE DEVICES HAVE BLOWN UP THE ENEMY DETECTOR!

BUT, IT IS TOO LATE! IT WILL HAVE SENT ITS FATEFUL MESSAGE BACK BY NOW!

WE MUST BE TRUE TO OUR WORD! THE TIME FOR HIDING IS **OVER!** INTO THE SHIPS! EARTH CAN SHELTER US NO LONGER! WE'LL MEET OUR DESTINY IN THE ENDLESS VOID OF **SPACE!**

THEY SHALL FIND, TO THEIR DISMAY, THAT THE **KALLU** ARE NOT AS HELP-LESS AS THEY THINK!

NOW **GO!** YOU HAVE YOUR ORDERS!

MEANWHILE, THE VAST ENEMY SPACE ARMADA STREAKS TOWARDS THE SOLAR SYSTEM WITH THEIR COBALT THROTTLES WIDE OPEN!!

THE KALLU SHALL NOT ESCAPE US **AGAIN!** THIS TIME WE FIGHT UNTIL **ONE** OF OUR RACES EXISTS NO LONGER!

18.

AND, IN THE HIDDEN CITY BENEATH THE ARCTIC ICE...

TO THE *SHIPS!* THERE'S NOT A SECOND TO LOSE!

WE'LL BE SPACE-BORNE, WITH ALL OUR WEAPONS, BEFORE THEY REACH US! *THIS* TIME, IT IS *THEY* WHO WILL FLEE FOR THEIR LIVES!

IN A STEADY STREAM OF MEN AND MACHINES, THE KALLU RACE UP THEIR BOARDING RAMPS INTO THEIR GIGANTIC STARSHIPS, STILL HIDDEN BENEATH THE SURFACE OF EARTH...

WE HOPED WE COULD REMAIN HIDDEN TILL THEY *LEFT* THIS PART OF THE UNIVERSE!

BUT NOW, THEY'VE *FOUND* US! WE'RE *FORCED* TO FIGHT! WE'VE NO CHOICE BUT TO *DESTROY* THEM FOREVER!

AT THE PRESS OF A BUTTON, SILENT, HIDDEN LAUNCH-PAD COVERS SWING OPEN ON THE SURFACE, AS THE KALLU SHIPS POINT THEIR NOSES SKYWARD! AND THEN...

OUR DESTINATION IS SECTOR 18-G, 1200 LIGHT YEARS FROM EARTH! IT IS *THERE* WE SHALL ENGAGE THE ENEMY IN FINAL BATTLE!

ATTENTION, ALL UNITS! DEPARTURE TIME IS... *NOW!*

SO SWIFTLY, SO SILENTLY, DOES THE KALLU FLEET BLAST INTO SPACE THAT IT IS *GONE* BEFORE THE FINAL ROCKET CAN CAUSE THE SLIGHTEST BLIP TO APPEAR ON ANY EARTH RADAR DEVICE!

19.

WHILE IN THE DESERTED CITY BELOW, ONE LONE SHADOW FALLS OVER THE EMPTY LIFELESS STREETS... AND ONE LONE VOICE SOFTLY WHISPERS...

THEY ARE GONE! ALL THAT REMAINS IS A FLEETING MEMORY IN THE MINDS OF... THE AVENGERS!

AND THEN, THE DRAMATIC FIGURE OF THE MOST MYSTERIOUS ENTITY IN THE KNOWN UNIVERSE... *THE WATCHER*... SLOWLY TAKES SHAPE AMID THE STRANGE DESOLATION...!

TWO ALIEN RACES... ABOUT TO BATTLE FOR SURVIVAL WITH *EARTH* AS THEIR BATTLEGROUND! IT WOULD HAVE MEANT THE END OF MANKIND!

BUT, THE HUMAN RACE HAS NOW BEEN SPARED... BECAUSE OF ONE DYING GIRL!

NONE BUT THE *WATCHER* CAN COMPREHEND THE WORKINGS OF FATE!

AND, EVEN *I*, WHO HAVE OBSERVED FOR AGES... WHO TRAVEL THROUGH GALAXIES THE WAY LESSER RACES TRAVERSE THE SURFACE OF THEIR OWN PLANETS... EVEN *I* CANNOT KNOW WHAT THE FUTURE WILL BRING!

PERHAPS THE KALLU WILL TRIUMPH... OR, THEY MAY SUFFER ANNIHILATION! BUT, HUMANITY WILL NEVER KNOW!

NOW, *I* MUST DEPART TO OBSERVE THE FINAL OUTCOME... FOR I AM.. THE *WATCHER!* AS FOR THE GIRL MEN CALL THE *WASP*... MANY HAVE PRAYED FOR HER...

..AND, THE POWER OF PRAYER IS *STILL* THE GREATEST EVER KNOWN IN THIS END-LESS, ETERNAL UNIVERSE!

THEN, EVEN THE WATCHER FADES INTO SPACE...

THE OPERATION IS... OVER!

FOUR OF THE EARTH'S MIGHTIEST CRUSADERS WATCH THE WEARY SURGEON WITH BURNING EYES... NONE DARING TO BE THE FIRST TO SPEAK... UNTIL...

TELL US, DOCTOR... WE.. WE *HAVE* TO KNOW..!

THE OPERATION WAS SUCCESSFUL! THE GIRL WILL RECOVER!

LET US NOW LEAVE THE AVENGERS! STRONG MEN SHOULD NOT BE SEEN WITH TEARS IN THEIR EYES! NOR SHOULD THEY BE DISTURBED AS THEY LIFT THEIR FACES HEAVEN-WARD, IN SOLEMN, GRATEFUL THANKSGIVING!

THE END 20.

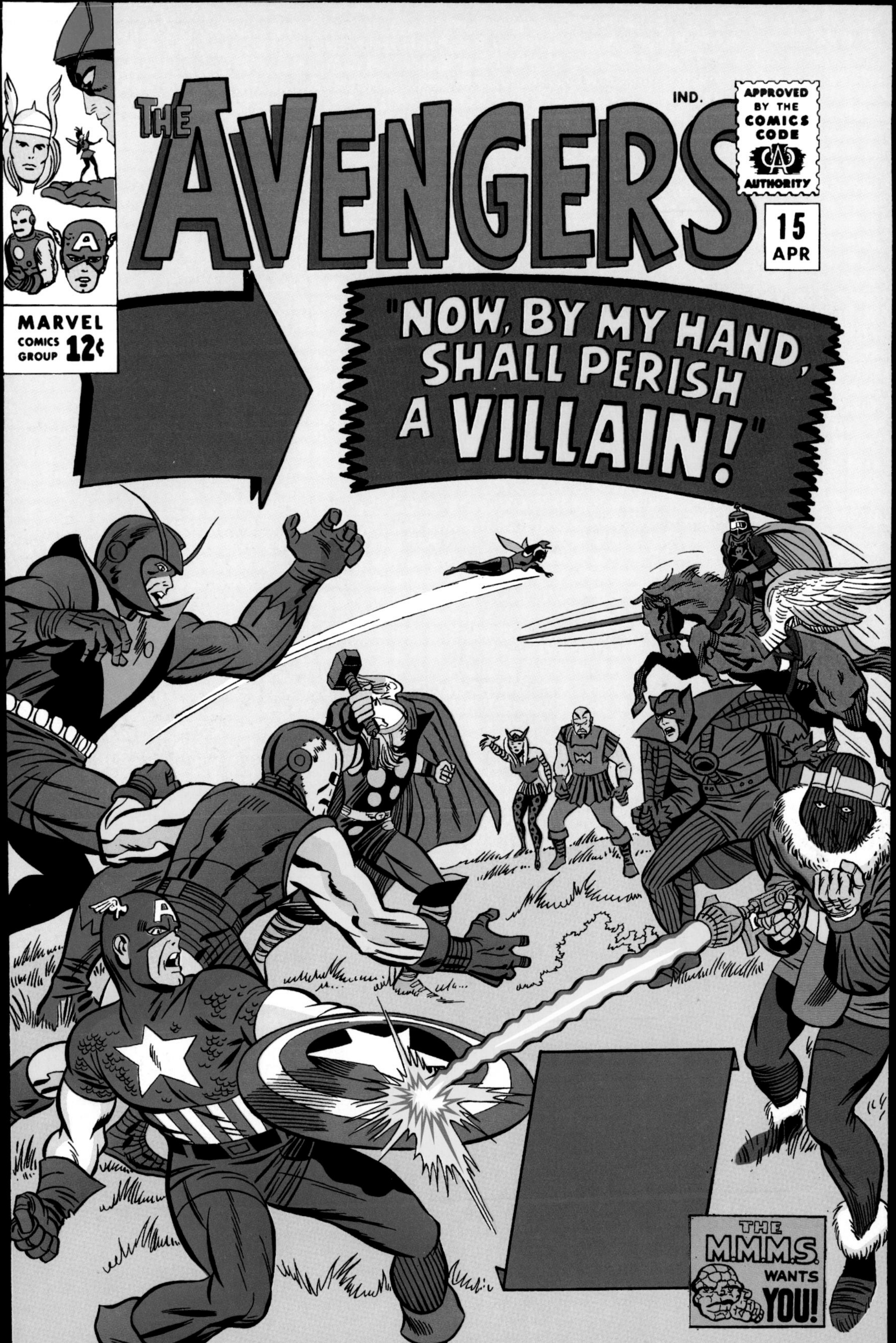

THE AVENGERS
IND.
APPROVED BY THE COMICS CODE AUTHORITY
15
APR
MARVEL COMICS GROUP 12¢
"NOW, BY MY HAND, SHALL PERISH A VILLAIN!"
THE M.M.M.S. WANTS YOU!

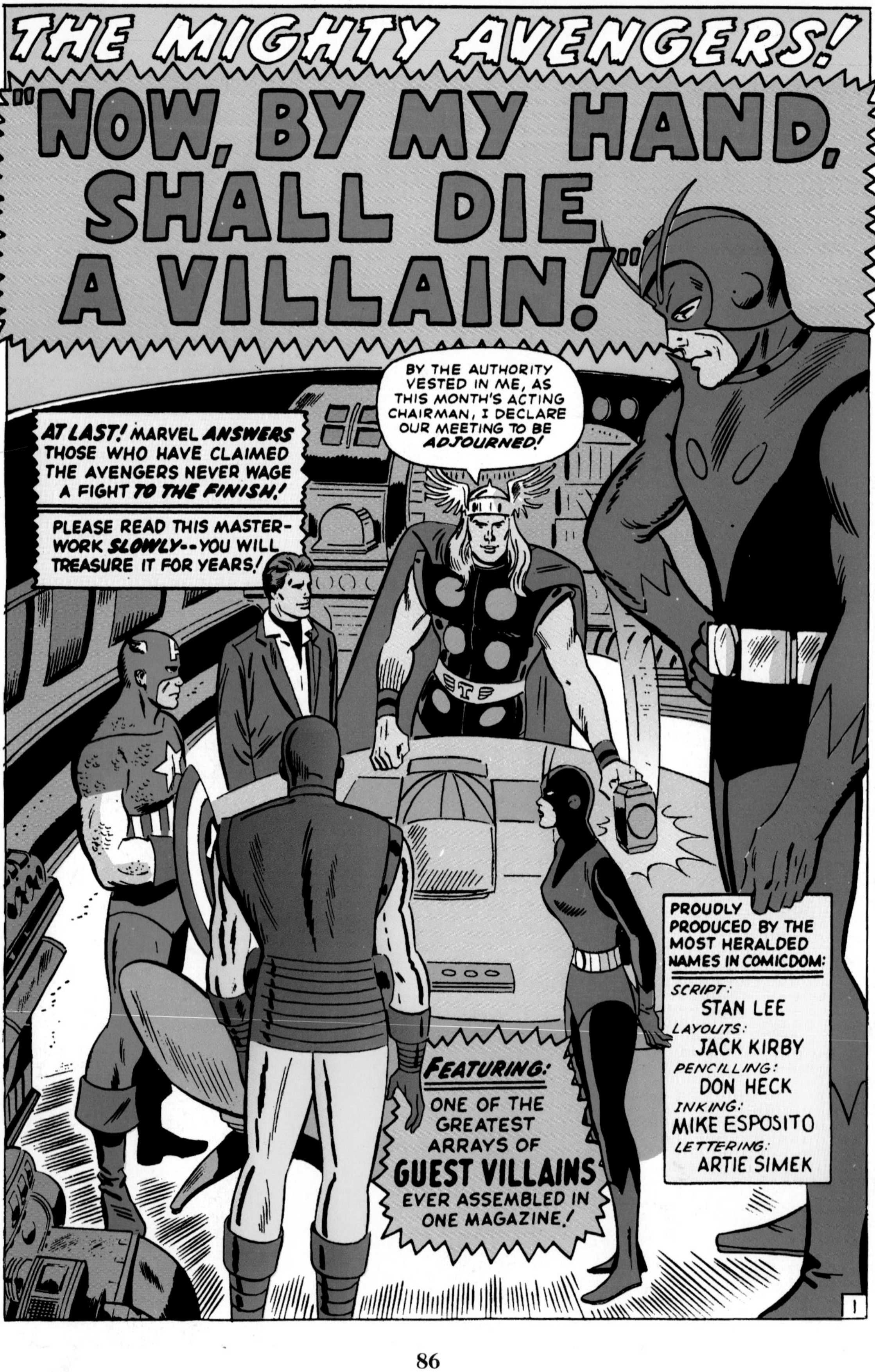
THE MIGHTY AVENGERS!
"NOW, BY MY HAND, SHALL DIE A VILLAIN!"
BY THE AUTHORITY VESTED IN ME, AS THIS MONTH'S ACTING CHAIRMAN, I DECLARE OUR MEETING TO BE ADJOURNED!
AT LAST! MARVEL ANSWERS THOSE WHO HAVE CLAIMED THE AVENGERS NEVER WAGE A FIGHT TO THE FINISH!
PLEASE READ THIS MASTER-WORK SLOWLY--YOU WILL TREASURE IT FOR YEARS!
PROUDLY PRODUCED BY THE MOST HERALDED NAMES IN COMICDOM:
SCRIPT: STAN LEE
LAYOUTS: JACK KIRBY
PENCILLING: DON HECK
INKING: MIKE ESPOSITO
LETTERING: ARTIE SIMEK
FEATURING: ONE OF THE GREATEST ARRAYS OF GUEST VILLAINS EVER ASSEMBLED IN ONE MAGAZINE!
1

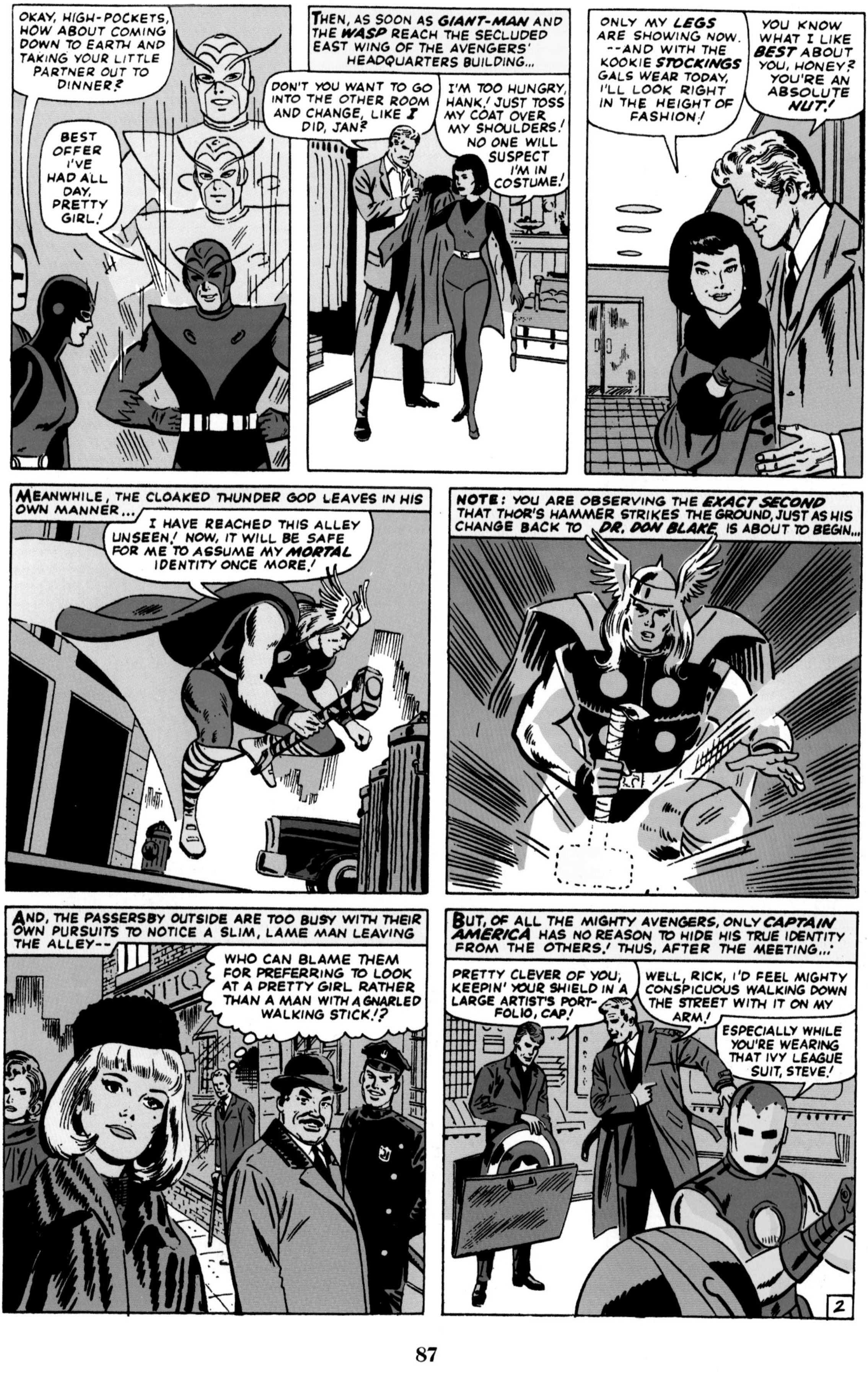
OKAY, HIGH-POCKETS, HOW ABOUT COMING DOWN TO EARTH AND TAKING YOUR LITTLE PARTNER OUT TO DINNER?
BEST OFFER I'VE HAD ALL DAY, PRETTY GIRL!
THEN, AS SOON AS GIANT-MAN AND THE WASP REACH THE SECLUDED EAST WING OF THE AVENGERS' HEADQUARTERS BUILDING...
DON'T YOU WANT TO GO INTO THE OTHER ROOM AND CHANGE, LIKE I DID, JAN?
I'M TOO HUNGRY, HANK! JUST TOSS MY COAT OVER MY SHOULDERS! NO ONE WILL SUSPECT I'M IN COSTUME!
ONLY MY LEGS ARE SHOWING NOW. --AND WITH THE KOOKIE STOCKINGS GALS WEAR TODAY, I'LL LOOK RIGHT IN THE HEIGHT OF FASHION!
YOU KNOW WHAT I LIKE BEST ABOUT YOU, HONEY? YOU'RE AN ABSOLUTE NUT!
MEANWHILE, THE CLOAKED THUNDER GOD LEAVES IN HIS OWN MANNER...
I HAVE REACHED THIS ALLEY UNSEEN! NOW, IT WILL BE SAFE FOR ME TO ASSUME MY MORTAL IDENTITY ONCE MORE!
NOTE: YOU ARE OBSERVING THE EXACT SECOND THAT THOR'S HAMMER STRIKES THE GROUND, JUST AS HIS CHANGE BACK TO DR. DON BLAKE IS ABOUT TO BEGIN...
AND, THE PASSERSBY OUTSIDE ARE TOO BUSY WITH THEIR OWN PURSUITS TO NOTICE A SLIM, LAME MAN LEAVING THE ALLEY--
WHO CAN BLAME THEM FOR PREFERRING TO LOOK AT A PRETTY GIRL RATHER THAN A MAN WITH A GNARLED WALKING STICK!?
BUT, OF ALL THE MIGHTY AVENGERS, ONLY CAPTAIN AMERICA HAS NO REASON TO HIDE HIS TRUE IDENTITY FROM THE OTHERS! THUS, AFTER THE MEETING...
PRETTY CLEVER OF YOU, KEEPIN' YOUR SHIELD IN A LARGE ARTIST'S PORT-FOLIO, CAP!
WELL, RICK, I'D FEEL MIGHTY CONSPICUOUS WALKING DOWN THE STREET WITH IT ON MY ARM!
ESPECIALLY WHILE YOU'RE WEARING THAT IVY LEAGUE SUIT, STEVE!
2

YOU TWO RUN ALONG! I WANT TO STAY BEHIND AND MAKE SURE ALL OUR ELECTRONIC EQUIPMENT IS FUNCTIONING PROPERLY!

STRANGE HOW *IRON MAN* IS ALWAYS LAST TO LEAVE! WELL, I GUESS IT'S NONE OF *MY* BUSINESS--!

OKAY, AVENGER! KEEP YOUR TRANSISTORS DRY!

BUT, THE REASON WHY THE GOLDEN AVENGER CHOOSES TO REMAIN BEHIND IS SOON MADE VERY CLEAR--TO *US*--!

I WAS AFRAID THEY'D *NEVER* LEAVE! IT'S TIME FOR ME TO RE-CHARGE MY LIFE-SAVING CHEST DEVICE--!

--BUT, I COULD HARDLY DO IT IN VIEW OF THE OTHERS, THUS REVEALING MYSELF AS *TONY STARK,* THE MAN FROM WHOM *IRON MAN* "BORROWS" THIS MANSION FOR THEIR MEETINGS!

IT CERTAINLY IS A PLEASURE TO HAVE THINGS NICE AND *PEACEFUL* FOR A CHANGE!

HOWEVER, THE HANDSOME MILLIONAIRE MIGHT BE FAR LESS RELAXED IF HE COULD WITNESS A SCENE WHICH IS NOW TAKING PLACE IN THE HEART OF THE AMAZON JUNGLE...

TOO LONG HAVE I REMAINED HERE IN HIDING! THE TIME HAS COME FOR *ZEMO* TO STRIKE BACK ONCE AGAIN AT THE ACCURSED *AVENGERS!!*

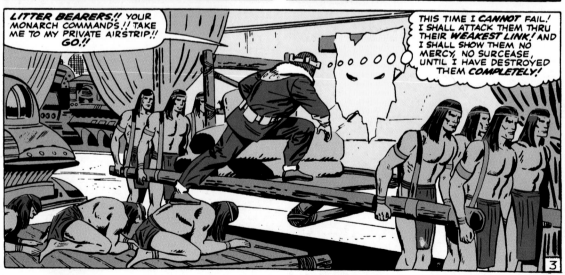

LITTER BEARERS!! YOUR MONARCH COMMANDS!! TAKE ME TO MY PRIVATE AIRSTRIP!! *GO!!*

THIS TIME I *CANNOT* FAIL! I SHALL ATTACK THEM THRU THEIR *WEAKEST LINK!* AND I SHALL SHOW THEM NO MERCY, NO SURCEASE, UNTIL I HAVE DESTROYED THEM *COMPLETELY!*

3

A SHORT TIME LATER...

YOU HAVE YOUR ORDERS! **OBEY** THEM! YOU KNOW THE PENALTY FOR **FAILURE!**

WE SHALL NOT FAIL! WE HAVE REHEARSED IT TOO MANY TIMES! YOUR PLAN IS **FOOL-PROOF!** HEIL, ZEMO!

OF ALL THE MURDEROUS NAZI WAR CRIMINALS, ONLY **ZEMO** HAS MANAGED TO ESCAPE COMPLETELY! BUT, IT'S ONLY A MATTER OF TIME BEFORE THE **AVENGERS** DESTROY HIM-- OR **HE** DESTROYS THEM!

IT'S **DONE!** NOTHING CAN STOP MY PLAN **NOW!** SOON I'LL HAVE MY **REVENGE** ON CAPTAIN AMERICA--ON **ALL** OF THEM, FOR THE WAY THEY'VE HOUNDED ME ALL THESE MONTHS!

BACK IN NEW YORK, IN A QUIET HOTEL ROOM, THE VALIANT MAN, WHOM THE WORLD KNOWS AS **CAPTAIN AMERICA,** ATTEMPTS TO FIND THE WORDS TO USE IN AN IMPORTANT LETTER...

Colonel Nick Fury
The Pentagon
Washington, D.C.

Dear Col. Fury
  You won't remember me, but we met in combat during the war!
  I'm anxious to get back into harness again, and I've heard that you are engaged in important counter-espionage ___ for the army

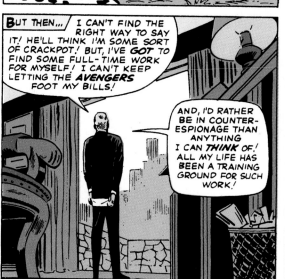

BUT THEN...

I CAN'T FIND THE RIGHT WAY TO SAY IT! HE'LL THINK I'M SOME SORT OF CRACKPOT! BUT, I'VE **GOT** TO FIND SOME FULL-TIME WORK FOR MYSELF! I CAN'T KEEP LETTING THE **AVENGERS** FOOT MY BILLS!

AND, I'D RATHER BE IN COUNTER-ESPIONAGE THAN ANYTHING I CAN **THINK** OF! ALL MY LIFE HAS BEEN A TRAINING GROUND FOR SUCH WORK!

FINALLY, STEVE ROGERS DECIDES TO MAIL THE LETTER! AND, AS HE DROPS IT IN THE CORNER MAILBOX, HE SEES...

IN THAT CAR--THE **ENCHANTRESS**-- AND THE **EXECUTIONER!** I'D KNOW THEM **ANYWHERE!!**

US MAIL

THEIR VERY **PRESENCE** IS A THREAT TO THE CITY! I'VE GOT TO **FOLLOW** THEM!!

4

TRAFFIC'S MOVING TOO FAST! CAN'T GRAB THEIR CAR! BUT-- I DON'T WANT TO *LOSE* THEM! I CAN SEE WHERE THEY'RE HEADED FROM UP *HERE!*

I'M IN *LUCK!* THE TRAFFIC'S *HEAVY* UP AHEAD-- THEY'VE HAD TO SLOW DOWN!

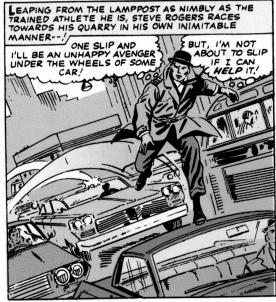

LEAPING FROM THE LAMPPOST AS NIMBLY AS THE TRAINED ATHLETE HE IS, STEVE ROGERS RACES TOWARDS HIS QUARRY IN HIS OWN INIMITABLE MANNER--!

ONE SLIP AND I'LL BE AN UNHAPPY AVENGER UNDER THE WHEELS OF SOME CAR!

BUT, I'M NOT ABOUT TO SLIP IF I CAN *HELP* IT!

UH OH-- THEY'RE PICKING UP *SPEED* NOW! I'VE GOT TO DO THE *SAME* IF I DON'T WANT TO *LOSE* THEM!

WHAT *IS* IT, ENCHANTRESS?? WHY DO YOU TURN TO LOOK BEHIND YOU THAT WAY?

MY SORCERER'S INTUITION *WARNED* ME WE'RE BEING FOLLOWED! AND I WAS *RIGHT!*

I KNOW *NOT* WHO OUR PURSUER IS, BUT HE SHALL FOLLOW US NO LONGER!!

ONE SIMPLE SPELL IS ALL I REQUIRE!

THEN, BEFORE STEVE ROGERS CAN SWING HIMSELF TO THE NEXT LAMPPOST--!

UHHH! THE *CABLE* SNAPPED!!

IT CAN ONLY BE THE *ENCHANTRESS'* DOING! I'LL NEVER CATCH THEM *NOW!*

5

LATER, IN AN IMPERIALLY FURNISHED PRIVATE BUILDING IN THE HEART OF THE CITY...

I GROW *BORED* WITH THIS INACTION! HOW MUCH LONGER NEED WE WAIT?

OUR WAITING IS *OVER!* SEE--THE COMMUNICATOR IS GLOWING RIGHT *NOW!*

THE TIME HAS *COME!* MY PLAN IS IN OPERATION! YOU BOTH REMEMBER WHAT YOU ARE TO DO?!

WORRY ABOUT *YOURSELF,* ZEMO! IMMORTALS *NEVER* FORGET!

THEN THE TIME HAS COME AT *LAST*-- FOR US TO *CRUSH THE AVENGERS!!*

THE FACT THAT THEY HAVE BEATEN US IN THE PAST-- PURELY BY *LUCK,* OF COURSE, WILL MAKE OUR TRIUMPH *DOUBLY* SWEET!

BUT, WE MUST NOT BE OVER-CONFIDENT! REMEMBER-- THEY ARE *STILL* THE MIGHTIEST FIGHTING TEAM ON EARTH!

AND, EVEN WHILE ZEMO AND THE TWO OUTCASTS FROM ASGARD FINALIZE THEIR PLANS...

I CALLED THIS EMERGENCY MEETING BECAUSE I SAW THE *ENCHANTRESS* AND THE *EXECUTIONER* IN THE CITY!

IT CAN ONLY MEAN *ONE* THING--!

A NEW *ATTACK* UPON US WILL COME AT ANY MINUTE!

SO *BE* IT! THEY SHALL FIND THE *AVENGERS* RESOLUTE AS EVER-- MIGHTY AS EVER!

WATCH OUT WHERE YOU SWING THAT *HAMMER,* GOLDEN BOY! THERE'S A *LADY* PRESENT!

BY THE WAY-- WHERE IS *RICK JONES?*

BUT, BEFORE ANYONE CAN ANSWER CAP... *LISTEN!!*

BRRRRR

THE ROAR OF A GIANT ENGINE-- COMING *CLOSER!*

WHAT CAN IT *BE??*

RUSHING OUTSIDE, READY FOR ANYTHING, THE AVENGERS SEE...

IT'S *RICK*-- BEING PULLED *SKYWARD!!!*

STAY *BACK!* I SHALL GO *AFTER* HIM!

RICK! RICK!!

GOING SO *FAST--* MY JETS CAN'T *CATCH* YOU--!!

SOMETHING'S PULLING ME UP INTO THE *AIR!!* C-CAN'T *STOP* MYSELF!!

LOOK! THERE'S A *PLANE* UP ABOVE! RICK IS HEADING RIGHT *TOWARDS* IT!

THAT'S THE ANSWER! SOME SORT OF INVISIBLE *RAY* IS PULLING RICK TO THE SHIP! --AT FANTASTIC SPEED!!

AVENGERS--*DISPERSE!!* THEY HAVE DROPPED A *MINE* DOWN UPON US!!

IT'S A *CONCUSSION-TYPE,* THOR!! IT'S READY TO BE *DETONATED!!*

I HAVE HURLED THE *WASP* AWAY-- AT LEAST *SHE* SHALL BE UNAFFECTED BY THE IMPACT!

AND THEN, IT *HAPPENS...*

WHOOM!

MOMENTARILY STUNNED BY THE AWESOME BLAST, THE TWO HEROIC FIGURES PLUMMET EARTHWARD, UNTIL-- A PAIR OF GIGANTIC HANDS REACHES UP, AND...

GOT THEM!

RICK IS GONE!! THEY WERE TOO LATE TO SAVE HIM!!

CAP-- QUICK! THERE'S STILL A SLIM CHANCE! GIVE ME YOUR SHIELD--!

HERE IT IS, AVENGER! I THINK I KNOW WHAT YOU'RE PLANNING TO DO--! ONLY YOU CAN PULL IT OFF!

INDEED, ONLY A MAN OF GIGANTIC HEIGHT COULD HURL THE SPINNING SHIELD FAR ENOUGH, FAST ENOUGH, HIGH ENOUGH, TO REACH THE SPEEDING AIRCRAFT!

I'VE GOT TO STOP THE SHIP! I MUSTN'T MISS!!

BUT, THOUGH THE MASTER OF MANY SIZES SENDS HIS PROJECTILE UNERRINGLY TO ITS TARGET, AN ELECTRONIC FORCE FIELD AROUND THE CRAFT MAKES THE AVENGER'S EFFORT ALL IN VAIN!

AND, INSIDE THE SPEEDING SHIP...

ZEMO WILL REWARD US HANDSOMELY FOR CAPTURING THE BOY!

ZEMO! SO HE'S BEHIND THIS!

THAT KNOWLEDGE WILL DO YOU NO GOOD! NOTHING CAN SAVE YOU!

TIE HIM SECURELY! IT IS ALMOST TIME FOR PHASE TWO OF ZEMO'S MASTER PLAN TO DESTROY THE AVENGERS!

OUR "ATTRACTOR BEAM" HAS SERVED US WELL!

IT SERVED BETTER THAN THEY SUSPECT! I WAS ABLE TO SNEAK ABOARD ALSO, WHILE THEY DREW RICK INTO THE SHIP!

8

93

MEANWHILE, DOWN BELOW...

EASY, CAP! WE'LL GO **AFTER** THEM! I'LL REQUISITION ONE OF TONY STARK'S **HUNTER PLANES!**

THEY GOT **RICK!** IF ANYTHING HAPPENS TO THAT BOY--!!

WE'LL **GET** THEM, AVENGER! **THEY'RE** THE ONES WHO SHOULD BE WORRIED! REMEMBER--WE'VE NEVER FAILED **YET!**

HOW QUICKLY CAN WE GET THAT PLANE, IRON MAN?

HE'S REGAINED CONTROL OF HIMSELF! **GOOD!** NOW TO USE MY BUILT IN TELE-SPEAKER....!

I'LL ROTATE MY ARC BEAM LIGHT UNTIL I EXPOSE THE CONCEALED DIAL...

THE HUNTER PLANE WILL BE HERE WITHIN **MINUTES**, CAP!

IRON MAN CALLING! **URGENT!** BY AUTHORIZATION OF ANTHONY STARK, I HEREBY ORDER THE IMMEDIATE DISPATCH OF THE XL-750 ROCKET PLANE...

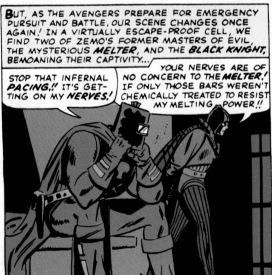

BUT, AS THE AVENGERS PREPARE FOR EMERGENCY PURSUIT AND BATTLE, OUR SCENE CHANGES ONCE AGAIN! IN A VIRTUALLY ESCAPE-PROOF CELL, WE FIND TWO OF ZEMO'S FORMER MASTERS OF EVIL, THE MYSTERIOUS **MELTER**, AND THE **BLACK KNIGHT**, BEMOANING THEIR CAPTIVITY...

STOP THAT INFERNAL **PACING!!** IT'S GETTING ON MY **NERVES!**

YOUR NERVES ARE OF NO CONCERN TO THE **MELTER!** IF ONLY THOSE BARS WEREN'T CHEMICALLY TREATED TO RESIST MY MELTING POWER!!

WE WERE ALLOWED TO KEEP OUR ARMORED COSTUMES BECAUSE A SCIENTIFIC DELEGATION FROM WASHINGTON IS ON THE WAY TO STUDY US-- AND WE'VE NO WAY TO **STOP** THEM!

DON'T TOUCH THAT WALL!! IT WILL RELEASE A SPECIAL GAS IF WE TRY TO SHATTER IT! THE AUTHORITIES ARE TAKING NO **CHANCES** WITH US!

9

BUT THEN, SUDDENLY...

LOOK AT THAT *GLOW*-- GETTING LARGER AND LARGER,!! IS IT ANOTHER TRAP TO HOLD US HERE??

NO! IT'S JUST THE *OPPOSITE!* EVERY-THING ABOUT IT SHRIEKS OF *SORCERY!*

THE WALL IS *FADING AWAY*-- RIGHT BEFORE OUR EYES!

I *KNEW* IT! ZEMO SENT THE *EXECUTIONER* AND THE *ENCHANTRESS* TO SET US FREE!

WE HAVE YOUR WEAPONS--AND YOUR WINGED HORSE! *HURRY* --BEFORE THE GUARDS COME AFTER YOU!

ONCE WE'RE *FREE* AGAIN, IT WILL TAKE MORE THAN MERE *GUARDS* TO CAPTURE US ONCE MORE!

WE HAVE *ORDERS* FOR YOU--FROM *ZEMO!* LISTEN CAREFULLY--!

WE HAVE CAPTURED AND HIDDEN *RICK JONES!* THE AVENGERS WILL BE AFTER US WITHIN SECONDS! YOU MUST INTERCEPT THEIR PLANE AND *DESTROY* IT! ALL THIS IS PART OF ZEMO'S MASTER PLAN!

SAY *NO MORE!*

I UNDERSTAND *FULLY*--AND MY LANCE HUNGERS FOR BATTLE! THEY WON'T ESCAPE ME!

I'LL REMAIN BELOW--WITH MY *MELTING BEAM* READY FOR USE WHEN THEY LEAST EX-PECT IT!

THEY HAVE OUTWITTED US IN THE PAST-- BUT *THIS* TIME NOTHING CAN SAVE THEM! NOW *GO!* DESTROY THEIR SHIP!!

I'VE WAITED TOO LONG FOR THIS MOMENT-- AND NOW, WITH THE ELEMENT OF *SURPRISE* ON MY SIDE, I CANNOT FAIL!

THERE IT *IS,!!* THE AVENGERS' ROCKET HUNTER PLANE! A FITTING TARGET FOR MY INVINCIBLE LANCE!

IRON MAN-- *LOOK!* DEAD AHEAD--THE *BLACK KNIGHT!*

WHERE DID HE *COME* FROM?

NO TIME FOR THAT NOW! HE'S *ATTACKING* US!

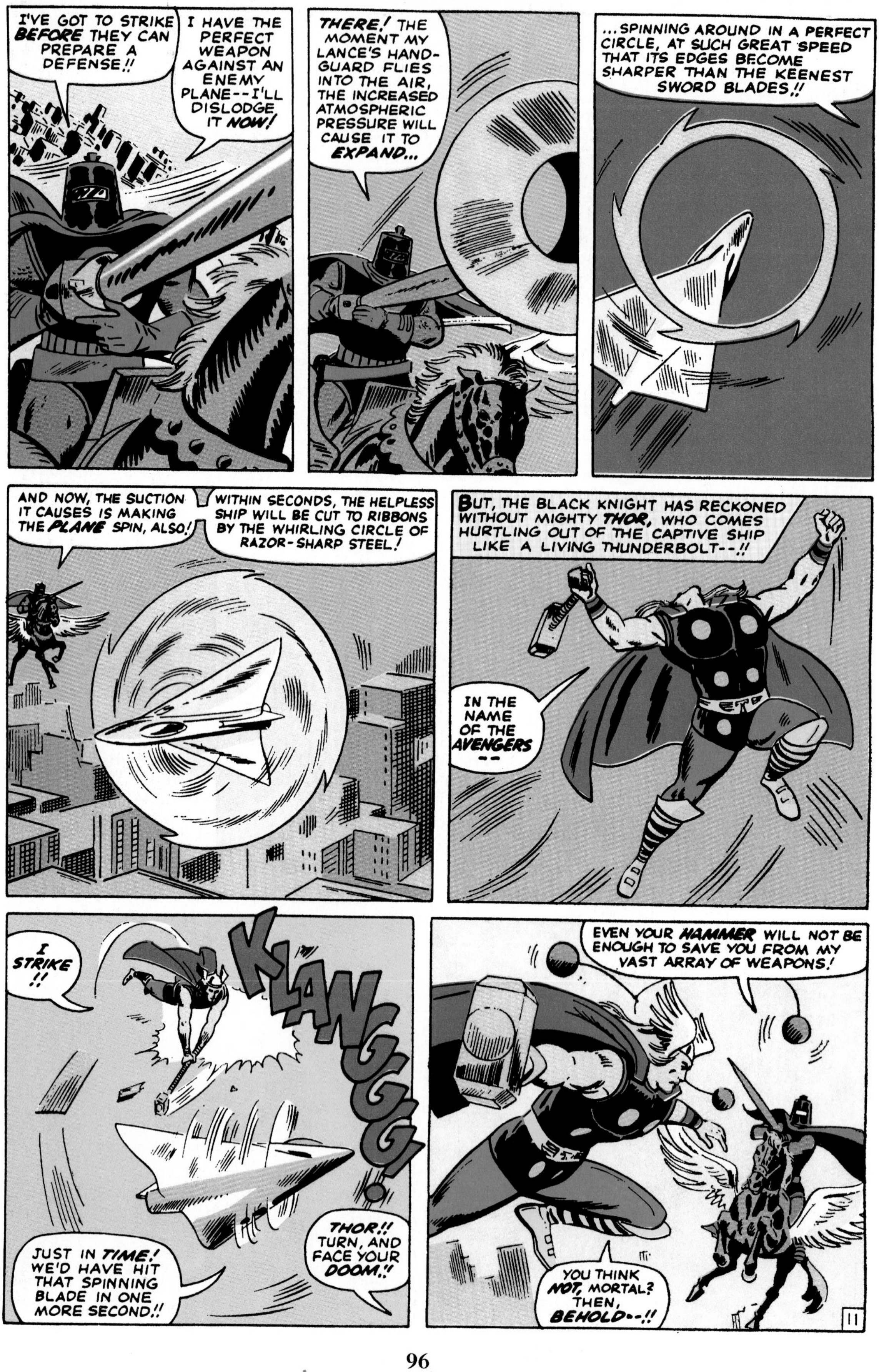
I'VE GOT TO STRIKE BEFORE THEY CAN PREPARE A DEFENSE!!
I HAVE THE PERFECT WEAPON AGAINST AN ENEMY PLANE--I'LL DISLODGE IT NOW!
THERE! THE MOMENT MY LANCE'S HAND-GUARD FLIES INTO THE AIR, THE INCREASED ATMOSPHERIC PRESSURE WILL CAUSE IT TO EXPAND...
...SPINNING AROUND IN A PERFECT CIRCLE, AT SUCH GREAT SPEED THAT ITS EDGES BECOME SHARPER THAN THE KEENEST SWORD BLADES!!
AND NOW, THE SUCTION IT CAUSES IS MAKING THE PLANE SPIN, ALSO!
WITHIN SECONDS, THE HELPLESS SHIP WILL BE CUT TO RIBBONS BY THE WHIRLING CIRCLE OF RAZOR-SHARP STEEL!
BUT, THE BLACK KNIGHT HAS RECKONED WITHOUT MIGHTY THOR, WHO COMES HURTLING OUT OF THE CAPTIVE SHIP LIKE A LIVING THUNDERBOLT--!!
IN THE NAME OF THE AVENGERS --
I STRIKE !!
KLANGGG!
JUST IN TIME! WE'D HAVE HIT THAT SPINNING BLADE IN ONE MORE SECOND!!
THOR!! TURN, AND FACE YOUR DOOM!!
EVEN YOUR HAMMER WILL NOT BE ENOUGH TO SAVE YOU FROM MY VAST ARRAY OF WEAPONS!
YOU THINK NOT, MORTAL? THEN, BEHOLD--!!
11

MY WHIRLING MALLET CAN LIFT ME *ABOVE* YOUR DEADLY BOLAS!! AND NOW, THE OFFENSIVE IS *MINE*!!

FASTER, MY TRUSTY STEED! WE MUST LURE THE THUNDER GOD AWAY WHILE THE *MELTER* STRIKES FROM BELOW WITH HIS AWESOME POWER!

AND, IN THE STILL-SPINNING SHIP...

THERE! SHE'S UNDER MY CONTROL AGAIN! I'LL HAVE HER UNDER WAY IN SECONDS!

LOOK OUT! THERE'S DANGER *BELOW!*

WHO *SAID* THAT?

I DID! I WAS *SPYING* ON THEM! THE *MELTER* IS ABOUT TO--*OH!!* TOO *LATE!!*

A *MELTING BEAM!!* MISSED US BY *INCHES!!*

KEEP THE SHIP AIRBORNE, AVENGERS! I'LL JET OUT THRU THE HOLE HE CUT WITH HIS BEAM AND *TACKLE* HIM!

THERE HE *IS* --ATOP THAT SKYSCRAPER MAST BELOW! IF I CAN JUST AVOID HIS DEADLY BEAM LONG ENOUGH--!

MADE IT!! OKAY, MELTER-- WAVE THE WHITE FLAG, OR MY TRANSISTOR FORCE-RAY WILL HURL YOU FROM HERE TO KINGDOM COME!

I *DARE* NOT SURRENDER! I'VE GOT TO STRIKE *AGAIN*--SOMEHOW!

ZITT!

12

SUPPORTED BY HIS DELICATELY BALANCED CLOAK, THE MYSTERIOUS *MELTER* ALMOST SEEMS TO BE FLYING AS HE DODGES AMONGST THE BUILDING LEDGES, TRYING TO LURE *IRON MAN* TO ONE CERTAIN SPOT!

HE'S FAST-- BUT I'LL GET HIM SOONER OR LATER!

I'VE GOT TO MAKE HIM REACH THE EDGE OF THE ROOF--!

I *DID* IT! *NOW*-- ALL I NEED DO IS MELT THE SUPPORTS ON WHICH THAT WATER TOWER STANDS--!

THE *WATER TOWER!!* SO, *THAT'S* WHAT YOU WERE AFTER, EH?

ZITTT!

I'M *SURPRISED* AT YOU, FELLA! THESE *POWER TRANSISTORS* OF MINE AREN'T HERE FOR *SHOW!*

WHOOM!

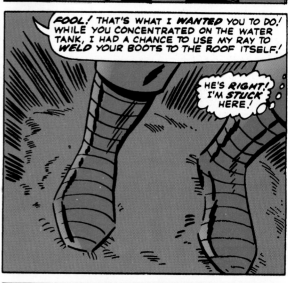

FOOL! THAT'S WHAT I *WANTED* YOU TO DO! WHILE YOU CONCENTRATED ON THE WATER TANK, I HAD A CHANCE TO USE MY RAY TO *WELD* YOUR BOOTS TO THE ROOF ITSELF!

HE'S *RIGHT!* I'M *STUCK* HERE!

AND NOW THAT I HAVE YOU WHERE I WANT YOU-- AND YOU'RE *HELPLESS* TO DODGE ME-- I'LL TURN MY MELTING RAY TO *FULL INTENSITY,* AND FINISH YOU OFF FOREVER!

MEANWHILE, A STRANGELY IRRESISTIBLE FORCE FIELD FROM BELOW HOLDS TONY STARK'S XL-750 HUNTER ROCKET PLANE MOTIONLESS IN THE SKY ABOVE, AS IT SHAKES IN A DESPERATE THOUGH FUTILE EFFORT TO FREE ITSELF...

IT'S NO USE, BIG FELLA! THE SHIP WON'T RESPOND!

SOMETHING'S AFFECTING IT FROM BELOW, CAP! STAY AT THE CONTROLS WHILE I LEAP TO THE GROUND!

LEAP TO THE *GROUND??* *HOW??*

13

JUST **WATCH** ME!!

HANK--**DON'T**!! YOU'LL BE **KILLED**!! **HANK!**

STAY **BACK,** WASP! I **KNOW** WHAT I'M DOING!

I'VE GOT TO **GROW**-- TO MY **LARGEST** **SIZE**-- WHILE I'M **FALLING**--!!

THERE! BY TIMING IT JUST RIGHT, IT'S **NOTHING** FOR A 100-FOOTER TO LAND ASTRIDE TWO ROOF-TOPS--LIKE **THIS!**

THEN, SCANNING THE CROWD IN THE STREET BELOW, THRU HIS MANY TIMES NORMAL-SIZED EYES, THE TOWERING TITAN SOON PICKS OUT--

I **THOUGHT** SO! THE **ENCHANT-RESS**-- AND THE **EXECUTIONER** --JUST AS CAP **SAID!**

SHE MUST HAVE BEEN HOLDING OUR PLANE IN ONE OF HER MYSTIC **SPELLS!** UH OH! THEY **SEE** ME!

HOLD IT, YOU TWO! THE **AVENGERS** WANT YOU!!

NEWSREEL M.M.M.S. MEET

THIS IS **ONE** TIME WHEN A LITTLE **WASP** CAN BE MORE EFFECTIVE THAN AN ENORMOUS **GIANT!** JUST SO LONG AS THEY DON'T **SEE** ME SPILL THIS CAN OF GREASE BENEATH THEM...!

BY THE SEVEN RINGS OF SATURN!!! WHO IS RESPONSIBLE FOR **THIS???**

14

NOW TO USE MY "WASP'S STING" AGAINST THE ENCHANTRESS BEFORE SHE SEES -- OH! TOO LATE!

THE WASP! A SIMPLE SPELL WILL BE ENOUGH FOR SO TINY A FOE!

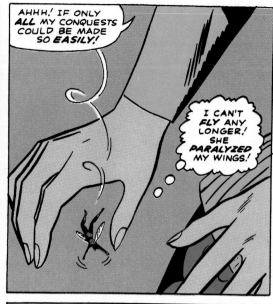

AHHH.! IF ONLY ALL MY CONQUESTS COULD BE MADE SO EASILY!

I CAN'T FLY ANY LONGER! SHE PARALYZED MY WINGS!

BUT SUDDENLY, A RAGING, EAR-SHATTERING, THUNDEROUS CRY RINGS OUT--!!

DROP HER -- IN THE NAME OF THE AVENGERS!!

IT'S THE GIANT ONE! LEAVE THE WASP--WE HAVE OTHER TASKS TO COMPLETE!

AGREED! BUT SHE KNOWS THE BOY IS ON HIS WAY TO ZEMO! WE MUST BE CAREFUL!

MEANTIME, THE MIGHTY ROCKET PLANE, NOW FREED FROM THE SPELL OF THE ENCHANTRESS, ZOOMS SKYWARD AGAIN....!

ONLY ZEMO COULD BE BEHIND THIS NEW ATTACK!

RICK JONES MEANS NOTHING TO HIM! HE'S ONLY BAIT FOR THE TRAP WHICH ZEMO MUST HAVE WAITING FOR ME!

AND HE WON'T BE DISAPPOINTED! I'M GOING AFTER HIM--ALONE! THIS TIME OUR FIGHT WILL BE-- TO THE FINISH!!

15

FLYING AT MANY TIMES THE SPEED OF SOUND, THE XL-750 REACHES THE AMAZON JUNGLE WITHIN MINUTES...

RRRRRrrrr

ZEMO WILL *SHOW* HIMSELF, SOONER OR LATER!

ZEMO! HE'S *HERE!* I HAVE HIM ON OUR *RADAR!*

THEN WHAT ARE YOU *WAITING* FOR, YOU *FOOL??* YOU *KNOW* MY ORDERS.!!

BRING HIM DOWN.! *BRING HIM DOWN!* HE MUST NOT ESCAPE ME AGAIN.!

INSTANTLY, A MIGHTY BARRAGE OF HIDDEN RAPID-FIRE ANTI-AIRCRAFT GUNS BREAKS THE OMINOUS JUNGLE STILLNESS....!

BUT, THE LIGHTNING-FAST HUNTER PLANE IS FAR FROM HELPLESS...!

I'VE *FOUND* HIM!

FIRST, I'LL SILENCE HIS GUNS WITH MY OWN ROCKET ATTACK.!!

WHOOM!

JUST THEN, BEFORE CAP CAN CEASE FIRING, A LARGE GLASS CAGE IS RAISED FROM A HIDDEN UNDERGROUND PIT DIRECTLY INTO THE LINE OF FIRE--.!

RICK! IT'S *RICK.!!*

THIS WAS ZEMO'S TRAP.! HE WANTED *ME* TO BE THE ONE TO CAUSE RICK'S DEATH.! AND, HEAVEN HELP ME -- IT ALMOST *HAPPENED.!!*

THE ROCKET FIRE BROKE OPEN MY CAGE.!!

16

MEANWHILE, BACK IN THE CITY, THE FATEFUL BATTLE STILL RAGES, UNCHECKED...

MY ONLY CHANCE IS TO STAY NEAR THE ROOFTOPS, WHERE THOR DARES NOT LOOSE THE FULL FURY OF HIS HAMMER!

HAH! MY FLYING STEED CAN VAULT OVER AN OBSTACLE, BUT YOU CAN'T CHECK YOUR FLIGHT SO EASILY, THUNDER GOD!

HE'S RIGHT! I'M ABOUT TO CRASH INTO THAT BUILDING!

BUT, BY TURNING IN MID-AIR, I CAN STRIKE WITH MY FEET, THUS BOUNCING OFF AROUND THE WALL AND CONTINUING ON MY WAY!

THUP!

WHILE, ON THE GROUND, THE INSIDIOUS MELTER WAITS HIS CHANCE...

NOW!! WHA-- I SHOULD HAVE KNOWN! THE ONE THING MY MELTING BEAM CANNOT AFFECT!! THOR'S HAMMER!

I WAS HOPING I'D FIND YOU AGAIN, BUSTER!

BACK, YOU IRON CLOD!! YOU CANNOT DEFY ME! YOUR ARMOR IS NOT ENCHANTED AS THOR'S HAMMER IS!

MAYBE NOT! BUT YOUR MELTING BEAM IS USELESS UNLESS IT HITS ITS TARGET!

AND MY JETS MAKE ME MUCH TOO FAST FOR YOU, SONNY!

HE'S RIGHT! I'VE GOT TO JOIN THE OTHERS! I NEED THEIR POWER TO HOLD HIM OFF WHILE I TAKE CAREFUL AIM WITH MY INVINCIBLE BEAM!

WHEN WILL YOU COSTUMED CLOWNS LEARN THAT THE GOOD GUYS ALWAYS WIN?

17

BUT, LUCK SEEMS TO BE WITH THE "BAD GUYS", FOR-- JUST THEN--

MELTER! QUICKLY-- ON TO THE CAR! WE'LL HELP YOU ESCAPE!

JUST IN TIME! IRON MAN ALMOST HAD ME TRAPPED!

ALMOST--BAH! I SAW THE WHOLE THING! YOU WERE FINISHED!

AND SO ARE YOU, EXECUTIONER! ALL OF YOU!

GIANT-MAN!!

IT'S THE END OF THE LINE FOR ZEMO'S MASTERS OF EVIL!

WHOOM!

I'VE GOT TO KEEP THEM ON THE RUN-- SO SHE'S NO TIME FOR A NEW SPELL!

HE FLATTENED THAT CAR WITH ONE STRIKE!

NO MATTER! I'M STILL HIS MASTER! ALL I NEED IS A WEAPON!

I'LL FINISH HIM! MY LANCE IS WEAPON ENOUGH!

NOT WHEN I CAN USE THIS FLATTENED CAR AS A SHIELD!

SPEAKING OF SHIELDS-- WHAT HAPPENED TO CAPTAIN AMERICA??

QUICKLY-- REGROUP! STAND TOGETHER FOR MAXIMUM POWER!

BAH! EVEN WITHOUT A WEAPON, MY STRENGTH CAN DEFEAT ANY AVENGER!

EXCEPT MIGHTY THOR, BRAGGART!

IT LOOKS LIKE THE SHOWDOWN, AT LAST!

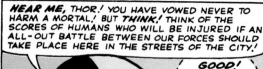

HEAR ME, THOR! YOU HAVE VOWED NEVER TO HARM A MORTAL! BUT THINK! THINK OF THE SCORES OF HUMANS WHO WILL BE INJURED IF AN ALL-OUT BATTLE BETWEEN OUR FORCES SHOULD TAKE PLACE HERE IN THE STREETS OF THE CITY!

GOOD! YOU ARE CONFUSING HIM!

HE'S RIGHT! WE'RE ALMOST EQUALLY MATCHED! THE DAMAGE COULD BE UNIMAGINABLE!

THEY CARE NOTHING FOR HUMAN SAFETY! DO NOT RELAX YOUR VIGILANCE! THEY SEEK TO CATCH US OFF-GUARD!

BAH! IF STEALTH CANNOT DEFEAT YOU --I'LL TURN AGAIN TO BRUTE FORCE!!

AVENGERS, ASSEMBLE!!!

BUT, AS THE MIGHTY RALLYING CRY IS SOUNDED, ONE AVENGER IS A CONTINENT AWAY--UNABLE TO HEAR!

RICK!! RICK, BOY-- ARE YOU ALL RIGHT??

SURE, CAP! BUT I WOULDN'T WANT A STEADY DIET OF THIS KINDA JAZZ!

I THINK YOU'LL BE SAFE NOW, LAD! YOU WERE JUST A MEANS TO AN END-- I'M THE ONE ZEMO WANTS TO DESTROY!

BUT, CAP-- YOU'RE ALL ALONE-- AND ZEMO HAS WEAPONS-- MEN-- EVERYTHING IN HIS FAVOR!

NOT EVERYTHING, RICK! THERE'S ONE WEAPON WE'RE ARMED WITH WHICH HE CAN NEVER POSSESS!

A THING CALLED-- JUSTICE!

HE LANDED!! THERE'S NO ESCAPE FOR HIM NOW!! I'VE GOT HIM!! DEATH TO CAPTAIN AMERICA!

STAND BACK, RICK! THIS IS THE MOMENT I'VE WAITED YEARS FOR!!

NO, ZEMO! IT WON'T BE AS EASY AS YOU THINK!! AND YOUR MEN WON'T HELP YOU! THIS IS OUR FINAL SHOWDOWN-- IT HAS TO BE JUST YOU AND ME!!

YOU'RE A FOOL TO THE END! HOW CAN YOUR SHIELD HELP YOU NOW?!!

19

HAH! IN YOUR *DESPERATE NERVOUSNESS*, YOU *MISSED* ME!

I WASN'T *AIMING* FOR YOU! I KNEW YOUR DISINTEGRATOR PISTOL COULD DESTROY MY SHIELD! I WAS AIMING FOR A MORE *VITAL* TARGET!

AND I *HIT* IT -- I HIT THAT *ONE CERTAIN ROCK!*

CLANG!

I *KNEW* IT! HE'S GONE *MAD!*

NO, YOU MURDERER! *NOT* MAD! JUST SKILLFUL ENOUGH TO HIT THE ONE ROCK WHICH COULD CAUSE THE OTHERS TO FALL IN SUCH A WAY AS TO *CUT YOU OFF* FROM YOUR WARRIORS!

A WASTE OF TIME! THAT CHEAP VAUDEVILLE TRICK CANNOT SAVE YOU NOW!

CAP, WATCH OUT! HE'S STILL HOLDING HIS DISINTEGRATOR!

NOT MERELY *HOLDING* IT! I AM ABOUT TO *USE* IT! AND -- *THUS DIES* CAPTAIN AMERICA!

BUT THEN, BEFORE ZEMO'S FINGER CAN SQUEEZE THE TRIGGER, CAP TILTS HIS GLITTERING SHIELD SO THAT THE SUN'S RAYS CATCH IT AT JUST THE RIGHT ANGLE, *BLINDING* HIS FOE!

MY EYES!! I CAN'T *SEE!!*

BUT I *CAN,* ZEMO! AND NOW--!

CONFUSED, BEWILDERED, FILLED WITH FEAR, THE HOODED MENACE FIRES BLINDLY, AS CAPTAIN AMERICA COMES CLOSER -- CLOSER --

ZZSSST

STAY BACK -- BACK--!

BUT, IN HIS UNTHINKING PANIC, ZEMO'S BLAST HITS A SUPPORTING ROCK ABOVE HIM, CAUSING ANOTHER FATAL *ROCKSLIDE....*!

AGGHHHHH...!

CAP!! LOOK OUT--!!

DON'T WORRY, RICK! MY *SHIELD* WILL SAVE ME!

BUT *NOTHING* CAN SAVE THE MASTER OF VILLAINY!

YOU CAN REST EASIER NOW, BUCKY -- WHEREVER YOU MAY BE! YOUR DEATH -- HAS BEEN -- *AVENGED!*

NO MAN CAN PERPETRATE EVIL WITHOUT PAYING THE PRICE! IF DESTINY COULD SPEAK, IT WOULD SAY..."BY MY HAND, SHALL ALWAYS DIE -- A VILLAIN!"

THE END

BUT, THOUGH ZEMO SHALL MENACE MANKIND NO MORE, THE MOST SPECTACULAR BATTLE OF ALL TIME AWAITS THE AVENGERS IN NEW YORK! AND, THE OUTCOME OF THAT BATTLE SHALL BRING A *CHANGE* IN THE LINE-UP OF THE AVENGERS, AS YOU WILL SEE AND MARVEL AT, NEXT ISSUE!

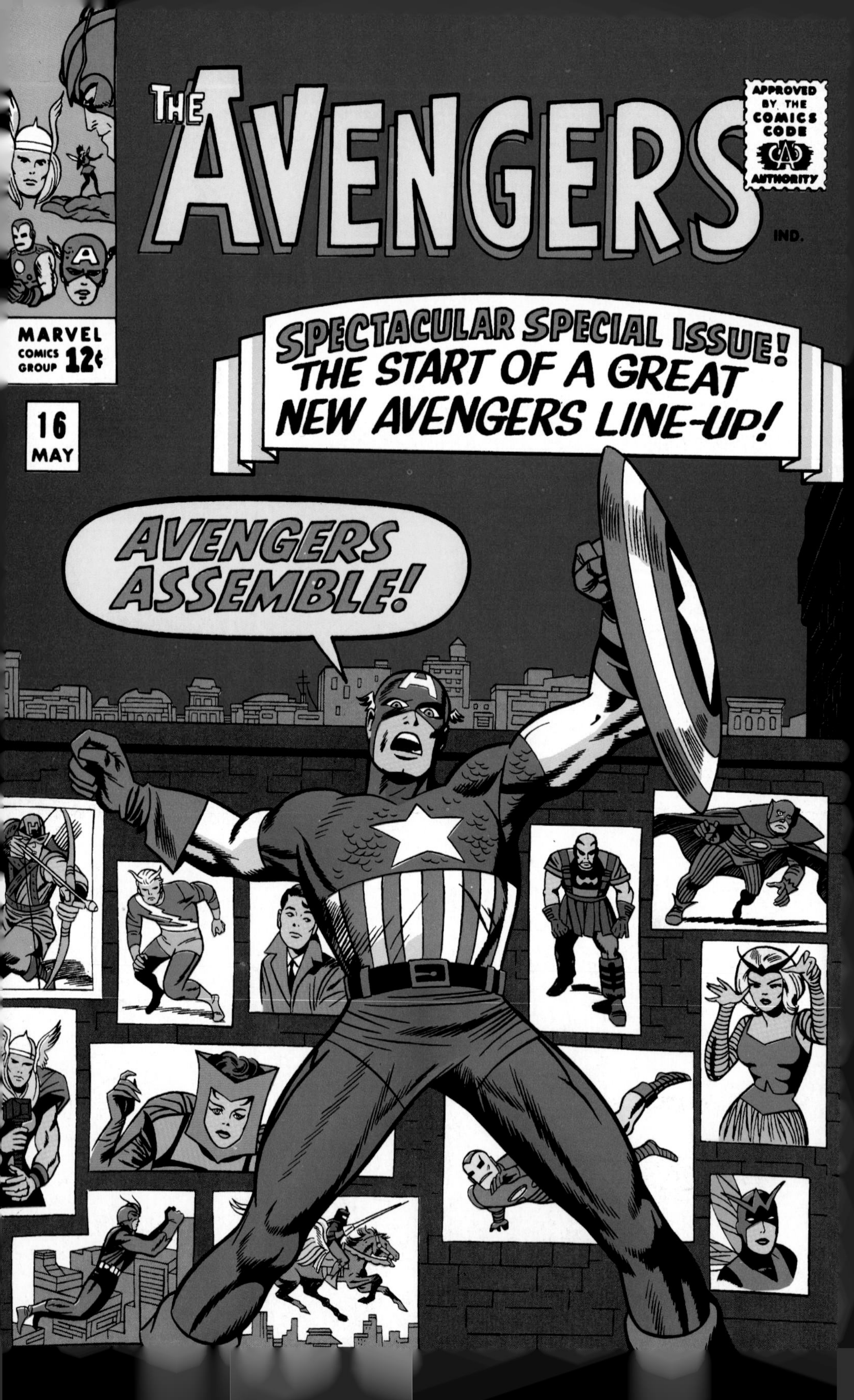

THE AVENGERS
APPROVED BY THE COMICS CODE AUTHORITY
IND.
MARVEL COMICS GROUP 12¢
16 MAY
SPECTACULAR SPECIAL ISSUE! THE START OF A GREAT NEW AVENGERS LINE-UP!
AVENGERS ASSEMBLE!

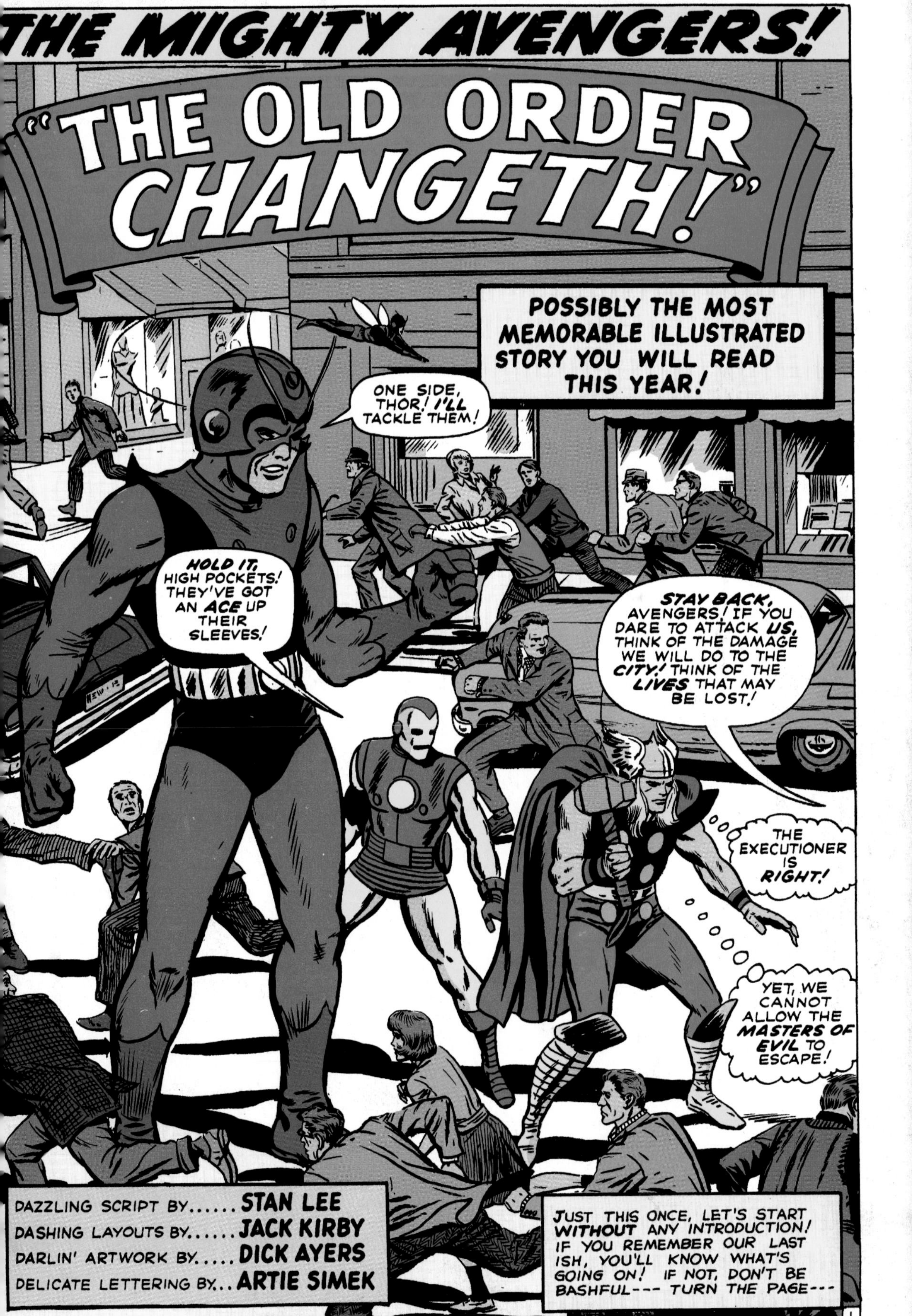
THE MIGHTY AVENGERS!
"THE OLD ORDER CHANGETH!"
POSSIBLY THE MOST MEMORABLE ILLUSTRATED STORY YOU WILL READ THIS YEAR!
ONE SIDE, THOR! I'LL TACKLE THEM!
HOLD IT, HIGH POCKETS! THEY'VE GOT AN ACE UP THEIR SLEEVES!
STAY BACK, AVENGERS! IF YOU DARE TO ATTACK US, THINK OF THE DAMAGE WE WILL DO TO THE CITY! THINK OF THE LIVES THAT MAY BE LOST!
THE EXECUTIONER IS RIGHT!
YET, WE CANNOT ALLOW THE MASTERS OF EVIL TO ESCAPE!
DAZZLING SCRIPT BY...... STAN LEE
DASHING LAYOUTS BY...... JACK KIRBY
DARLIN' ARTWORK BY..... DICK AYERS
DELICATE LETTERING BY... ARTIE SIMEK
JUST THIS ONCE, LET'S START WITHOUT ANY INTRODUCTION! IF YOU REMEMBER OUR LAST ISH, YOU'LL KNOW WHAT'S GOING ON! IF NOT, DON'T BE BASHFUL--- TURN THE PAGE---
1

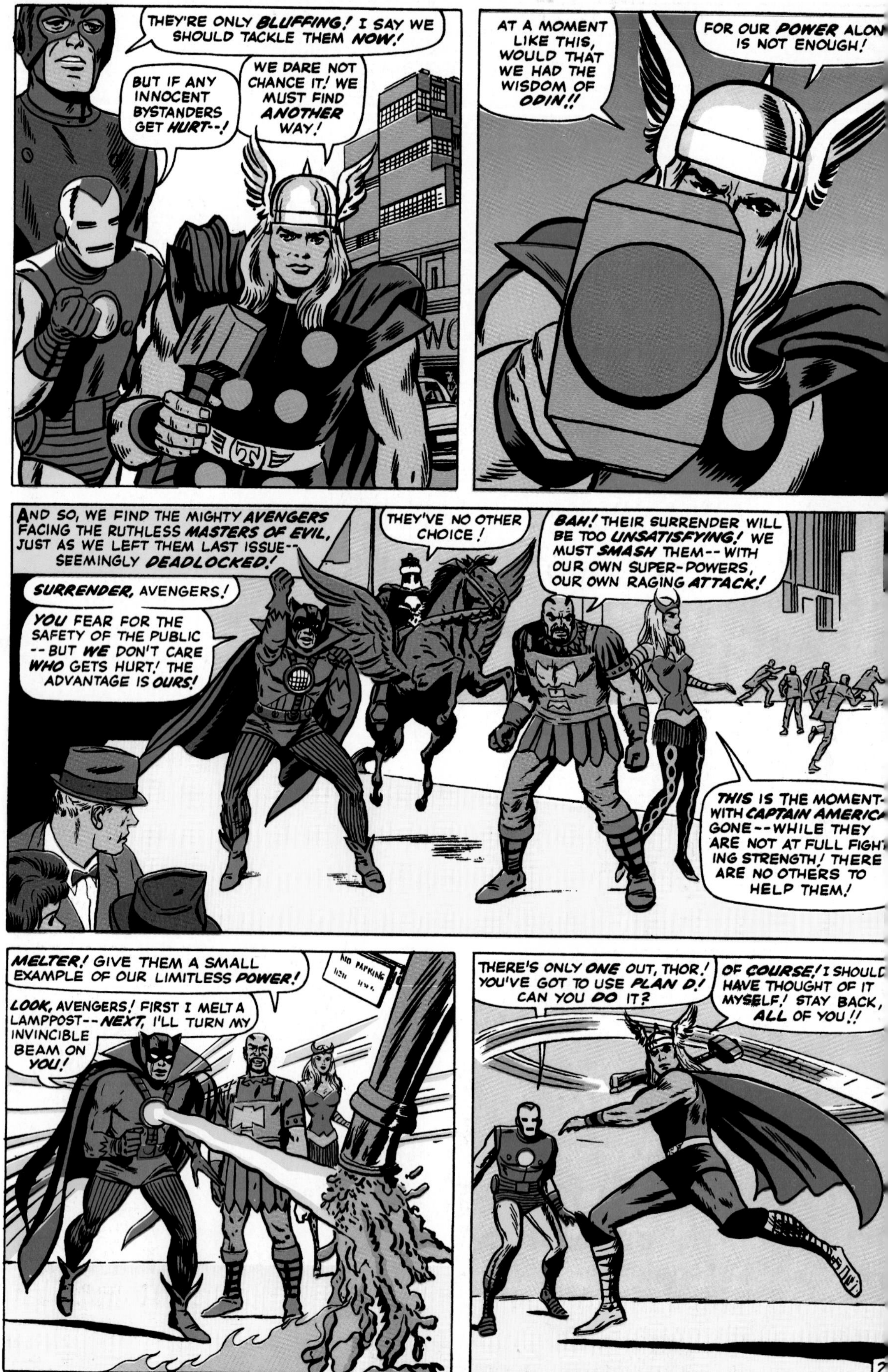
THEY'RE ONLY BLUFFING! I SAY WE SHOULD TACKLE THEM NOW!
BUT IF ANY INNOCENT BYSTANDERS GET HURT--!
WE DARE NOT CHANCE IT! WE MUST FIND ANOTHER WAY!
AT A MOMENT LIKE THIS, WOULD THAT WE HAD THE WISDOM OF ODIN!!
FOR OUR POWER ALON IS NOT ENOUGH!
AND SO, WE FIND THE MIGHTY AVENGERS FACING THE RUTHLESS MASTERS OF EVIL, JUST AS WE LEFT THEM LAST ISSUE-- SEEMINGLY DEADLOCKED!
SURRENDER, AVENGERS!
YOU FEAR FOR THE SAFETY OF THE PUBLIC --BUT WE DON'T CARE WHO GETS HURT! THE ADVANTAGE IS OURS!
THEY'VE NO OTHER CHOICE!
BAH! THEIR SURRENDER WILL BE TOO UNSATISFYING! WE MUST SMASH THEM-- WITH OUR OWN SUPER-POWERS, OUR OWN RAGING ATTACK!
THIS IS THE MOMENT- WITH CAPTAIN AMERICA GONE--WHILE THEY ARE NOT AT FULL FIGHT ING STRENGTH! THERE ARE NO OTHERS TO HELP THEM!
MELTER! GIVE THEM A SMALL EXAMPLE OF OUR LIMITLESS POWER!
NO PARKING
LOOK, AVENGERS! FIRST I MELT A LAMPPOST--NEXT, I'LL TURN MY INVINCIBLE BEAM ON YOU!
THERE'S ONLY ONE OUT, THOR! YOU'VE GOT TO USE PLAN D! CAN YOU DO IT?
OF COURSE! I SHOULD HAVE THOUGHT OF IT MYSELF! STAY BACK, ALL OF YOU!!
2

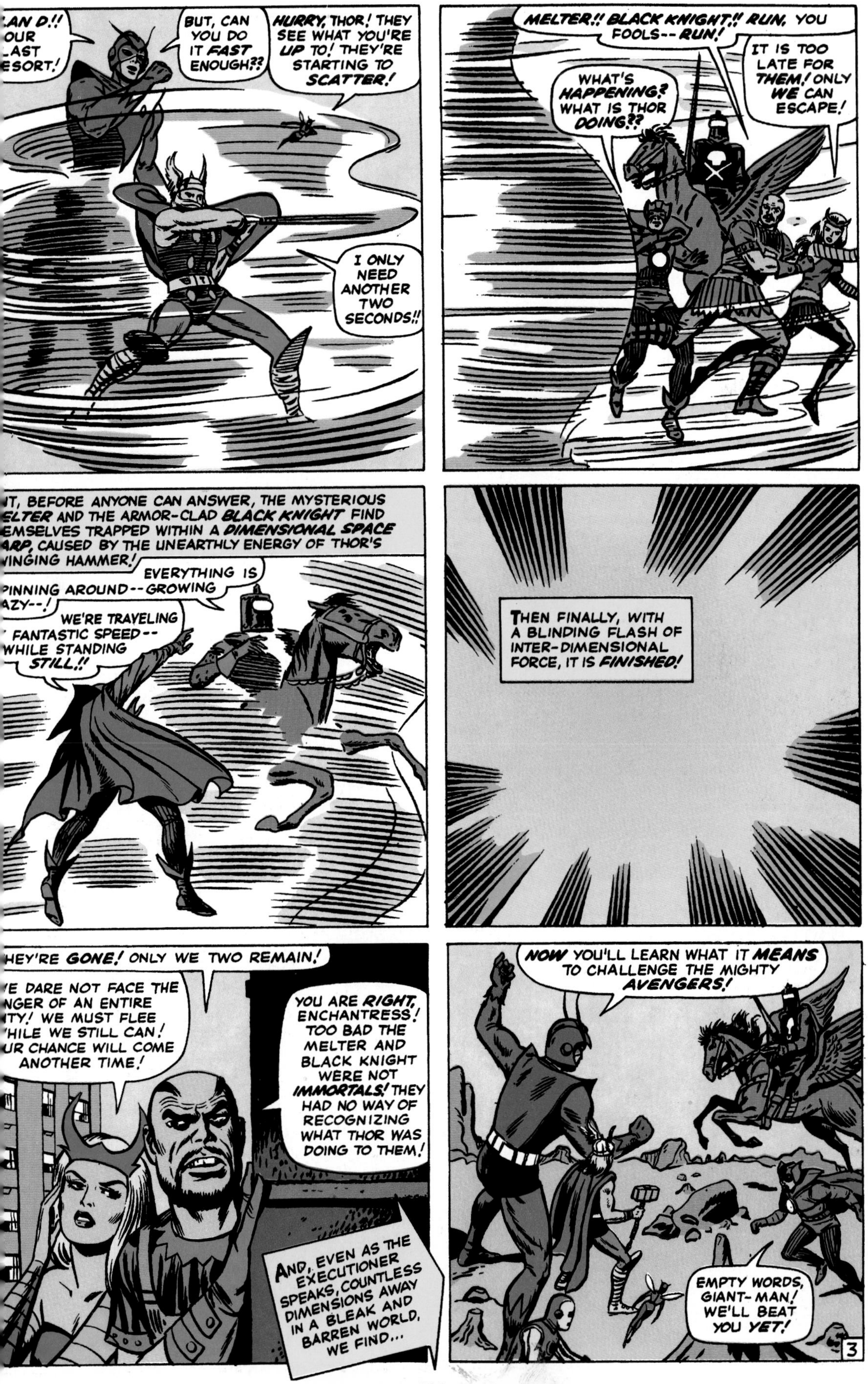

AN D.!! OUR LAST ESORT!
BUT, CAN YOU DO IT FAST ENOUGH??
HURRY, THOR! THEY SEE WHAT YOU'RE UP TO! THEY'RE STARTING TO SCATTER!
I ONLY NEED ANOTHER TWO SECONDS!!
MELTER!! BLACK KNIGHT!! RUN, YOU FOOLS-- RUN!
WHAT'S HAPPENING? WHAT IS THOR DOING??
IT IS TOO LATE FOR THEM! ONLY WE CAN ESCAPE!
IT, BEFORE ANYONE CAN ANSWER, THE MYSTERIOUS ELTER AND THE ARMOR-CLAD BLACK KNIGHT FIND EMSELVES TRAPPED WITHIN A DIMENSIONAL SPACE ARP, CAUSED BY THE UNEARTHLY ENERGY OF THOR'S WINGING HAMMER!
EVERYTHING IS PINNING AROUND--GROWING AZY--!
WE'RE TRAVELING FANTASTIC SPEED-- WHILE STANDING STILL!!
THEN FINALLY, WITH A BLINDING FLASH OF INTER-DIMENSIONAL FORCE, IT IS FINISHED!
HEY'RE GONE! ONLY WE TWO REMAIN!
E DARE NOT FACE THE NGER OF AN ENTIRE ITY! WE MUST FLEE HILE WE STILL CAN! UR CHANCE WILL COME ANOTHER TIME!
YOU ARE RIGHT, ENCHANTRESS! TOO BAD THE MELTER AND BLACK KNIGHT WERE NOT IMMORTALS! THEY HAD NO WAY OF RECOGNIZING WHAT THOR WAS DOING TO THEM!
AND, EVEN AS THE EXECUTIONER SPEAKS, COUNTLESS DIMENSIONS AWAY IN A BLEAK AND BARREN WORLD, WE FIND...
NOW YOU'LL LEARN WHAT IT MEANS TO CHALLENGE THE MIGHTY AVENGERS!
EMPTY WORDS, GIANT-MAN! WE'LL BEAT YOU YET!
3

WE KNOW YOU ARE SWORN NEVER TO TAKE HUMAN LIFE!

BUT WE'RE NOT BOUND BY ANY SUCH STUPID OATH! SO THE ODDS ARE STILL IN OUR FAVOR!!

USE YOUR BEAM, MELTER--FULL FORCE! I'LL ATTACK WITH MY ATOMIC LANCE!!

THEY DIDN'T EXPECT THIS! IT'S TOO LATE TO STOP US! WE'VE GOT THEM!

BUT THEN...

MY LANCE HAD NO EFFECT! AND THE RECOIL BOWLED US OVER!! HOW?? WHY??

WE WERE HOPING YOU'D ASK!!

MY BEAM!! IT BACKFIRED-- IF I HADN'T STOPPED IT IN TIME, I'D HAVE BEEN KILLED!

AND WE WOULDN'T WANT THAT TO HAPPEN, WOULD WE??

DIDN'T IT EVER OCCUR TO YOU THAT CERTAIN NATURAL LAWS ARE REVERSED IN DIFFERENT DIMENSIONS?? WE GAMBLED THAT YOU WOULD ATTACK US BEFORE YOU REALIZED THAT YOUR OWN WEAPONS WOULD TRAP YOU HERE!

STOP SQUIRMING! I'M SORRY THERE ISN'T TIME TO HAVE YOU GIFT-WRAPPED!

LET ME KNOW IF THIS IS TOO TIGHT, MELTER! IF IT IS, I'LL CRY MYSELF TO SLEEP!

AND NOW, LET US RETURN TO OUR OWN DIMENSION IN THE SAME MANNER AS WE DEPARTED--!

I FEEL AS NECESSARY AS A BUMP ON A LOG RIGHT NOW--AND I PROBABLY LOOK LIKE ONE, TOO!

SAY, I WONDER HOW CAPTAIN AMERICA MADE OUT WITH ZEMO IN SOUTH AMERICA?

4

AND, AS THE AVENGERS LEAVE THE ALIEN DIMENSION, THEY HAVE NO WAY OF KNOWING THAT CAPTAIN AMERICA HAS ALREADY CONCLUDED HIS LAST BATTLE WITH THE MURDEROUS ZEMO--A BATTLE WHICH HAS ENDED IN THE ARCH-VILLAIN'S DEATH.*

SO IT'S OVER AT LAST! I SHOULD FEEL A SENSE OF ELATION, BUT--I DON'T!

ALL I FEEL IS A STRANGE EMPTINESS, AND A NUMB SENSE OF DISBELIEF!

BUT YOU WON, CAP! WITH EVERYTHING AGAINST YOU-- ON HIS OWN HOME GROUNDS-- YOU BEAT HIM!

AS SHOWN IN AVENGERS #15 -- STAN.

MIGHTY IS THE RED, WHITE AND BLUE AVENGER! ALL HAIL OUR NEW CHIEFTAIN ALL HAIL CAPTAIN AMERICA!

ON YOUR FEET, ALL OF YOU! YOU'RE FREE MEN NOW! NO LONGER NEED YOU KNEEL IN HOMAGE TO A TYRANT!

MAYBE THEY CAN HELP US RETURN HOME, CAP!

NO, RICK! ALL WE NEED IS THIS JET! LUCKILY, IT WASN'T DAMAGED IN THE BATTLE!

WHA--? HOLD IT, LAD! I HEAR SOMETHING BEHIND US! SOUNDS LIKE TROUBLE!

SHOTS!! TAKE COVER, RICK! I WAS AFRAID OF THIS! IT'S ZEMO'S MERCENARIES! THEY WANT THE PLANE FOR THEMSELVES!

SPANNGG!

WHEW! THAT WAS A CLOSE ONE!

GET THEM! THERE'S ONLY ENOUGH ROOM ON THAT PLANE FOR US!

THEY HAVE NO CHANCE AGAINST AUTOMATIC GUNS! SHOW THEM NO MERCY!

THE COSTUMED ONE IS MAD! HE'S CHARGING RIGHT TOWARDS US!

MAD, AM I ?? WE'LL SEE ABOUT THAT!!

WHUMMP!

HOLD 'EM, CAP! I'LL SCOOP UP THEIR POPGUNS!

5

YOU HAVEN'T STOPPED US *YET!* I'LL FINISH YOU OFF WITH THIS *GRENADE!*

NOT WITH AN AIM LIKE *THAT* YOU WON'T!

DUCK, CAP!!

I'M 'WAY *AHEAD* OF YOU, SON!

BUT, AS FATE WOULD HAVE IT, THE HASTILY THROWN GRENADE, FALLING WIDE OF ITS MARK, STRIKES THE JET PLANE'S FUEL TANK INSTEAD!

WHOOM!

CAP! THEY'RE GETTIN' *AWAY!*

LET THEM GO, RICK! THERE'S NO PLACE FOR THEM TO RUN EXCEPT DEEPER INTO THE JUNGLE! AND THE NATIVES WILL BE *WAITING* FOR THEM THERE!

AS FOR *US...* I HAVE AN IDEA--!

BUT, LET US LEAVE CAPTAIN AMERICA AND RICK JONES ONCE AGAIN, AS WE RETURN TO AVENGERS HQ. IN A MANSION ON MANHATTAN'S UPPER EAST SIDE...

THE BLACK KNIGHT AND THE MELTER ARE BACK IN POLICE CUSTODY, AND THE EXECUTIONER AND ENCHANTRESS HAVE VANISHED AGAIN! *NOW* WHAT DO WE DO?

WAIT'LL I GET DOWN TO YOUR SIZE PARTNER! IT'S KINDA HARD TO *HEAR* YOU UP THERE! BY THE WAY, WHERE'S *THOR?*

HE CAN'T *BE* HERE TODAY! HE MUTTERED SOMETHING ABOUT A *TRIAL OF THE GODS,** AND RAN OFF!

*AS SHOWN IN *THOR #116*--ON SALE NOW *(HINT!)*--STAN

AND STILL NO WORD FROM CAP!

BUT HE DIDN'T WANT US TO BUTT IN-- HE SAID IT WAS A *PRIVATE* FIGHT!

THERE'S SOMETHING I'VE BEEN WANTING TO SAY--

--AND THIS SEEMS TO BE AS GOOD A TIME AS ANY TO *SAY* IT!

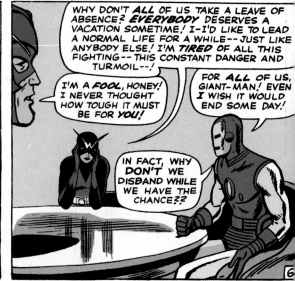

WHY DON'T *ALL* OF US TAKE A LEAVE OF ABSENCE? *EVERYBODY* DESERVES A VACATION SOMETIME! I-I'D LIKE TO LEAD A NORMAL LIFE FOR A WHILE-- JUST LIKE ANYBODY ELSE! I'M *TIRED* OF ALL THIS FIGHTING-- THIS CONSTANT DANGER AND TURMOIL--!

I'M A *FOOL,* HONEY! I NEVER THOUGHT HOW TOUGH IT MUST BE FOR *YOU!*

FOR *ALL* OF US, GIANT-MAN! EVEN *I* WISH IT WOULD END SOME DAY!

IN FACT, WHY *DON'T* WE DISBAND WHILE WE HAVE THE CHANCE??

BUT SUDDENLY... LOOK! SMOKE-- FILTERING INTO THE ROOM FROM UNDER THE DOOR! IT COULD BE AN ATTACK!

LET ME INVESTIGATE! I'M THE LEAST VULNERABLE IN MY ARMOR!

OH NO! WHY DID IT HAVE TO HAPPEN NOW-- OF ALL TIMES?!!

IT'S COMING FROM BEHIND THE DOOR! SOMETHING IS STUCK ONTO THE BACK! IT'S AN ARROW!

QUICKLY THEN! WHOEVER FIRED IT MUST STILL BE NEAR! LET'S GET HIM!

THE SMOKE IS SO DENSE I CAN HARDLY SEE!

I HAVE A FEELING I KNOW WHO FIRED THAT ARROW! AND, IF IT'S WHO I THINK IT IS, WE'LL HAVE A FIGHT ON OUR HANDS!

I WAS RIGHT!! IT'S-- HAWKEYE!!

LOOK! TONY STARK'S BUTLER IS TIED UP-- THAT'S HOW HE MANAGED TO GET IN!

STOP--ALL OF YOU!

I COME AS A FRIEND, NOT AS AN ENEMY!!

YOU?? A FRIEND??

YES! I WISH TO JOIN THE AVENGERS!! I NEVER INTENDED TO BE AN OUTCAST, OR AN ENEMY OF SOCIETY!

"I ALWAYS WISHED TO USE MY SKILLS, MY POWERS TO AID THE PUBLIC, BUT A CAPRICIOUS ACCIDENT OF FATE MADE THE POLICE THINK I WAS A MENACE!*"

STOP HIM! DON'T LET HIM GET AWAY!

I WANTED TO HELP THEM-- BUT THEY MISUNDERSTOOD!

* SEE IRON MAN #57--STAN.

7

113

THEN, BEFORE I COULD CLEAR MYSELF, I MET THE BEAUTIFUL *BLACK WIDOW*, AND FELL HOPELESSLY IN LOVE WITH HER! EVEN AFTER I LEARNED SHE WAS IN THE EMPLOY OF THE COMMUNISTS, I COULDN'T TEAR HER FROM MY HEART!

BUT THEN, JUST ONE WEEK AGO, THEY MADE HER *PAY* THE PRICE FOR TRYING TO DESERT HER RED MASTERS!

"I REACHED THE SCENE IN TIME TO *AVENGE* HER-- AFTER WHICH, THERE WAS NOTHING MORE TO DO BUT CALL THE AMBULANCE--AND FEEL MY SOUL SHRIVEL WITHIN ME AS I SAW THEM DRIVE HER AWAY!"

FATE ALWAYS EXACTS HER PRICE FOR PAST DEEDS! THERE WAS NO WAY TO ESCAPE--MY *DARLING!*

BUT, I'LL MAKE *UP* FOR WHAT WE'VE DONE! I'LL DEVOTE MY *LIFE* TO MAKING AMENDS

"SHE WAS STILL ALIVE WHEN THEY TOOK HER AWAY! I DIDN'T TRY TO LEARN WHAT HAPPENED AFTER THAT! I-- I WAS AFRAID TO FIND OUT!"

I *BELIEVE* YOU HAWKEYE! BUT-- THE *OTHER* AVENGERS MUST ALSO ACCEPT YOU FOR MEMBERSHIP!

WAIT! WHAT ARE YOU *DOING??*

I'M GOING TO PROVE MY WORTH TO *ALL* OF YOU!

YOU'VE FACED ME IN BATTLE, IRON MAN-- BUT *THEY* HAVEN'T! *THIS* WILL SHOW THEM MY SKILL!

IT WAS I WHO TIED UP YOUR BUTLER, SO IT'S ONLY FITTING THAT *I* BE THE ONE TO *FREE* HIM--*MY* WAY!

AT THE SAME SPLIT-SECOND, THREE ARROWS FIND THEIR MARK AS *ONE*, AND THE MOTIONLESS MAN IS FREE ONCE AGAIN!

ZZZZZZIT!

TWANNNNG!

SSSSSSSST!

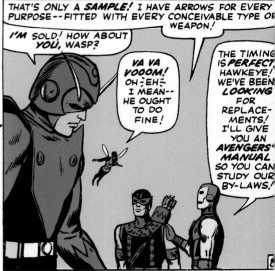

THAT'S ONLY A *SAMPLE!* I HAVE ARROWS FOR EVERY PURPOSE--FITTED WITH EVERY CONCEIVABLE TYPE OF WEAPON!

I'M SOLD! HOW ABOUT *YOU*, WASP?

VA VA VOOOM! OH--EH-- I MEAN-- HE OUGHT TO DO FINE!

THE TIMING IS *PERFECT*, HAWKEYE! WE'VE BEEN *LOOKING* FOR REPLACE-MENTS! I'LL GIVE YOU AN *AVENGERS'* MANUAL SO YOU CAN STUDY OUR BY-LAWS!

THE NEXT DAY, A NUCLEAR-POWERED REMOTE CONTROL UNDERSEA TV SCANNER PROBES THE OCEAN'S DEPTHS NEAR THE LAST KNOWN APPEARANCE OF THE REGAL SUB-MARINER...

AVENGERS CALLING PRINCE NAMOR! AVENGERS CALLING PRINCE NAMOR! DO YOU HEAR US, SUB-MARINER??

WITHIN MINUTES, THE HEREDITARY RULER OF THE KINGDOM OF ATLANTIS HEARS THE ULTRA-SONIC SOUNDINGS, AND ACCOMPANIED BY HIS PALACE GUARD, SWIMS AT INDESCRIBABLE SPEED TOWARDS THE SOURCE...

WHO CALLS THE SUB-MARINER?? WHO DARES INTRUDE UPON MY REALM??

THE AVENGERS DARE!! WE OFFER YOU A CHANCE TO WIN THE FRIENDSHIP AND RESPECT OF THE HUMAN RACE, NAMOR, INSTEAD OF ITS HATRED! WE OFFER YOU AN OPPORTUNITY TO RENOUNCE YOUR DREAMS OF CONQUEST, AND BECOME -- AN AVENGER!

RENOUNCE MY CLAIM TO DOMINION OVER THE SURFACE WORLD?? NEVER!

UNTIL MY PEOPLE ARE AGAIN RULERS OF EARTH'S LAND, AS WELL AS HER SEAS, I CAN NEVER ALLY MYSELF WITH ANY HUMANS -- EVEN THOUGH YOUR OFFER DOES ME HONOR!

SPOKEN LIKE THE PRINCE HE IS!

TOO BAD! HE'D HAVE MADE A GREAT AVENGER!

BUT, IN AN ISOLATED SWISS CHALET, HALF-WAY AROUND THE EARTH, A GRACEFUL BLACK-HAIRED BEAUTY WATCHES THE FASTEST HUMAN ON EARTH RACING TOWARDS HER FROM THE VALLEY BEYOND...

WANDA, MY SISTER! I HAVE THRILLING NEWS!!

WHAT IS IT, PIETRO? WHAT HAS HAPPENED??

SEE THE REPORT FROM AMERICA ON THE SECOND PAGE -- ABOUT THE AVENGERS!! READ IT, WANDA!

IT HAS BEEN LEARNED BY A RELIABLE SOURCE THAT THE MIGHTY AVENGERS HAVE ACCEPTED THE DASHING HAWK-EYE AS A PROBATIONARY MEMBER, AND ARE CONSIDERING OTHER APPLICANTS AS REPLACEMENTS....

THIS COULD BE OUR CHANCE, MY SISTER!

115

SILENTLY, THE DRAMATIC COUPLE RETURN TO THEIR ROOMS, ONLY TO REAPPEAR ON THE TERRACE MOMENTS LATER AS-- THE *SCARLET WITCH,* AND *QUICKSILVER!!*

YOU ARE THE OLDEST, PIETRO, AND I SHALL DO AS YOU SAY! BUT, I THOUGHT WE HAD VOWED NEVER AGAIN TO USE OUR SUPER-POWERS FOR OTHERS!

ONLY BECAUSE WE HAD BEEN CRUELLY EXPLOITED BY *MAGNETO,* MY SISTER!

YES! I SHALL NEVER FORGET HOW HE ONCE SAVED OUR LIVES, AND THEN MADE US REPAY HIM BY SERVING HIS VILLAINOUS CAUSE IN HIS BAND OF *EVIL MUTANTS!* I STILL TREMBLE AT THE THOUGHT OF HIS POWER-- THE WAY HE RULED OVER ALL OF US!*

* AS SHOWN IN PRACTICALLY EVERY ISSUE OF *X-MEN--* STAN.

BECAUSE OF MAGNETO, WE WERE FORCED TO BATTLE THE VALIANT *X-MEN,* EVEN THOUGH OUR HEARTS SECRETLY FAVORED THE JUSTICE OF THEIR CAUSE! BUT, WHY DID YOU NOT JOIN *THEM,* WHEN YOU HAD THE CHANCE??

BECAUSE I WISHED TO *FORGET* THAT WE ARE *HOMO SUPERIOR--* BORN WITH POWERS DENIED TO ORDINARY, HUMAN BEINGS!

BUT, THE *AVENGERS* MIGHT ACCEPT US WITHOUT CARING THAT WE ARE *DIFFERENT--* WITHOUT ALWAYS REMINDING US-- WE'RE *MUTANTS!!*

I SHALL DO AS YOU WISH, MY BROTHER!

AND SO, THAT VERY AFTER-NOON, A FATEFUL LETTER IS WRITTEN TO THE WORLD'S MIGHTIEST SUPER-TEAM...

The Avengers
New York City
U.S.A.
Attention: Acting Chairman.
My sister and I are
interested in
your

10

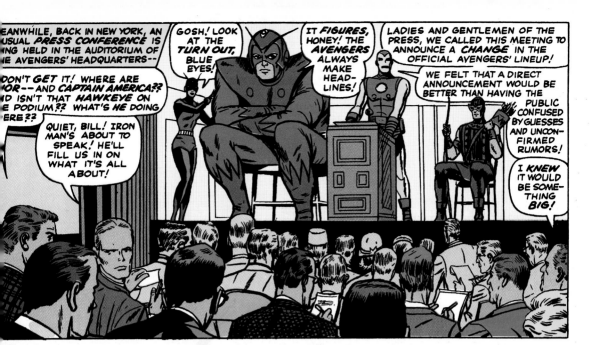

MEANWHILE, BACK IN NEW YORK, AN UNUSUAL *PRESS CONFERENCE* IS BEING HELD IN THE AUDITORIUM OF THE AVENGERS' HEADQUARTERS--

GOSH! LOOK AT THE *TURN OUT,* BLUE EYES!

IT *FIGURES,* HONEY! THE *AVENGERS* ALWAYS MAKE HEADLINES!

LADIES AND GENTLEMEN OF THE PRESS, WE CALLED THIS MEETING TO ANNOUNCE A *CHANGE* IN THE OFFICIAL AVENGERS' LINEUP!

WE FELT THAT A DIRECT ANNOUNCEMENT WOULD BE BETTER THAN HAVING THE PUBLIC CONFUSED BY GUESSES AND UNCONFIRMED RUMORS!

I *DON'T GET* IT! WHERE ARE *THOR*-- AND *CAPTAIN AMERICA*?? AND ISN'T THAT *HAWKEYE* ON THE PODIUM?? WHAT'S *HE* DOING HERE??

QUIET, BILL! IRON MAN'S ABOUT TO SPEAK! HE'LL FILL US IN ON WHAT IT'S ALL ABOUT!

I *KNEW* IT WOULD BE SOMETHING *BIG!*

AND NOW, IT GIVES ME GREAT PLEASURE TO ANNOUNCE THE *FIRST NEW AVENGERS' REPLACEMENT* IN MANY MONTHS! I TAKE PRIDE IN PRESENTING THE MAN KNOWN AS-- *HAWKEYE!*

HAWKEYE HAS SUCCESSFULLY PASSED OUR RIGOROUS SERIES OF QUALIFICATIONS TESTS, AND HAS BEEN THOROUGHLY INVESTIGATED AND APPROVED BY THE FEDERAL SECURITY AGENCY AT OUR REQUEST!

HAWKEYE! I'VE READ ABOUT HIS PROWESS WITH THAT BOW HE USES! HE'LL MAKE A GREAT AVENGER!

IRON MAN! YOU USED THE WORD *"REPLACEMENT"!* DOES THAT MEAN SOME AVENGERS ARE *RESIGNING?*

SAY! THAT'S *RIGHT!* IS THAT THE REASON *THOR* AND *CAPTAIN AMERICA* AREN'T WITH YOU?

I'M AFRAID THAT ANY INFORMATION ABOUT OUR TWO ABSENT AVENGERS IS *RESTRICTED* FOR THE PRESENT! BUT, I *CAN* TELL YOU THIS MUCH--

WE ARE IN THE PROCESS OF INTERVIEWING *OTHER* APPLICANTS FOR MEMBERSHIP, AND WILL ANNOUNCE THEIR ACCEPTANCE AS SOON AS IT IS FINAL!

THAT'S ALL FOR NOW, LADIES AND GENTLEMEN! THANK YOU FOR ATTENDING!

WISH I *KNEW* ABOUT CAP AND THOR MYSELF!!

THEN, AFTER THE PRESS HAS DEPARTED...

WELCOME TO OUR RANKS, HAWKEYE! MAY YOUR CAREER WITH US BE A FRUITFUL ONE!

I'M GRATEFUL TO ALL OF YOU FOR YOUR TRUST IN ME! I VOW TO DO NOTHING THAT WILL EVER DISCREDIT THE NAME OF THE *AVENGERS!*

11

117

SPOKEN LIKE A TRUE AVENGER, HAWKEYE! WE EXPECT GREAT THINGS OF YOU, AND SOMEHOW I DON'T THINK WE'LL BE DISAPPOINTED!

MY ONLY REGRET IS THAT YOU PLAN A LEAVE OF ABSENCE! I WOULD RELISH THE THRILL OF BATTLING SIDE-BY-SIDE WITH THE THREE OF YOU!

SO WOULD WE, HAWKEYE!

SPEAK FOR YOURSELF, IRON MAN! I'D RELISH A VACATION!

I'VE BEEN PROMISING THE WASP A VACATION FOR MONTHS, AND I CAN'T DISAPPOINT HER AGAIN! BUT REMEMBER--WE'RE ONLY TAKING A LEAVE OF ABSENCE! WE'RE NOT PLANNING TO RESIGN FOREVER!

MAYBE YOU'RE NOT, HIGH POCKETS--BUT IF I CAN EVER GET YOU NEAR A JUSTICE OF THE PEACE, LOOK OUT!

YOU'D BETTER WATCH YOUR STEP, BIG FELLA, OR SAY! HERE'S THE NOON MAIL! LET'S SEE IF WE HAVE ANY MORE APPLICATIONS FOR MEMBERSHIP

IT LOOKS MIGHTY HEAVY! I'LL JUST GET THE MAIL BAG OVER HERE BY REVERSING MY TRANSISTORIZED REPELLOR BEAMS! I HATE TO GET OUT OF PRACTICE!

OKAY, PRETTY GIRL, LET'S ROLL UP OUR SLEEVES! WE'VE GOT A LOT OF MAIL OPENING TO DO!

U.S. MAIL

SOME JOB FOR SUPER-HEROES! ≈SIGH≈!

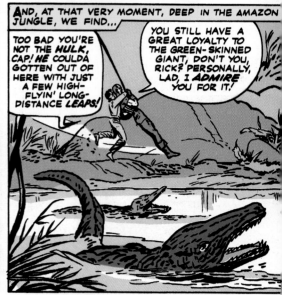

AND, AT THAT VERY MOMENT, DEEP IN THE AMAZON JUNGLE, WE FIND...

TOO BAD YOU'RE NOT THE HULK, CAP! HE COULDA GOTTEN OUT OF HERE WITH JUST A FEW HIGH-FLYIN' LONG-DISTANCE LEAPS!

YOU STILL HAVE A GREAT LOYALTY TO THE GREEN-SKINNED GIANT, DON'T YOU, RICK? PERSONALLY, LAD, I ADMIRE YOU FOR IT!

WOW! LOOK AT THE SIZE OF THAT BOA CONSTRICTOR, CAP!

HE WON'T BOTHER US IF WE DON'T BOTHER HIM! BUT--HOLD IT! I HEAR SOMETHING IN THAT CLEARING!

A WHITE MAN--BEING ATTACKED BY A LEOPARD!! TOO FAR FOR ME TO REACH HIM IN TIME! ONLY ONE THING TO DO--!

N-NO! NO!

CLANNG!

YOU *SAVED* ME, SEÑOR! THE LEOPARD FLEES IN PAIN!

SAY! IF YOU SPEAK ENGLISH, WE MUST BE GETTING NEAR CIVILIZATION!

THAT'S RIGHT, RICK! WE'RE ON THE BORDER OF A COASTAL PLANTATION!

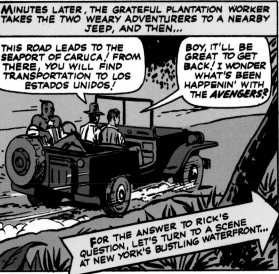

MINUTES LATER, THE GRATEFUL PLANTATION WORKER TAKES THE TWO WEARY ADVENTURERS TO A NEARBY JEEP, AND THEN...

THIS ROAD LEADS TO THE SEAPORT OF CARUCA! FROM THERE, YOU WILL FIND TRANSPORTATION TO LOS ESTADOS UNIDOS!

BOY, IT'LL BE GREAT TO GET BACK! I WONDER WHAT'S BEEN HAPPENIN' WITH THE *AVENGERS?*

FOR THE ANSWER TO RICK'S QUESTION, LET'S TURN TO A SCENE AT NEW YORK'S BUSTLING WATERFRONT...

HERE COME *QUICKSILVER* AND THE *SCARLET WITCH* NOW!

IT FEELS FUNNY TO BE DRIVIN' YOU TO MEET SOMEONE WHO ISN'T A BEAUTIFUL SOCIETY GAL, BOSS!

I THINK YOU'LL FIND THAT THE *SCARLET WITCH* IS FAR FROM UNATTRACTIVE, HAPPY!

MY NAME IS ANTHONY STARK! I AM A *FRIEND* OF THE AVENGERS -- IN FACT, THEY HOLD THEIR MEETINGS IN A BUILDING WHICH I LEASE TO THEM FOR THAT PURPOSE! THEY ASKED ME TO MEET YOU HERE AND TAKE YOU TO THEIR HEADQUARTERS!

THAT IS KIND OF YOU, MR. STARK! MY NAME IS *PIETRO*, AND THIS IS MY SISTER, *WANDA!*

PERHAPS WE ARE BETTER KNOWN AS *QUICKSILVER*, AND THE *SCARLET WITCH!*

THE *REPORTERS* WHO ARE HERE BEAR WITNESS TO YOUR FAME, MY FRIENDS!

WOULD YOU REMOVE YOUR COATS FOR A PICTURE, PLEASE? THANKS-- THAT'S *GREAT!*

IS IT TRUE YOU'RE GOING TO BE THE NEXT TWO *AVENGERS* REPLACEMENTS??

WE *HOPE* TO BECOME AVENGERS -- IF THEY WILL *HAVE* US!

13

YOU'VE BATTLED THE *X-MEN* IN THE PAST! BUT THEY'VE PUBLICLY STATED THAT YOU ARE NO LONGER TO BE CONSIDERED MENACES TO SOCIETY!

COULD WE HAVE A LITTLE DEMONSTRATION OF YOUR POWER, QUICKSILVER? IT WOULD MAKE A GREAT PICTURE SERIES FOR OUR SUNDAY SUPPLEMENT!

I DO NOT APPROVE OF PUBLIC DEMONSTRATIONS ...AND YET--

PERHAPS IT WILL HELP TO CONVINCE THE *AVENGERS* OF OUR VALUE! I SHALL *DO* IT!

SECONDS LATER...

NO MATTER *HOW* FAST YOUR CHAUFFEUR DRIVES, MY BROTHER WILL BEAT HIM TO YOUR HOME, MR. STARK!

THIS IS TOO *EASY!* I'LL TRY TO MAKE IT MORE INTERESTING--!

INCREDIBLE! THE POLICE HAVE CLEARED THE HIGHWAY, ALLOWING US TO GO AT TOP SPEED, AND YET--

HE'S RACING AROUND US AS THOUGH WE'RE STANDING *STILL!*

DID YOU JUST SEE SOMETHING RACE BY, DEAR?

YES! AS FAST AS A *COMET!* IT LOOKED LIKE A HUMAN B-- OH, NO! THAT'S *IMPOSSIBLE!*

I'LL STOP AND GET MY BEARINGS NOW, SO THAT I DO NOT GET LOST IN THIS UNFAMILIAR NEIGHBORHOOD!

FINALLY...

I HAVEN'T SEEN HIM FOR TEN MINUTES, BOSS! DO YOU THINK WE LEFT 'IM BEHIND? I WAS MAKIN' PRETTY GOOD TIME!

NOT A CHANCE, HAPPY! THERE HE IS, UP AHEAD, WAITING FOR US! HE BEAT US WITH *EASE!*

THEN, AFTER THE NEWSMEN HAVE RUSHED AWAY WITH THEIR PHOTOS...

YOU'RE NOT EVEN BREATHING HARD! I HAVE A FEELING THE AVENGERS WILL BE VERY EAGER TO MEET YOU!

AND, THEY SHALL FIND MY SISTER'S *HEX POWER* EQUALLY INTERESTING!

14

THUS, THE COLORFUL MUTANTS ARE USHERED INTO TONY STARK'S MANSION, WHERE THEY AWAIT THEIR COMING INTERVIEW...

IS IT REALLY TRUE THAT THE AVENGERS ARE BREAKING UP, MR. STARK?

NOT AT ALL, WANDA! IN FACT, FAR FROM IT! SOME OF THE MEMBERS MERELY WANT TO TAKE LEAVES OF ABSENCE!

BUT, THEY CANNOT DO IT UNTIL SATISFACTORY REPLACEMENTS ARE FOUND!

AND I BELIEVE THAT YOU TWO WILL QUALIFY IN THAT RESPECT! WELL, I MUST LEAVE YOU NOW! SINCE I'M NOT OFFICIALLY AN AVENGER, THERE'S NOTHING MORE I CAN DO HERE!

BUT, IF YOU SHOULD BE ACCEPTED, YOU CAN ALWAYS COUNT ON ME FOR ANY ASSISTANCE WHICH MY WEALTH WILL ALLOW ME TO FURNISH! GOOD LUCK TO YOU BOTH!

THANK YOU, MR. STARK!

I TRUST OUR INTERVIEW WILL BE SOON! I AM ANXIOUS TO MEET THE FAMOUS AVENGERS!

ONCE OUT OF SIGHT, TONY STARK ENTERS A PRIVATE ROOM, AND THEN...

AND NOW, I'LL SEE TO IT THAT THEY AREN'T KEPT WAITING TOO LONG!

EVEN WE AVENGERS DON'T REVEAL OUR SECRET IDENTITIES TO EACH OTHER! IT'S SAFER THIS WAY!

AND THEN, WITH A SMOOTH AND PRACTICED SKILL, THE DASHING MILLIONAIRE DONS HIS POWERFUL ARMOR, TRANSFORMING HIMSELF INTO THE AWESOME FIGURE OF IRON MAN...

HAWKEYE, QUICKSILVER, AND THE SCARLET WITCH HAVE VALUABLE SKILLS! THEY'LL MAKE PERFECT AVENGERS!

BUT, WITH THOR GONE -- AND GIANT-MAN AND ME LEAVING, I WONDER IF THEY WILL HAVE THE RAW STRENGTH WHICH THEY'LL NEED?

IF ONLY WE COULD FIND THE HULK! IF WE COULD CONVINCE HIM TO REJOIN!

MEANTIME, A SMALL SPEEDY PLANE LANDS AT LA GUARDIA FIELD AFTER AN EMERGENCY FLIGHT FROM SOUTH AMERICA...

TELL GENERAL CURTISS I'M GRATEFUL TO HIM FOR HAVING US FLOWN TO THE STATES SO QUICKLY, LIEUTENANT!

HE WAS GLAD TO DO IT -- ESPECIALLY AFTER THE STATE DEPARTMENT VERIFIED YOUR A-1 PRIORITY!

THAT AVENGERS' ID CARD SURE CARRIES A LOT OF WEIGHT, EH, CAP?

RENTING A CAR AT THE AIRPORT, CAPTAIN AMERICA AND HIS TEEN-AGE COMPANION EAGERLY HEAD FOR AVENGERS' HQ....

BOY! WAIT'LL THEY FIND OUT THAT ZEMO IS DEAD! AND YOU DID IT ALL BY YOUR LONESOME!

MEN WITH GALLANT RECORDS SUCH AS THE AVENGERS ARE NOT EASILY IMPRESSED, RICK!

THERE WAS A JOB TO BE DONE, AND I DID IT! THAT'S ALL!

15

MINUTES LATER, REACHING TONY STARK'S EAST SIDE MANSION, THEY FIND...

THERE'S A HUGE **CROWD** IN FRONT OF OUR HEADQUARTERS! SOMETHING MUST HAVE **HAPPENED** DURING OUR ABSENCE! I DON'T LIKE THE **LOOKS** OF IT!

YOU PARK THE CAR AND THEN COME IN TO MEET ME, RICK! I WANT TO GET INSIDE WITHOUT WASTING A SECOND!

BUT, HOW WILL YOU EVER GET THRU THAT **CROWD**, CAP? THERE MUST BE **HUNDREDS** OF 'EM!

BS TV

I DIDN'T SAY ANYTHING ABOUT GETTING **THRU** THEM, LAD!

THERE ARE **OTHER** WAYS TO ACCOMPLISH THE SAME OBJECTIVE--

OF COURSE, IT HELPS TO BE ABLE TO USE THE RESILIENT STEEL HOOD OF A CAR AS A **SPRINGBOARD**--

ESPECIALLY, IF YOU'VE SPENT YEARS MASTERING THE DANGEROUS AND DIFFICULT ART OF COMBAT GYMNASTICS!

FINALLY, OUTSIDE THE AVENGERS' CONFERENCE ROOM...

GOSH, CAP, THEY'RE STILL TALKIN' ABOUT THAT LEAP OF YOURS! YOU SURE GAVE THAT CROWD SOMETHIN' TO WRITE HOME ABOUT!

LUCKILY, THERE IS NO EMERGENCY INSIDE, RICK! THAT'S WHY I WAITED FOR YOU! NOW, LET'S GO IN AND GIVE OUR REPORT, AND FIND OUT THE REASON FOR THE GATHERING OUTSIDE!

16

WHAT'S IT, CAP? WHAT'S GOIN' ON IN HERE?

I'M NOT SURE, RICK! THERE SEEM TO BE SOME *NEWCOMERS* AT THE ROUND TABLE--ONE OF THEM, A COSTUMED GIRL, IS MAKING AN *ACCEPTANCE* SPEECH!

MY BROTHER AND I ARE DEEPLY GRATEFUL FOR THE TRUST YOU HAVE PLACED IN US, AND WE ACCEPT OUR POSITIONS WITH GREAT PRIDE...

HOLD IT, ALL OF YOU! LOOK--LOOK WHO'S *HERE!*

HELLO, AVENGERS! APPARENTLY, THERE'S BEEN SOME *CHANGES* MADE SINCE I LEFT!

CAP! THANK HEAVENS YOU'RE SAFE!

YOU'RE A SIGHT FOR SORE EYES, CAP!

AND WHAT AM *I*--A FEVER BLISTER?

BOY, ARE WE GLAD TO SEE *YOU,* YOU OL' SHIELD-SPINNIN' SCALLIWAG!

EASY, BLUE *EYES!* IF YOU *DROP* HIM, WE MAY LOSE 'T ON OUR *VACATION!*

WHOA THERE, BIG BOY! I APPRECIATE YOUR ENTHUSIASM, BUT--

--I'D BE JUST AS IMPRESSED BY A *HANDSHAKE!* C'MON, LET ME DOWN BEFORE YOU END UP WITH AN AIR-SICK AVENGER!

EASY, YOU BIG CLOWN! KNOCK IT OFF! I WANT TO HEAR ALL ABOUT CAP'S BATTLE WITH *ZEMO!*

HOW DIFFERENT IS THEIR COMRADESHIP FROM THE FEAR AND DISTRUST OF THE EVIL MUTANTS!

I FEEL WE SHALL BE MOST HAPPY HERE IN THE COMPANY OF ADVENTURERS SUCH AS *THESE,* MY SISTER!

THE MINUTES PASS SWIFTLY AS CAP RELATES THE EVENTS LEADING UP TO THE DEATH OF ZEMO, AND THEN...

AND *NOW,* AVENGERS, I BELIEVE *YOU* HAVE SOME REPORTS FOR RICK AND ME!

RIGHT YOU ARE, CAP! SAY HELLO TO OUR THREE NEWEST MEMBERS --THE SCARLET WITCH, QUICK-SILVER, AND HAWKEYE!

THEN, AFTER THE INTRODUCTIONS HAVE BEEN COMPLETED...

NATURALLY, GIANT-MAN, THE WASP, AND MYSELF MADE UP A MAJORITY, SO WE HAD THE AUTHORITY TO ACCEPT THE NEW MEMBERS EVEN WITHOUT YOU AND THOR BEING PRESENT!

YOU CHOSE WISELY, AVENGER, BUT WON'T WE NOW HAVE *TOO MANY* MEMBERS?

NOT REALLY, CAP! YOU SEE, HIGH-POCKETS, THE WASP, AND I ARE *LEAVING!*

WHAT ??!!....

YOU MEAN YOU'RE *BREAKING UP* THE *AVENGERS?!!* IT *CAN'T* BE! WHY? HOW--?

EASY, OLD FRIEND! WE'RE MERELY TAKING A LEAVE OF ABSENCE! DON'T FORGET, WE'VE BEEN PART OF THE TEAM *LONGER* THAN YOU-- AND *EVERYBODY* NEEDS A REST SOONER OR LATER!

THEN, *THAT'S* WHY YOU ACCEPTED THE OTHER THREE FOR MEMBERSHIP! THEY'RE GOING TO BE YOUR *REPLACE-MENTS!!*

MEANWHILE, OUTSIDE THE MULTI-MILLION DOLLAR RESIDENCE, A SMALL ARMY OF NEWS-MEN, AS WELL AS AN EAGER, CURIOUS PUBLIC ANXIOUSLY AWAIT WORD FROM INSIDE...

KEEP BACK, FOLKS! WE SHOULD BE GETTING A REPORT 'MOST ANY MINUTE NOW!

THERE HASN'T BEE[N] THIS MUCH PUBLIC INTEREST SINCE TH[E] LAST PRESIDENTIA[L] ELECTION!

BUT, THE AFFAIRS OF THE *AVENGERS* ARE OF GREAT CONCERN TO *OTHERS* BESIDES THE AVERAGE LAW-ABIDING CITIZENS! OTHERS, SUCH AS--

WILL THE AVENGERS BECOME WEAKER-- OR STRONGER?

NO MATTER *HOW* THEY CHANGE THEIR ROSTER, THEY MUST BE *DESTROYED!*

I ALMOST DEFEATED THEM ONCE-- NEXT TIME I SHALL NOT FAIL!

I MUST FOLLOW EVERY DEVELOPMENT --FOR SOON I SHALL STRIKE AGAIN!

THE AVENGERS!! I SHALL NEVER REST UNTIL THEY HAVE BEEN DESTROYED FOREVER!

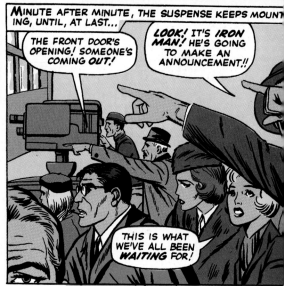

MINUTE AFTER MINUTE, THE SUSPENSE KEEPS MOUNT[-]ING, UNTIL, AT LAST...

THE FRONT DOOR'S OPENING! SOMEONE'S COMING *OUT!*

LOOK! IT'S *IRON MAN!* HE'S GOING TO MAKE AN ANNOUNCEMENT!!

THIS IS WHAT WE'VE ALL BEEN *WAITING* FOR!

LADIES AND GENTLEMEN, MAY I HAVE YOUR ATTENTION?

I'D LIKE TO PUT A STOP TO THE WILD RUMORS AND SPECULATION WHICH SEEM TO BE GOING AROUND!

I'VE BEEN ASKED TO ANNOUNCE THAT THERE WILL BE A *NEW LINE-UP* IN THE RANKS OF THE *AVENGERS* UNTIL FURTHER NOTICE!

EFFECTIVE IMMEDIATELY, *CAPTAIN AMERICA,* HAVING SENIORITY OVER THE OTHERS, WILL BE THE SPOKESMAN FOR THE GROUP, WHICH INCLUDES *HAWKEYE, QUICKSILVER,* AND THE *SCARLET WITCH.*

THEY WILL APPEAR IN PERSON TO CONFIRM WHAT I HAVE SAID IN A VERY FEW MINUTES! THANK YOU!

WELL, IT'S *DONE!* I MADE THE ANNOUNCEMENT! NOW, IT'S UP TO *YOU!*

HE DIDN'T MENTION *MY* NAME, CAP! I GUESS I'LL--I'LL *NEVER* BE A FULL-FLEDGED AVENGER!

ALL IN GOOD TIME, RICK!

YOU SEEM DOWN-HEARTED, IRON MAN --PERHAPS YOU'D LIKE TO *RECONSIDER* YOUR DECISION?

NO! I *MUST* LEAVE! I HAVE MANY --PERSONAL REASONS!

BUT, I SUDDENLY REALIZE HOW MUCH MY MEMBERSHIP HAS *MEANT* TO ME --HOW MUCH I'LL *MISS* YOU--! IT IS NOT EASY TO STOP BEING-- AN *AVENGER!*

YOU'LL *NEVER* STOP BEING AN AVENGER! SOONER OR LATER, YOU'LL REJOIN THE RANKS--AND YOUR PLACE WILL ALWAYS BE WAITING FOR YOU!

WE'LL LIVE UP TO THE PROUD TRADITION WHICH YOU, THOR, GIANT-MAN AND THE WASP HAVE ESTABLISHED! WE'LL NEVER BRING DIS-HONOR TO OUR NAME!

I *KNOW* YOU WON'T--*ANY* OF YOU! BUT, THERE IS ONE NAME YOU OMITTED!

WHEN THE AVENGERS WERE FIRST FORMED, THE *HULK* WAS A MEMBER, ALSO! I HOPE THAT YOU CAN FIND HIM, SOME DAY--AND CONVINCE HIM TO BECOME AN ALLY AGAIN!

DESPITE ALL YOUR SKILLS, AWESOME *STRENGTH* SUCH AS HIS COULD BE YOUR GREATEST ASSET! THE LAST WORD OF ADVICE I CAN LEAVE WITH YOU IS-- *FIND THE HULK!*

AND NOW, IT'S TIME FOR YOU TO APPEAR BEFORE THE PUBLIC, AS A TEAM, FOR THE FIRST TIME! GOOD LUCK TO YOU ALL!

HERE THEY *COME!!*

IT'S THE NEW AVENGERS! HOORAY!!

STRANGE THAT *CAPTAIN AMERICA,* WHO SEEMS TO POSSESS NO NOTICE-ABLE SUPER POWER, SHOULD BE CHOSEN AS OUR LEADER! OH WELL....!

I'VE DONE ALL I CAN! THE LIME-LIGHT BELONGS TO *YOU* NOW! THE MANTLE HAS BEEN PASSED TO A NEW AND YOUNGER GROUP--MAY YOU ALL WEAR IT WITH PRIDE, AND HONOR!

IT *HAS* TO BE THIS WAY! THE RANKS OF THE AVENGERS WILL ALWAYS NEED REPLENISHING! THE OLD MUST EVER GIVE WAY TO THE NEW! AND YET--!

AND YET, SO LONG AS I MAY LIVE, I'LL NEVER FORGET THE WORDS-- *AVENGERS ASSEMBLE!!* I'LL NEVER FORGET WHAT THEY *STOOD* FOR!

19

IT'S TIME! ARE YOU READY?

WE'RE READY, AVENGER! THANKS FOR DOING IT FOR US! SOMEHOW, WE COULDN'T QUITE FACE THE TASK!

I NEVER THOUGHT I'D SEE GIANT-MAN WITH TEARS IN HIS EYES!

NOW, AS WE EACH RETURN TO OUR OWN PRIVATE LIVES-- AND OUR OWN PERSONAL CAREERS-- I WANT TO SAY IT'S BEEN AN HONOR FIGHTING AT YOUR SIDE, IRON MAN!

I'M SURE YOU BOTH KNOW THAT GOES FOR ME, TOO-- IN SPADES! IF ONLY THOR COULD BE HERE! BUT, THERE'S NO TELLING WHEN HE'LL RETURN--! HE MENTIONED THE MOST DIFFICULT BATTLE OF HIS LIFE WHEN HE LEFT FOR THE PLACE HE CALLS ASGARD!

I-I THINK WE'D BETTER GO NOW-- BEFORE I RUIN MY M-MASCARA!

AND SO, WITHOUT ANY FURTHER WORDS, THE GOLDEN AVENGER AND TOWERING TITAN, TOGETHER WITH THE WONDERFUL, FLYING WASP, TAKE THEIR LEAVE OF EACH OTHER, EACH DEPARTING BY A SEPARATE EXIT... EACH RESPECTING THE OTHER'S SECRET IDENTITY TILL THE VERY END!

IT'LL BE A LONG TIME BEFORE WE MEET ANOTHER MAN-- ANOTHER FRIEND-- WHO CAN COMPARE WITH THE ONE WHO CALLS HIM-SELF-- IRON MAN!

GIANT-MAN-- AND THE WASP! I'LL NEVER FORGET THEM AS LONG AS I LIVE!

WHERE TO, BOSS?

THE FACTORY, HAPPY! I WANT TO LOSE MYSELF IN MY WORK FOR A WHILE-- A LONG WHILE!

AND SO, AS THE NEW AVENGERS ACCEPT THE CHEERS OF THE CROWD, A NEW ERA BEGINS!

SAY IT, CAP! LET'S HEAR IT, JUST ONCE MORE!

ALL RIGHT! THIS IS FOR YOU--! AVENGERS ASSEMBLE!!

RIGHT NOW THE CROWDS ARE WITH US! BUT, WITHOUT THOR, GIANT-MAN, AND IRON MAN, DO WE HAVE ENOUGH STRENGTH TO JUSTIFY THEIR CONFIDENCE?? I WONDER?

NEXT ISSUE! THE ACTION-PACKED THRILLER YOU'VE BEEN WAITING FOR! "THE SEARCH FOR THE HULK!!"

MONTHS IN PREPARATION! TRULY AN EPIC! 'NUFF SAID!

THE END

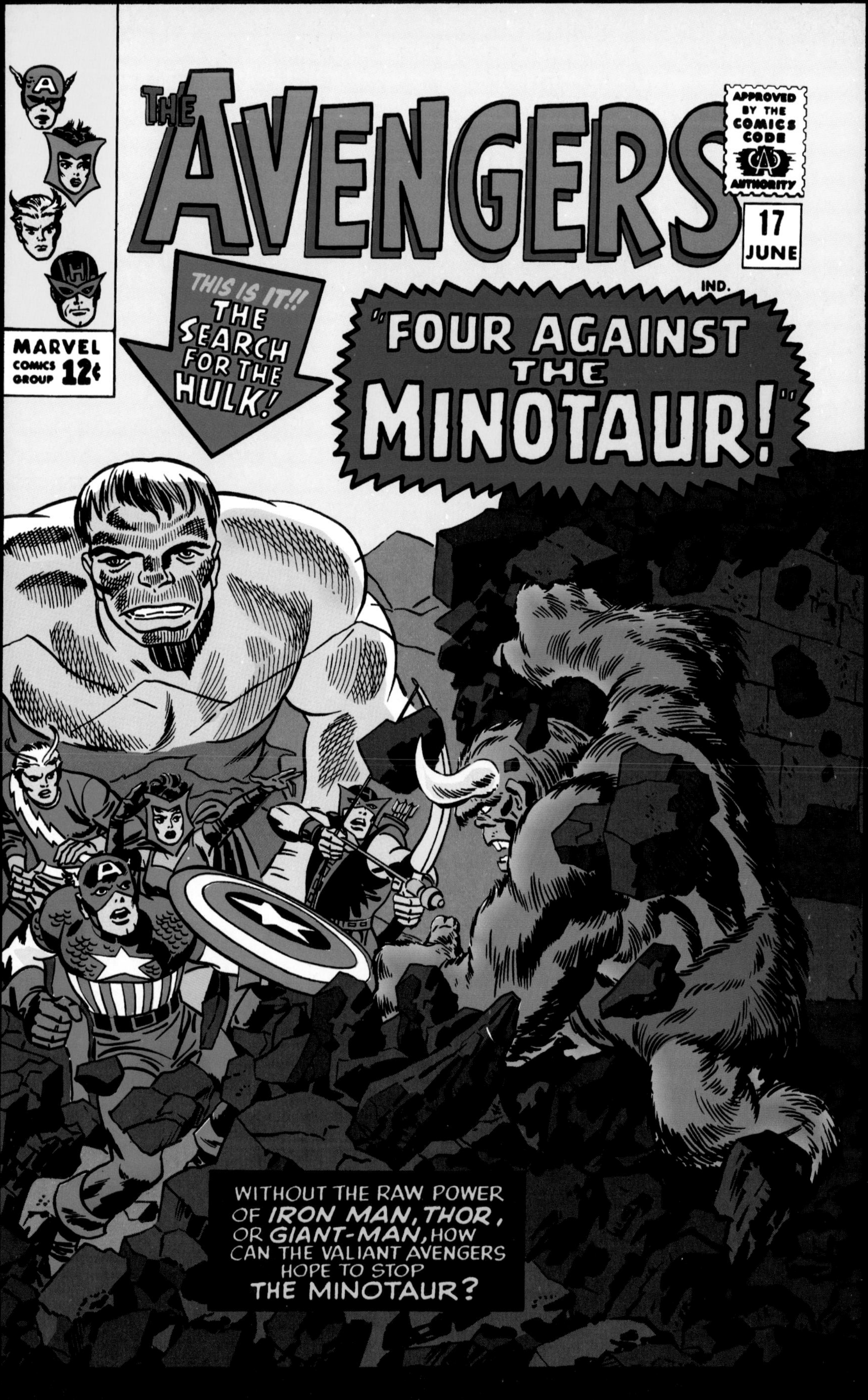
THE AVENGERS
APPROVED BY THE COMICS CODE AUTHORITY
17
JUNE
MARVEL COMICS GROUP 12¢
IND.
THIS IS IT!! THE SEARCH FOR THE HULK!
"FOUR AGAINST THE MINOTAUR!"
WITHOUT THE RAW POWER OF IRON MAN, THOR, OR GIANT-MAN, HOW CAN THE VALIANT AVENGERS HOPE TO STOP THE MINOTAUR?

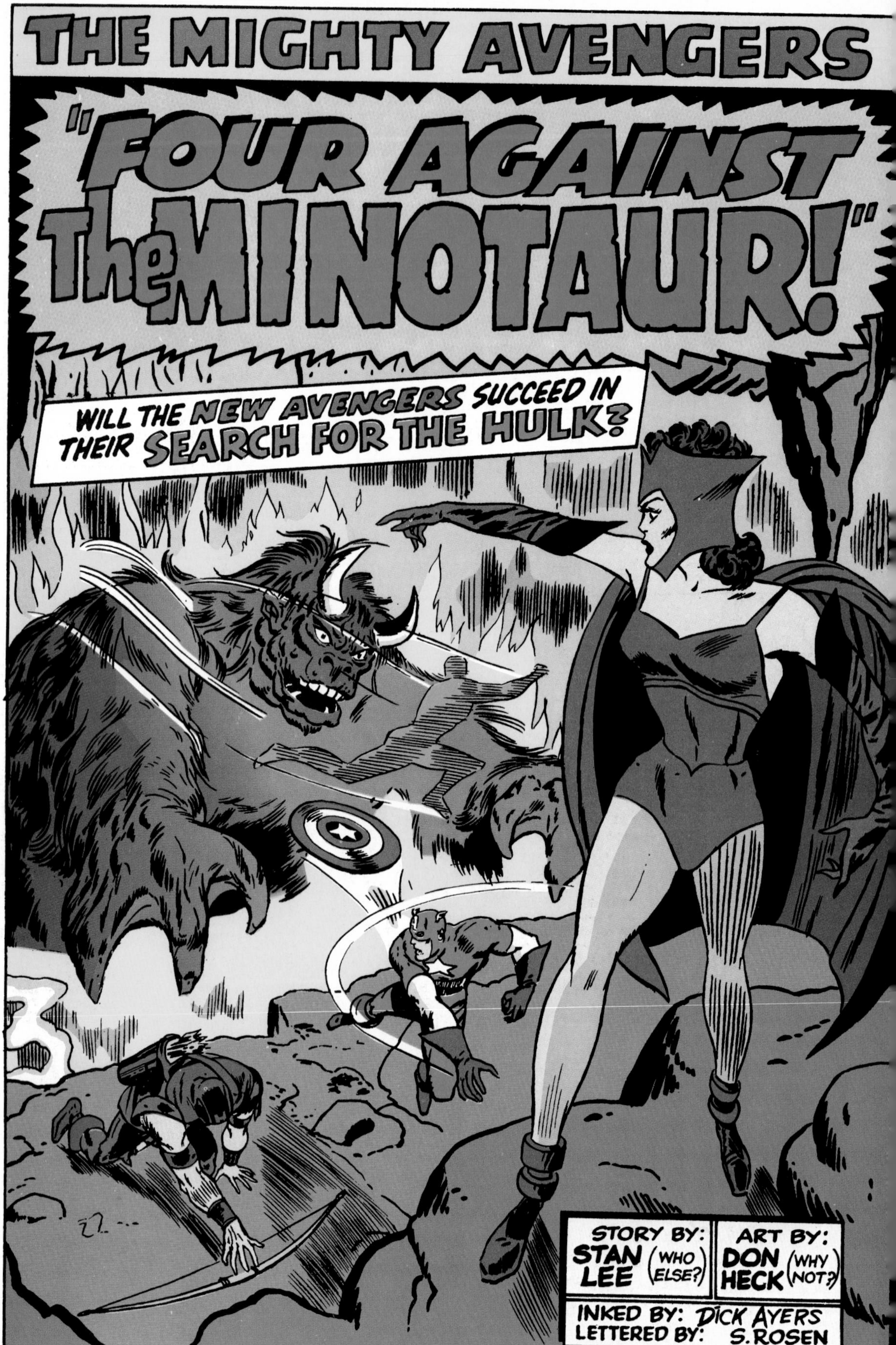
THE MIGHTY AVENGERS
"FOUR AGAINST The MINOTAUR!"
WILL THE NEW AVENGERS SUCCEED IN THEIR SEARCH FOR THE HULK?
STORY BY: STAN LEE (WHO ELSE?)
ART BY: DON HECK (WHY NOT?)
INKED BY: DICK AYERS
LETTERED BY: S. ROSEN

YOU ARE WITNESSING A MOMENTOUS MOMENT IN AVENGERS' HISTORY...THE FIRST SCHEDULED MEETING OF THE *NEW* AVENGERS!

FAIR! THOSE THREE JOHNNY-COME-LATELIES ARE NOW OFFICIAL MEMBERS ...AND CAP *STILL* WON'T LET *ME* BE A FULL-FLEDGED UNIFORMED AVENGER!

NOW THAT I'VE SHOWN YOU THE SECRET UNDERGROUND FORTRESS BENEATH TONY STARK'S MANSION, ARE THERE ANY QUESTIONS?

THERE ARE NONE FROM THE *SCARLET WITCH,* CAPTAIN AMERICA!

I MUST BE PATIENT! WITH MY GREAT *SPEED,* IT IS ONLY A MATTER OF TIME BEFORE *QUICK-SILVER* REPLACES CAPTAIN AMERICA AS *LEADER* OF THIS GROUP!

DOES HE REALLY EXPECT SOMEONE AS YOUNG AND POWERFUL AS *HAWK-EYE* TO TAKE ORDERS FROM A RELIC OF WORLD WAR TWO... LIKE *HIMSELF* ?!

SINCE THERE ARE NO FURTHER QUESTIONS, WE SHALL BEGIN OUR FIRST MISSION...WE MUST *FIND THE HULK!* FOR, WITHOUT *THOR, IRON MAN* AND *GIANT-MAN* IN OUR ROSTER, WE NEED THE POWER WHICH ONLY *HE* CAN PROVIDE!

I KNOW WHAT *EACH* OF THEM IS THINKING! THEY FEEL THAT I AM THE WEAKEST OF ALL! THEY THINK ONE OF *THEM* SHOULD BE THE LEADER! I CAN SEE IT IN THEIR EYES!

ESPECIALLY *HAWKEYE!* HE HAS NEVER TAKEN ORDERS FROM ANYONE BEFORE!

LOOK, HOTSHOT! SUPPOSE WE *VOTE* FOR OUR LEADER ?!

AT EASE, YOU IMITATION ROBIN HOOD! WHEN *YOU'VE* BEEN AN AVENGER AS LONG AS *I* HAVE, *THEN* YOU'LL HAVE THE RIGHT TO SPEAK OUT THAT WAY!

AND YOU CAN *LIKE* IT OR *LUMP* IT, PAL!

CAPTAIN AMERICA IS *RIGHT!* ONLY *HE* HAS THE EXPERIENCE TO LEAD US... FOR THE *PRESENT,* AT ANY RATE!

OKAY! WE CAN *WAIT!*

THEY'RE YOUNG, HOT-HEADED... AMBITIOUS! I HOPE I CAN HANDLE THEM, RICK!

YOU'LL DO IT FINE, CAP!

CAPTAIN AMERICA IS NO WEAKLING! I SHALL *ENJOY* BEING AN AVENGER!

2.

A FEW HOURS LATER...

BULLETIN! IT HAS JUST BEEN CONFIRMED THAT THE MIGHTY AVENGERS ARE CONDUCTING AN INTENSIVE SEARCH FOR THE INCREDIBLE HULK! A USUALLY RELIABLE SOURCE...

...HAS TOLD THIS NETWORK THAT THE AVENGERS ARE PREPARED TO OFFER A FULL PARTNERSHIP TO THE MYSTERIOUS GREEN-SKINNED STRONG MAN WHO IS REPORTED TO BE THE MOST POWERFUL HUMAN ON THE FACE OF THE EARTH!

NEWSPAPERS THROUGHOUT THE FREE WORLD CARRY THE STORY IN BANNER HEADLINES...!

HULK

WORLD-WIDE SEARCH BEGINS FOR THE HULK!

IF YOU SEE THIS MAN, CALL YOUR LOCAL OPERATOR AND ASK FOR A DIRECT LINE TO AVENGERS...

BUT, EVEN AS THE SEARCH PROCEEDS WITH GRIM INTENSITY, THE GREEN-SKINNED GOLIATH IS BEING WHISKED THROUGH THE SKY ON A FANTASTIC JOURNEY INTO CAPTIVITY BY ONE OF THE WORLD'S STRANGEST VILLAINS...! *

*AS SEEN IN THE CURRENT ISSUE OF ASTONISH #69 "THE LAIR OF THE LEADER!"...STAN.

MEANWHILE, NOT SUSPECTING THE FATE OF THE ONE THEY SEEK, CAPTAIN AMERICA CONTINUES THE INDOCTRINATION OF HIS NEW ALLIES...

HOW MUCH MORE OF THIS SIGHT-SEEING? WHEN DO WE GO INTO ACTION?

SOONER THAN YOU THINK, HAWKEYE! WHILE WE AWAIT NEWS OF THE HULK, I HAVE A LITTLE "TREAT" FOR YOU!

BEING AN AVENGER MEANS MORE THAN SIGNING AUTOGRAPHS AND TAKING BOWS! WE NEVER STOP TRAINING,...AS YOU SHALL SEE!

IT SEEMS TO ME THAT YOU NEVER STOP TALKING, EITHER!

WITHOUT ANOTHER WORD, THE RED-WHITE-AND-BLUE AVENGER USHERS THE TRIO INTO A VAST CHAMBER, THE SIGHT OF WHICH ALMOST STAGGERS THE SENSES...!

VERY WELL, HAWKEYE! THE TIME FOR TALKING IS *PAST!* THIS IS OUR "PLAY ROOM"! IT IS FITTED WITH EVERY CONCEIVABLE ELECTRONIC DEVICE TO SIMULATE ANY POSSIBLE ATTACK THAT MIGHT BE MADE ON US!

ONLY ONE AS WEALTHY AND AS BRILLIANT AS *ANTHONY STARK* COULD HAVE CREATED ALL THIS! IT IS A PITY THAT *HE* HAS NO SUPER-POWERS, FOR SOMEHOW I FEEL THAT HIS IS THE GUIDING GENIUS BEHIND THE AVENGERS!

AND YET, MY BROTHER, HAVE YOU FORGOTTEN THAT *IRON MAN*, ONE OF THE GREATEST OF ALL AVENGERS, IS SAID TO BE IN THE EMPLOY OF TONY STARK! PERHAPS IT IS *IRON MAN* HIMSELF WHO IS THE POWER BEHIND STARK!

WHAT ARE WE SUPPOSED TO *DO*... GASP IN AMAZEMENT? AS FOR *ME*, I'VE SEEN MORE IMPRESSIVE SIGHTS IN *DISNEYLAND!*

HAWKEYE, I'M GOING TO GIVE YOU A CHANCE TO PUT YOUR *MUSCLE* WHERE YOUR *MOUTH* IS....!

GO ON, CAP... *TRY* ME! I'VE BEEN *HOPING* YOU WOULD!

A SPLIT-SECOND LATER, A SIZZLING *STUN-RAY* SHOOTS TOWARD HAWKEYE, BUT THE AMAZING ARCHER MOVES WITH THE *SPEED OF THOUGHT*, AND...

THIS IS *KID STUFF* TO ME! WHATEVER THAT RAY IS, MY COUNTER-BLAST ARROW WILL CHECK IT!

HE'S AS GOOD AS HE CLAIMS TO BE! HE MOVES LIKE A PANTHER!

4.

BUT THEN...

HAWKEYE...*LOOK OUT!* THOSE TWO OTHER RAYS WOULD HAVE HIT YOU IF YOU HADN'T BEEN PUSHED OUT OF THE WAY!

NOW WHAT...??!

WELL DONE, QUICKSILVER! THE PURPOSE OF *THAT* TEST WAS TO SEE HOW QUICKLY YOU WOULD MOVE TO AID A FELLOW AVENGER BUT YOUR TASK ISN'T *OVER* YET!

HE'S *RIGHT!* ONLY MY GREAT SPEED CAN SAVE ME FROM THESE *ADDITIONAL* RAYS, WHICH KEEP SHOOTING OUT, EVIDENTLY ATTRACTED BY MY OWN HEARTBEAT!

WHAT MAKES YOU THINK I *NEEDED* HELP?? ONE HIGH-PITCHED SONAR-SCREECH ARROW WILL DESTROY THE MAIN ELECTRIC CONTROL OF ALL THESE TRAPS!

HE *DID* IT! IF I CAN JUST KEEP A TIGHT REIN ON HIM, HAWKEYE WILL BE AN AVENGER TO BE PROUD OF! HE'S A BORN FIGHTER!

YOU DESTROYED THOSE DEVICES BEFORE I HAD A CHANCE TO SHOW WHAT *I* COULD DO, HAWKEYE!

YOU DON'T HAVE TO DO *ANYTHIN* GORGEOUS! JUS' STAND THERE AND LET U *LOOK* AT YOU

THEN SUDDENLY...

WHAT GIVES?! I THOUGHT THE TEST WAS *OVER!*

CRASH!

IT *IS* OVER! BE ON GUARD, *ALL* OF YOU! I DON'T KNOW *WHAT* THIS IS...OR WHO IS *CONTROLLING* IT!!

AVENGERS! I - BRING - MESSAGE - FROM - MY - MASTER!

IT — CONCERNS — HULK...!

HAWKEYE! QUICKSILVER! SCARLET WITCH! STAY BACK! HE'S REACHING FOR ME! IT COULD BE A TRAP! I'LL HANDLE IT!

WANDA! DID YOU SEE CAPTAIN AMERICA DODGE THAT BLOW??

YES, MY BROTHER! THOUGH HE DOES NOT POSSESS YOUR GREAT SPEED, HE MOVES WITH THE POWER AND PRECISION OF A COILED STEEL SPRING!

AND I CALLED HIM A WORLD WAR TWO RELIC! I'M LUCKY HE DIDN'T FLATTEN ME WITH THAT SHIELD OF HIS!

KLANGGG!·

NO USE! I CAN'T FIGHT HIM THIS WAY! IT'S LIKE TRYING TO PUT A DENT INTO A BATTLESHIP WITH A CORKSCREW!

CAP CAN'T KEEP DODGING HIM FOREVER!

WE'VE GOT TO HELP HIM!

WELL, WHAT ARE WE WAITING FOR??

6.

MY BLASTER ARROW WON'T PENETRATE! I'VE GOT TO TRY SOMETHING ELSE!

WHILE YOU'RE TRYING, I'LL JUST GRAB A PIECE OF STEEL TO USE AS A CROWBAR AGAINST THAT THING!

AT LAST *I* CAN HELP! MY *HEX POWER* WILL SLOW THE MONSTER UP FOR A WHILE! LET IT HAPPEN *NOW!*

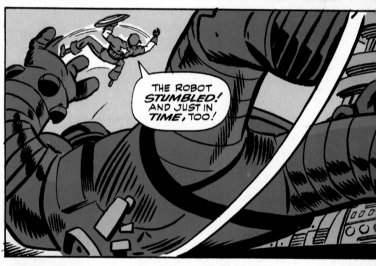

THE ROBOT *STUMBLED!* AND JUST IN *TIME,* TOO!

THIS IS THE CHANCE I NEEDED! *STAY BACK... I'LL* FINISH HIM OFF NOW!

MOVING WITH DAZZLING SPEED, QUICKSILVER USES THE STEEL SHAFT HE HOLDS TO PRY OPEN THE ROBOT'S MAIN CONTROL PANEL...

I *DID* IT! THERE ARE HIS MASTER CONTROLS! NOW, IF I CAN JUST *JAM* THEM...!

YOU'VE DONE *ENOUGH*, QUICKSILVER! HAWKEYE'S *ARROW* CAN FINISH THE JOB! *NOW*, AVENGER... DON'T MISS!!

MISS?? THERE'S NO SUCH WORD IN MY LANGUAGE, CAP! JUST *WATCH* ME, PARTNER!

TWANNNG!

YOU'LL - FIND - *HULK* - IN - DESERT - DESERT - DESERT -

ALTHOUGH HE'S *KAPUT*, HIS MESSAGE TAPE IS STILL RUNNING..!

IF ONLY WE KNEW WHO *SENT* HIM HERE!

SO, THE HULK IS IN THE *DESERT*, EH?

IT COULD BE A *TRAP!* BUT *THAT* WON'T STOP US!

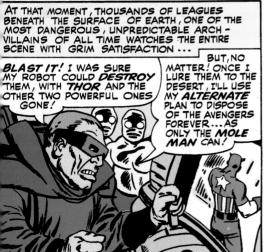

AT THAT MOMENT, THOUSANDS OF LEAGUES BENEATH THE SURFACE OF EARTH, ONE OF THE MOST DANGEROUS, UNPREDICTABLE ARCH-VILLAINS OF ALL TIME WATCHES THE ENTIRE SCENE WITH GRIM SATISFACTION...

BLAST IT! I WAS SURE MY ROBOT COULD *DESTROY* THEM, WITH *THOR* AND THE OTHER TWO POWERFUL ONES GONE!

BUT, NO MATTER! ONCE I LURE THEM TO THE DESERT, I'LL USE MY *ALTERNATE* PLAN TO DISPOSE OF THE AVENGERS FOREVER... AS ONLY THE *MOLE MAN* CAN!

THEY WILL NOT BE ABLE TO RESIST THE *BAIT* I HAVE DANGLED BEFORE THEM... THE CHANCE THAT THEY MIGHT FIND THE *HULK* HERE!

BUT THEY SHALL FIND INSTEAD, THE ONE LIVING CREATURE THAT *NONE* CAN DEFEAT!! GO, MY MINDLESS SUBTERRANEAN SLAVES... PREPARE THE *MINOTAUR* FOR HIS NEXT VICTIMS!!

8.

MINUTES LATER, THE AVENGERS' NEWEST MODEL JET-STREAM CRUISER HEADS DUE WEST...

IF IT *IS* A TRAP, WHO COULD BE *SETTING* IT FOR US?

NO POINT IN GUESSING! WE'VE TOO MANY ENEMIES!

IT COULD BE ANY ONE OF A *DOZEN!*

LATER...

THE DESERT'S A MIGHTY BIG PLACE, CAP! HOW DO YOU KNOW WHERE TO LOOK?

I'M PLAYING A *HUNCH* HAWKEYE! I'M HEADING FOR THE SPOT WHERE THE HULK HELPED US FIGH THE *LAVA MEN,* MANY MONTHS AGO! *

*AVENGERS #5... STAN

THIS IS THE PLACE! I'LL LAND THE SHIP BEFORE WE'RE TRACKED BY RADAR FROM THE MISSILE BASE NEARBY!

GOOD IDEA! THEY'D JUST WASTE OUR TIME WITH A LOT OF RED TAPE!

THEN, SECONDS AFTER THE GREAT SHIP HAS LANDE

I'VE RACED ACROSS A TEN MILE AREA! NO SIGN OF HIM!

BUT, AT YOUR GREAT SPEED, PERHAPS YOU *MISSED* HIM!

WHAT DO WE DO *NEXT?*

MY BROTHER MISSES *NOTHING,* CAPTAIN AMERICA!

BUT, LITTLE DO THE AVENGERS SUSPECT HOW CLOSE THEY ARE TO THE ONE THEY SEEK! FOR, JUST A FEW MINUTES EARLIER, ON THE MESA JUST BEYOND THEM, A SILENT AIRSHIP HAS DESCENDED AND ENTERED A SECRET, CAMOUFLAGED OPENING...

SAFE AT LAST! NO ONE WILL FIND ME NOW! NO ONE WILL EVER KNOW THAT THE *HULK* IS MY PRISONER IN MY HIDDEN RETREAT!

AND, MINUTES LATER, AS THE AVENGERS CONTINUE TO SEARCH VAINLY OVERHEAD, THE RAMPAGING *HULK* HOLDS HIS CAPTOR AT BAY IN A LIFE-AND-DEATH STRUGGLE WHICH GROWS EVER MORE DESPERATE...

AND, STILL UNAWARE OF THE DRAMA TRANSPIRING WITHIN THE SILENT MESA BEHIND THEM, THE AVENGERS ATTEMPT TO FORMULATE A NEW PLAN... A PLAN WHICH WILL BE DESTINED TO DIE A'BORNING!

IT SEEMS MY HUNCH DIDN'T PAN OUT! PERHAPS WE SHOULD RETURN AND EXAMINE THE GIANT ROBOT FOR CLUES!

I HAVE A MAP OF THIS AREA! LET ME TRY TO COVER A LARGER DISTANCE, USING MY TOP SPEED!

IT'S WORTH A TRY WHILE WE'RE HERE!

THEY ARE EXACTLY WHERE I WANT THEM! THIS IS THE MOMENT...

NOW!!

IT WAS A TRAP! WE'RE PLUNGING DOWN... INTO A BOTTOMLESS CHASM!

MY SPEED IS USELESS TO US NOW!

WE STILL HAVE A CHANCE! HAWK-EYE! YOUR SUCTION-TIPPED ARROW!! QUICK!!

OF COURSE! I SHOULD HAVE THOUGHT OF IT!

THE REST OF YOU... REACH OUT... CATCH HIS CABLE AS YOU FALL!

HE'S NEVER AT A LOSS! HE TAKES COMMAND EVERYWHERE... NO MATTER WHAT!

IT WORKED! THIS WILL GET US SAFELY TO THE BOTTOM!

BUT, WHAT NEW DANGER AWAITS US DOWN THERE?

WHATEVER IT IS, WE'LL FACE IT... AS AVENGERS!!

THERE'S NOT MUCH FURTHER TO GO! I CAN SEE THE BOTTOM NOW!

10.

137

FINALLY, AT THE END OF THE PERILOUS DESCENT...

I'LL RACE AHEAD AND SEE WHAT AWAITS US!

HAVE A CARE, MY BROTHER! DO NOT TAKE FOOLHARDY CHANCES, PIETRO!

IF YOU'RE WORRIED ABOUT HIS SAFETY, DOLL, YOU SURE PICKED THE WRONG OUTFIT FOR HIM TO JOIN!

STAY WITHIN EARSHOT OF US, QUICK-SILVER! WE'LL FOLLOW!

BUT, SCANT SECONDS AFTER THE MASTER OF SPEED HAS VANISHED AROUND A BEND...

AVENGERS!! AVENGERS!!

HE'S FOUND SOMETHING! LET'S MOVE!!

HE SOUNDS LIKE A MAN IN SHOCK! I DON'T LIKE IT!

PIETRO! WHAT IS IT? WHAT DID YOU SEE?

TELL ME I WAS DREAMING! SAY I IMAGINED IT! IT CAN'T BE REAL! IT CAN'T BE! NOTHING SO HORRIBLE CAN EXIST!

EASY, AVENGER! PULL YOURSELF TOGETHER! WHATEVER IT WAS, WE'LL HANDLE IT! NOW TELL ME... WHAT DID YOU SEE?

I..I CAN'T DESCRIBE IT! BUT, LOOK FOR YOUR-SELF! I HEAR IT COMING NOW!

THAT HEAVY TREAD! THAT DEAFENING ROAR! EVEN THE WALLS OF THIS SUB-TERRANEAN CAVE ARE SHAKING! WHAT IN THE NAME OF CREATION CAN IT BE?

THERE IT IS! YOU WERE RIGHT, QUICKSILVER! QUICK... EVERYONE BEHIND ME! I'VE GOT TO FACE IT FIRST!

138

AND THEN, LIKE THE EVIL EMBODIMENT OF EVERY LEGENDARY MONSTER SINCE THE BEGINNING OF TIME, SHEER HATRED, SHEER MENACE BLAZING IN ITS EYES, THE *MINOTAUR* APPEARS!!

A *MINOTAUR*!! THE MOST DREADED CREATURE OF GREEK MYTHOLOGY! HALF-MAN, HALF-BULL, TRAPPED UNDER THE EARTH, WAITING FOR ITS HUMAN VICTIMS!!

THAT MUST BE THE APPARITION WHICH *INSPIRED* THE ANCIENT LEGENDS! BUT...HOW CAN WE *BATTLE* IT?!

THE SAME AS WE BATTLE ANY *OTHER* DANGER...WITH COURAGE AND SKILL! AND TWO WORDS, RINGING ON OUR LIPS...

AVENGERS, ASSEMBLE!

CLANG!

CLANG!

CLANG!

MY SHIELD HAD *NO EFFECT!* HE DIDN'T EVEN *FEEL* IT!

STEP ASIDE, CAP! THE AVENGERS ARE A *TEAM*, NOT A SOLO ACT!

NO MATTER *HOW* BIG HE IS, MY *BLAST ARROW'LL* STOP HIM!

12.

IF I SAY SO MYSELF, IT LOOKS LIKE IT'S *BYE-BYE MINOTAUR!!*

WELL, BEAUTIFUL, I GUESS THERE'S NO NEED TO WONDER WHO SHOULD GET THE "BEST PLAYER AWARD" ON *THIS* TEAM!

LOOK OUT!! BEHIND YOU!!

SKRUNNNCH!

HE *SURVIVED* THE BLAST! IF NOT FOR WANDA'S WARNING, I'D HAVE BEEN *KAPUT!!*

QUICK! TO THE NARROW END OF THE TUNNEL... *ALL* OF YOU!

IT'S OUR ONLY CHANCE! MAYBE HE CAN'T *GET* AT US THERE!

THAT *RUMBLING* UP AHEAD! *WAIT!* COME *BACK!* IT'S A *ROCKSLIDE!!* YOU'LL BE *CRUSHED!*

WE CAN'T GO *FORWARD*... AND THE MINOTAUR'S *BEHIND* US! MAYBE WE SHOULD LOOK FOR A NEW HOBBY!

PIETRO! HE WAS *AHEAD* OF US! THAT ROCKSLIDE... OH, *NO!!* PIETRO... MY BROTHER... *PIETRO!!!*

13.

140

BUT THE AVENGER KNOWN AS *QUICKSILVER* IS FAR TOO *FAST* TO HAVE BEEN CAUGHT BY THE FALLING ROCKS! HOWEVER, HE, TOO, IS PLAGUED BY WORRY....!

WANDA! AND THE OTHERS! THEY WERE JUST BEHIND ME! DID THE ROCKSLIDE ENGULF THEM?? IF...IF ONLY I COULD DIG MY WAY THROUGH!!

NOW I REALIZE WHY CAPTAIN AMERICA IS SO ANXIOUS TO FIND THE *HULK!* AT A MOMENT LIKE THIS, ONLY STRENGTH SUCH AS *HIS* COULD PREVAIL!

HOW IRONIC ARE THE WAYS OF FATE.!! FOR, AT THE SAME INSTANT THAT QUICKSILVER THINKS HIS NAME, THE RAMPAGING *HULK* IS USING HIS ALMOST LIMITLESS STRENGTH IN A DESPERATE BATTLE... LESS THAN ONE MILE AWAY.!!

EVEN *BATTLESHIP STEEL* CAN'T KEEP HIM OUT!

THE INCREDIBLE *HULK!* STRONGEST OF ALL EARTH'S MORTALS! ONE OF THE MOST MYSTERIOUS, AWESOME LIVING BEINGS OF ALL TIME! SO NEAR... AND YET, SO HOPELESSLY FAR AWAY.!!

AND, AS QUICKSILVER HIMSELF TRIES FRANTICALLY TO MOVE THE WALL OF BOULDERS ...

SOUNDS! BEHIND ME! SOMEONE IS THERE!

THERE IS *ONE* OF THEM! *GET HIM!*

BUT, THE MOLE MAN'S SUBTERRANEAN SLAVES SOON LEARN HOW DIFFICULT IT IS TO CATCH ... *QUICKSILVER!*

14.

141

THEN, AS PIETRO BEGINS TO MAKE SHORT SHRIFT OF HIS STARTLED, UNDEREARTH FOES, A HARSH, COMMANDING VOICE RINGS OUT...!

THE *GAS GUN*, YOU MINDLESS FOOLS! *USE THE GAS GUN!*

AND, WITH THE BLIND OBEDIENCE OF THE SUB-HUMANS THEY ARE, THE MOLEMAN'S SLAVES *OBEY*....!

WHOOOOSH!

MOMENTS LATER, WHEN HE RECOVERS CONSCIOUSNESS, THE LIGHTNING-FAST AVENGER FINDS HIMSELF FACE-TO-FACE WITH THE MERCILESS *MOLEMAN!*

SPEAK, DETESTED AVENGER! TELL ME THE SECRET OF YOUR *SPEED*, AND I MAY SPARE YOUR LIFE!

EVEN IF IT *WERE* A SECRET I COULD GIVE, I'D CHOOSE DEATH GLADLY BEFORE GIVING IT TO ONE AS EVIL AS *YOU!*

I HAVE STUDIED ALL THE AVENGERS' CASE HISTORIES! I *KNOW* WHO YOU ARE, AND HOW YOU DREAM OF ONE DAY CONQUERING THE SURFACE WORLD!

ARROGANT FOOL! I HAVE WAYS TO *MAKE* YOU TALK!

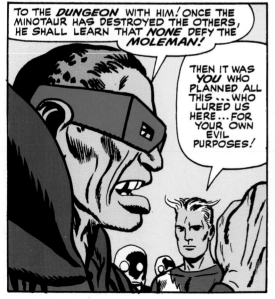

TO THE *DUNGEON* WITH HIM! ONCE THE MINOTAUR HAS DESTROYED THE OTHERS, HE SHALL LEARN THAT *NONE* DEFY THE *MOLEMAN!*

THEN IT WAS *YOU* WHO PLANNED ALL THIS ...WHO LURED US HERE...FOR YOUR OWN EVIL PURPOSES!

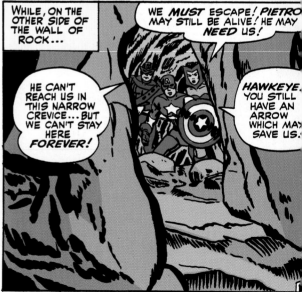

WHILE, ON THE OTHER SIDE OF THE WALL OF ROCK...

HE CAN'T REACH US IN THIS NARROW CREVICE...BUT WE CAN'T STAY HERE *FOREVER!*

WE *MUST* ESCAPE! PIETRO MAY STILL BE ALIVE! HE MAY *NEED* US!

HAWKEYE, YOU STILL HAVE AN ARROW WHICH MAY SAVE US!

HOW? IF MY *BLAST ARROW* DIDN'T STOP HIM...??

THINK, AVENGER! YOUR *FLARE* ARROW! IT'S OUR ONE HOPE!!

OF *COURSE!* I SEE WHAT CAPTAIN AMERICA MEANS!!

THE *MINOTAUR* HAS LIVED HERE IN THE SEMI-DARKNESS FOR *AGES!* THE SIGHT OF A SUDDEN BURST OF *LIGHT...!*

ARGGHH!

YEAH! YEAH! I GET THE MESSAGE! HERE *GOES!!*

BUT, YOU *KNOW* YOUR SHIELD CANNOT HARM THE MINOTAUR..!!

GOOD SHOT!! AND NOW, WE'LL *FIGHT* AGAIN! WE'LL FIGHT AS ONLY *AVENGERS* CAN!

HE'S NOT WHAT I'M AIMING AT..!!

YOU SLICED THROUGH THAT ROCK... OVERHEAD!!

NOW *WATCH..!*

ZNNZ'ZZAKKKKKK

16.

KRAKK!

GOOD! IT MADE HIM TURN, JUST AS I PLANNED!

NOW THAT HE'S IN THE RIGHT POSITION, I'LL CATCH MY SHIELD ON THE REBOUND, AND NEXT---

SKRUTCH!

IT WORKED! I KNEW HE'D BUTT AT ME IN A FIT OF RAGE... AND, BY DUCKING IN TIME, HE HIT THE HARD SHALE ABOVE ME!!

NOW QUICKLY, WANDA..USE YOUR HEX POWER!

I WAS JUST ABOUT TO DO THE VERY THING!! STAND BACK...!!

WELL, WADDAYA KNOW!! ALL SHE DOES IS POINT, AND THE WHOLE WALL OF SHALE FALLS FORWARD, LOCKING ITSELF AROUND THE MINOTAUR'S HORNS!!

WE DID IT! FOR ALL HIS SIZE AND STRENGTH, WE TRAPPED HIM AS THOROUGHLY AS IF HE WERE JUST SOME PENNY ANTE CROOK!

ARGGHHH!

HIS HORNS ARE IMBEDDED SO DEEPLY, THAT HE'LL LEAVE THEM STUCK IN THE ROCK EVEN IF HE DOES PULL FREE!

AND, WITHOUT HIS HORNS, DEATH WOULD QUICKLY FOLLOW!

AND NOW, WANDA, WE'LL NEED YOUR HEX POWER AGAIN TO REMOVE THOSE ROCKS AHEAD AND REACH YOUR BROTHER!

17.

144

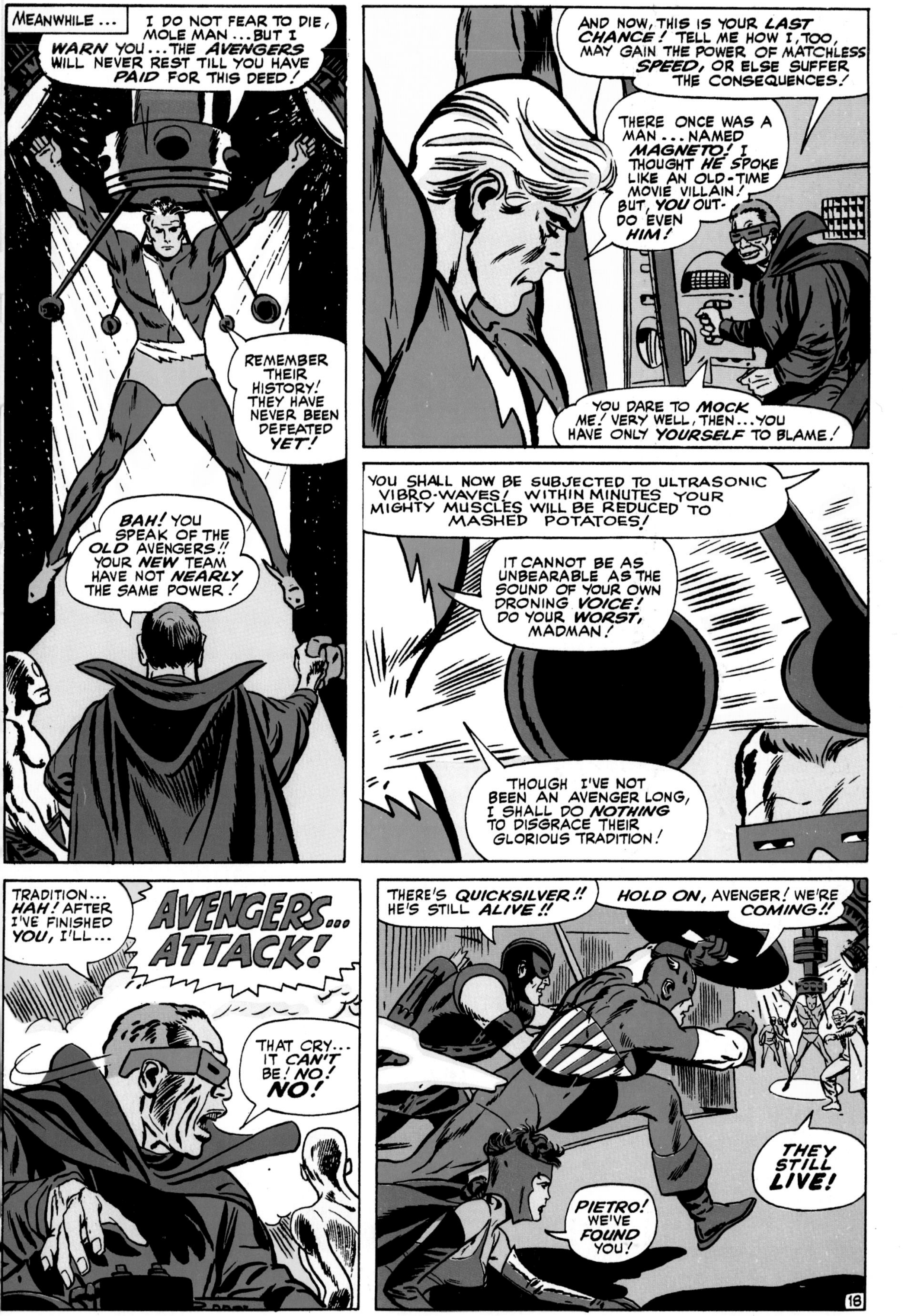
MEANWHILE ...
I DO NOT FEAR TO DIE, MOLE MAN ... BUT I WARN YOU ... THE AVENGERS WILL NEVER REST TILL YOU HAVE PAID FOR THIS DEED!
REMEMBER THEIR HISTORY! THEY HAVE NEVER BEEN DEFEATED YET!
BAH! YOU SPEAK OF THE OLD AVENGERS!! YOUR NEW TEAM HAVE NOT NEARLY THE SAME POWER!
AND NOW, THIS IS YOUR LAST CHANCE! TELL ME HOW I, TOO, MAY GAIN THE POWER OF MATCHLESS SPEED, OR ELSE SUFFER THE CONSEQUENCES!
THERE ONCE WAS A MAN ... NAMED MAGNETO! I THOUGHT HE SPOKE LIKE AN OLD-TIME MOVIE VILLAIN! BUT, YOU OUT-DO EVEN HIM!
YOU DARE TO MOCK ME! VERY WELL, THEN ... YOU HAVE ONLY YOURSELF TO BLAME!
YOU SHALL NOW BE SUBJECTED TO ULTRASONIC VIBRO-WAVES! WITHIN MINUTES YOUR MIGHTY MUSCLES WILL BE REDUCED TO MASHED POTATOES!
IT CANNOT BE AS UNBEARABLE AS THE SOUND OF YOUR OWN DRONING VOICE! DO YOUR WORST, MADMAN!
THOUGH I'VE NOT BEEN AN AVENGER LONG, I SHALL DO NOTHING TO DISGRACE THEIR GLORIOUS TRADITION!
TRADITION ... HAH! AFTER I'VE FINISHED YOU, I'LL ...
AVENGERS... ATTACK!
THAT CRY... IT CAN'T BE! NO! NO!
THERE'S QUICKSILVER!! HE'S STILL ALIVE!!
HOLD ON, AVENGER! WE'RE COMING!!
THEY STILL LIVE!
PIETRO! WE'VE FOUND YOU!
18

HURRY, HAWKEYE! THE MOLE MAN'S ESCAPING!

TWO WELL PLACED ARROWS WILL HAVE YOU FREE IN SECONDS, PARTNER!

TWANG!

DON'T WORRY, SPEEDY! HE WON'T GET FAR!

SO! HE TRIED TO HARM YOU WITH THAT MACHINE, MY BROTHER!

I'LL USE MY STRONGEST HEX ON IT. THE EVIL DEVICE SHALL NEVER AGAIN MENACE ANOTHER VICTIM.!!

PIETRO... WE DID IT!! UNDER THE LEADERSHIP OF CAPTAIN AMERICA, WE DEFEATED THE MINOTAUR!! AND WE FOUND YOU!

IT IS TO BE EXPECTED, MY SISTER!

WE ARE AVENGERS NOW!

HALT, MOLE MAN! THERE'S NO ESCAPE FOR YOU... SO LONG AS I CAN HURL MY SHIELD!

CLANG!

STOP HIM! DEATH TO CAPTAIN AMERICA!

OH, NO YOU DON'T! NOT WHILE OL' HAWKEYE HAS A STUN-BLAST ARROW LEFT!

THEY FIGHT LIKE RAGING FURIES!

I DISMISSED MY MAIN FORCE OF SUBTERRANEANS... THINKING THE MINOTAUR WOULD FINISH THEM OFF! BUT NOW...!

19

WHO GETS HIM **NOW,** CAP? OR, IS HE UP FOR **GRABS?**

WAIT! STAND YOUR **GROUND!** HE'S **UP** TO SOMETHING! THAT SWITCH HE JUST THREW...

LOOK! A GLASS ENCLOSURE IS RISING AROUND US! WE'RE IN THE **CENTER** OF IT!

I NEVER THOUGHT I'D HAVE TO RESORT TO **THIS!** BUT, THEY'RE TOO **MUCH** FOR ME! I'VE GOT TO FREE THEM... SEND THEM BACK TO THE SURFACE...BEFORE THEY **DESTROY** ME!

A SPLIT-SECOND LATER, A BLINDING **FLASH** FILLS THE HUGE UNDERGROUND CHAMBER, AND THEN...

WE'RE **MOVING!!** WHAT **HAPPENED?**

EASY, WANDA! THERE'S NOTHING TO FEAR!

HE CHOSE SENDING US TO THE SURFACE, RATHER THAN **FIGHTING** US!

THEN WE'VE **WON!!** WE'VE HAD OUR BAPTISM OF BATTLE!!

BUT, WHAT OF THE **HULK?** WE DIDN'T **FIND** HIM...!

OUR SEARCH FOR THE HULK WAS A **SUCCESS!** FOR WE **DID** FIND THE MOST IMPORTANT THING....!

WE FOUND OUR TRUE **STRENGTH** TOGETHER! WE FOUND THAT WE DON'T **NEED** ANY-ONE ELSE'S POWER!

YOU'RE **RIGHT,** CAP! FIGHTING TOGETHER AS A TEAM, WE'RE STRONG ENOUGH FOR **ANY** FOE!

AND, PERHAPS IT IS JUST AS WELL THAT THE NEW AVENGERS, INDEED, THE **MIGHTY** AVENGERS... DO NOT KNOW THAT EACH FLEETING SECOND IS TAKING THEM FURTHER FROM THE SPOT WHERE A MAN LIES DYING... A MAN WHO, JUST A FEW MOMENTS EARLIER, HAD BEEN... THE INCREDIBLE **HULK!**

HIS PULSE IS SO FAINT, THAT I--**NO!** IT STOPPED! THERE'S NO PULSE AT **ALL!**

BUT, UN-MINDFUL OF THE STRANGE TRICK WHICH FATE HAD PLAYED UPON THEM, THE AVENGERS RETURN TO THEIR HEADQUARTERS, LITTLE DREAMING HOW CLOSE THEY HAD BEEN TO THE ONE THEY SOUGHT....!

THEY'RE PLEASANT AND FRIENDLY **NOW**... BUT HOW WILL THEY STAND UP TO OUR FIRST **SET-BACK?** ONLY TIME CAN TELL!

YOU HAVE JUST FINISHED READING A MILESTONE IN ADVENTURE LORE! BUT, IT IS ONLY A FORETASTE OF WHAT IS TO COME! SO, BE WITH US AGAIN NEXT ISH WHEN THE STIRRING CRY "AVENGERS ASSEMBLE" ECHOES THROUGHOUT THE LAND!

THE END.

20.

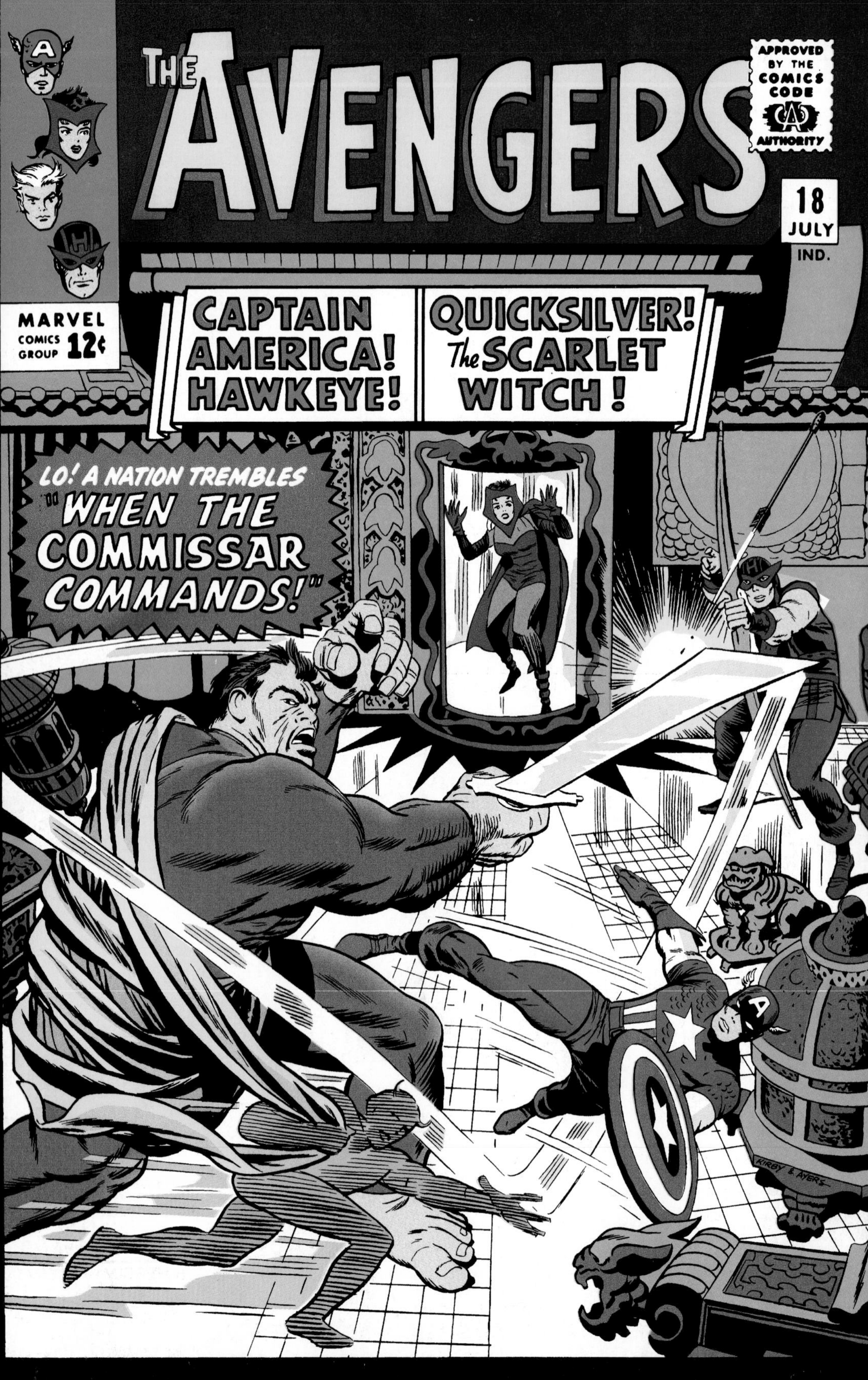
THE AVENGERS
APPROVED BY THE COMICS CODE AUTHORITY
18
JULY
IND.
MARVEL COMICS GROUP 12¢
CAPTAIN AMERICA! HAWKEYE!
QUICKSILVER! The SCARLET WITCH!
LO! A NATION TREMBLES
"WHEN THE COMMISSAR COMMANDS!"
KIRBY & AYERS

THE MIGHTY AVENGERS
"WHEN THE COMMISSAR COMMANDS!"
HIS MISSION: PROVE THAT THE REDS ARE SUPERIOR TO FREEDOM'S CHAMPIONS!
HIS METHOD: DEFEAT AN AMERICAN FIGHTING TEAM BY ANY AND ALL MEANS!
HIS MADNESS: WHEN SELECTING HIS FOES, HE DARED TO CHOOSE--THE AVENGERS!
SLYLY WRITTEN BY STAN LEE
SMOOTHLY DRAWN BY DON HECK
SUAVELY INKED BY DICK AYERS
SUPERBLY LETTERED BY ARTIE SIMEK
STOICALLY READ BY YOU (IF YOU'LL EVER TURN THE PAGE...!)
1

HIS FAME IS UNIVERSAL! HIS FEATS ARE LIVING LEGEND! HIS NAME IS HAILED WHEREVER FREEDOM RINGS! AND YET, *CAPTAIN AMERICA* SITS ALONE IN AVENGERS' HEADQUARTERS, HIS HEART HEAVY WITHIN HIM....!

IS *THIS* HOW I'M DESTINED TO SPEND THE REST OF MY DAYS--?

--RAMROD OF A MIGHTY FIGHTING TEAM, YET WITHOUT A PRIVATE LIFE TO CALL MY OWN!

EATING ANOTHER MAN'S FOOD-- ACCEPTING ANOTHER MAN'S SHELTER--*

--BROODING AWAY THE LONELY HOURS, WAITING FOR EACH NEW CALL TO ACTION!

*AS ALL MARVELDOM KNOWS, THE *AVENGERS* ARE BILLETED IN THE MANSION OF MILLIONAIRE TONY STARK-- *STAN*.

IF ONLY *NICK FURY* WOULD ANSWER THE LETTER I SENT HIM, REQUESTING AN APPOINTMENT IN HIS COUNTER-INTELLIGENCE UNIT--!

HOW MUCH *LONGER* CAN I GO ON THIS WAY--BEING A LIVING SYMBOL TO MILLIONS--AND YET, A FRUSTRATED ANACHRONISM TO *MYSELF!*

OUTSIDE MY WINDOW, THE *WORLD* PASSES BY-- A WORLD IN WHICH I HAVE *STILL* TO FIND MY RIGHTFUL PLACE-- MY OWN IDENTITY!

BUT, I DARE NOT *DESERT* THE AVENGERS--FOR, I AM *NEEDED* HERE! INTO *MY* HANDS THE TORCH HAS BEEN PASSED!

THOUGH *IRON MAN, THOR*, AND *GIANT-MAN* HAVE LEFT OUR RANKS I MUST REMAIN--TO GUIDE THE THREE WHO HAVE REPLACED THEM

2

AND NOW, LET US TURN TO THE AVENGERS' NEWEST MEMBERS, STARTING WITH *QUICKSILVER*, AND HIS SISTER, THE *SCARLET WITCH*...

DO NOT DISTURB ME NOW, WANDA! I AM WATCHING THE CIRCUS ACROBATS PERFORM!

THE CIRCUS! ALWAYS THE CIRCUS! BUT I HAVE SOMETHING *FOR* YOU PIETRO--!

I HAVE TWO TICKETS FOR "TWELFTH NIGHT" AT THE REPERTORY THEATRE!

IT'S FUNNY YOU SHOULD MENTION THAT...

I HAVE JUST BOUGHT TWO TICKETS TO -- THE *CIRCUS!*

ADMIT ONE CIRCUS

AND SO... ALL MY LIFE I HAVE DREAMED OF BEING AN *ACTRESS!* HOW I *LOVE* THE THEATER!

WHILE, ACROSS TOWN...

IF ONLY IT COULD BE *ME* UPON THAT TRAPEZE!

YOUR *HAND!!* QUICKLY -- YOUR *HAND!*

A SUDDEN *MUSCLE CRAMP!!* I CAN'T *REACH* YOU!

BUT, I'D NEVER *DARE!* WITH MY GREAT SPEED, MEN WOULD SOON SUSPECT THAT I AM A *MUTANT,* AND THEN --

WAIT! THEIR *TIMING* IS OFF! HE'S IN *TROUBLE!*

WOW! THEY PULL ALL THE STOPS TO MAKE IT LOOK *SCARY!*

3

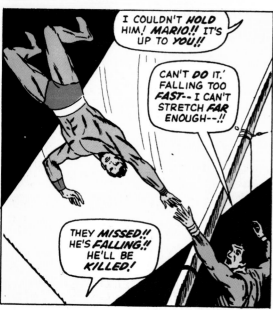

I COULDN'T *HOLD* HIM! *MARIO!!* IT'S UP TO *YOU!!*

CAN'T *DO* IT! FALLING TOO *FAST*-- I CAN'T STRETCH *FAR* ENOUGH--!!

THEY *MISSED!!* HE'S *FALLING!!* HE'LL BE *KILLED!*

HE'LL HIT THE GROUND WITHIN *SECONDS!* THERE'S NO *NET* TO STOP HIM!

HE-- HE HASN'T A *CHANCE!*

BUT, THE SEEMINGLY DOOMED ACROBAT *DOES* HAVE A CHANCE, AS A FIGURE LEAPS FROM THE STANDS-- MOVING SO FAST THAT HIS BODY IS NO MORE THAN AN ELUSIVE BLUR OF MOTION--!

LOOK! THE NET SEEMS TO BE *RISING*-- SHAPING ITSELF AS IF BY *MAGIC!*

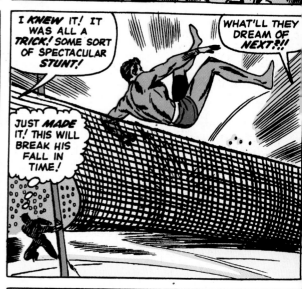

I *KNEW* IT! IT WAS ALL A *TRICK!* SOME SORT OF SPECTACULAR *STUNT!*

WHAT'LL THEY DREAM OF *NEXT?!!*

JUST *MADE* IT! THIS WILL BREAK HIS FALL IN TIME!

SECONDS LATER, AS THE OVERJOYED PERFORMER WALKS SAFELY AWAY...

I DON'T KNOW HOW IT HAPPENED-- BUT I'M NOT COMPLAINING!

YOU WERE VERY FORTUNATE, MY FRIEND!

WHILE, IN ANOTHER PART OF TOWN, THE AVENGER KNOWN AS *HAWKEYE* PREPARES FOR ONE OF HIS MOST DRAMATIC FEATS...

I'VE SPENT *WEEKS* IN THIS LAB, WORKING ON JUST *ONE* TYPE OF ARROW! AND NOW, I'LL LEARN WHETHER MY TIME HAS BEEN WASTED!

ZZZING!

PLANNG!

I **DID** IT! BY VIBRATING THE ARROW AT THE CORRECT FREQUENCY PITCH, I MADE IT ACTUALLY **LIFT** A ONE-TON **SAFE!**

I'VE **PROVEN** THAT WEIGHT MEANS **NOTHING--**

--PROVIDED THE ULTRA-SONIC VIBRATION IS PERFECTLY PITCHED!

NOW I'LL SEND A MOVING CREW TO REPLACE THE SAFE!

BUT, LET US TURN FROM THE AVENGERS, AND DIRECT OUR ATTENTION HALF-WAY AROUND THE WORLD, TO THE COMMUNIST-RULED PUPPET STATE OF **SIN-CONG--!**

YOU HAVE BEEN TOO **SLOW** IN PAYING YOUR TAXES! THIS IS A **BAD** THING!

THE STATE PROTECTS YOU FROM THE IMPERIALISTS! SO YOU MUST **PAY** THE STATE!

BUT, YOU HAVE TAKEN **EVERY-THING!** WE CAN PAY NO MORE!

WHO SPOKE THOSE TREASONOUS WORDS?! WHO DARES DEFY **MY** COMMAND?!

IS **THIS** HOW YOU REPAY THE GENEROSITY OF OUR BELOVED **COMMISSAR??** SEE HOW YOU HAVE **OFFENDED** HIM! BOW YOUR HEADS IN SHAME, UNDESERVING ONES!

5

HAS HE NOT PLEDGED HIS AWESOME STRENGTH, HIS UNLIMITED POWER, TO USE THEM IN *YOUR* BEHALF-- TO GUARD YOU FROM THE ACCURSED IMPERIALISTS??

BEHOLD HOW HE DISPLAYS HIS *MIGHT*-- TO PROVE HIS *LOVE* FOR YOU! AND YET, YOU *BETRAY* HIM!

SEE HOW I STAND READY TO *FIGHT* FOR YOU AGAINST THE SCHEMING CAPITALIST NATIONS!

BUT, WE DO NOT FEAR THE CAPITALISTS! THEY HAD BEEN OUR *FRIENDS*-- THEY HELPED *FEED* US, HELPED CLOTHE US, UNTIL *YOU* CAME TO POWER!

SO! YOU ARE *STILL* VICTIMS OF THEIR EVIL PROPOGANDA! BUT, I SHALL *CURE* YOU OF THAT ILLNESS! I SHALL *PROVE* THAT ONLY *WE* ARE YOUR FRIENDS! *THEY* ARE WEAK, AND HELPLESS!

BOW YOUR HEADS! BOW DOWN BEFORE THE KINDNESS, AND THE GENEROSITY OF YOUR BELOVED COMMISSAR! SOON YOU SHALL SEE THE *AMERICANS* BOW BEFORE ME, AS WELL!

AND SO WE LEAVE THE *"PROTECTOR OF THE WEAK"*, AS HIS FORBIDDING SHADOW FALLS OVER HIS HELPLESS SUBJECTS AND SPREADS LIKE A VIRUS ACROSS THE CONQUERED LAND...

6

HOURS LATER, AT *AVENGERS' HQ.*, WE FIND...

RADIO FREE SIN-CONG-- CALLING THE AVENGERS!! THE REDS ARE DESTROYING OUR LAND!! ONLY *YOU* CAN HELP! SOON, IT WILL BE TOO LATE--!

AT *LAST!* A CALL TO *ACTION!*

I THOUGHT SIN-CONG WAS COMMUNIST CON-TROLLED! BUT, IF AN UNDERGROUND FREEDOM MOVEMENT EXISTS--!

WE *READ* YOU, RADIO FREE SIN-CONG! THE *AVENGERS* SHALL BE ALERTED! OVER!

TIME IS OF THE ESSENCE! ANY MOMENT MAY BE OUR LAST! OVER-- AND OUT!

IF WE CAN SUCCESSFULLY COMPLETE THIS MISSION, IT MAY BE MY STEPPING STONE TO NICK FURY'S AGENCY! HE'LL *HAVE* TO CONSIDER ME!

IT'S WHAT I'VE BEEN *WAIT-ING* FOR--!

HE HAS BROKEN CONTACT, HONORABLE *COMMISSAR!*

HE HAS SWALLOWED THE BAIT! NOW, THEY WILL SURELY COME!

IF YOU DEFEAT THEM, EXCELLENCY, YOUR NAME SHALL BE REVERED THRUOUT ALL ·ASIA!

IF!! YOU DARE SAY *IF??!*

I SHALL CRUSH THEM AS I CRUSH THIS BLOCK OF GRANITE! THE TRAP IS *SET!*

7

AND, BACK IN THE STATES...

AVENGERS, ASSEMBLE!

EXACTLY ONE HOUR LATER, AFTER CAP'S BRIEFING...

ARE THERE ANY QUESTIONS?

COME *OFF* IT, GLAMOR PANTS! WE'RE NOT KIDS! WE GET THE MESSAGE!

HOLD YOUR TONGUE, HAWKEYE! *WE* DO NOT "*GET THE MESSAGE*"!

I THOUGHT OUR PURPOSE WAS TO BATTLE *CRIME!* WHY NEED WE CONCERN OURSELVES WITH INTERNATIONAL AFFAIRS?

I ECHO MY BROTHER'S QUESTION!

LET *ME* SPELL IT OUT FOR YOU! WE'RE SUPPOSED TO AVENGE *INJUSTICE,* RIGHT? WELL, WHEN *LIBERTY'S* THREATENED, JUSTICE GOES DOWN THE DRAIN! THAT'S *IT* IN A NUTSHELL!

BUT, IF YOU TWO HAVE SOMETHIN' *MORE* IMPORTANT TO DO, OL' WING-HEAD AND I CAN HANDLE IT *ALONE!*

YOU HAVE MADE YOUR POINT, AVENGER! WE SHALL FIGHT AS A *TEAM* -- AS ALWAYS.

I ALWAYS *THOUGHT* HAWK-EYE'S BARK WAS WORSE THAN HIS BITE!

LET US BEGIN!

8

AND SO... HAWKEYE, I APPRECIATE THE SUPPORT YOU GAVE ME WHEN--!

STOW IT, PAL! I JUST WANTED TO PROVE THAT *ANYONE* CAN ACT LIKE A SQUARE IF HE WORKS AT IT!

FINALLY, AT SIN-CONG AIRDROME, IN CENTRAL ASIA...

THE *COMMISSAR* SENDS HIS COMPLIMENTS! I AM TO BRING YOU *TO* HIM!

IT LOOKS *BAD!* THEY WERE *EXPECTING* US! COULD THEY HAVE INTERCEPTED THE UNDERGROUND'S RADIO MESSAGE??

CAN THOSE BEWILDERED-LOOKING, COSTUMED CAPITALISTS BE THE MIGHTY *AVENGERS?*

THE *COMMISSAR* WILL MAKE SHORT WORK OF THEM!

O AS THEY SAY-- FOR *OW!* WE'LL HAVE TO .AY THIS BY EAR TILL VE GET OUR BEARINGS!

I DON'T LIKE *GUNS* POINTED AT ME! 'SPECIALLY *COMMIE* GUNS!

NO NEED FOR YOUR *ARROW!* YOU ARE SAFE --FOR *NOW!*

INTO THE CAR--ALL OF YOU!

EXACTLY ONE HOUR LATER...

HEY ARE *HERE,* EXCELLENCY!

ON'T JUST *STAND* HERE, FOOL! PRE- PARE A SUITABLE *WELCOME!!*

SUCH SPLENDOR -- IN THE MIDST OF STARVING MILLIONS! IT STAGGERS THE SENSES!

KEEP YOUR WITS ABOUT YOU! *ANYTHING* CAN HAPPEN NOW!

REMAIN HERE! THE *COMMISSAR* WILL SEE YOU AT HIS PLEASURE!

YEAH? *MY* PLEASURE WOULD BE TO RAM THAT ARROGANT SMILE RIGHT DOWN YOUR THROAT!

KNOCK IT OFF, HAWKEYE! WE'RE NOT LOOKING FOR A BAR-ROOM BRAWL!

WHAT'S THAT *SOUND??* LIKE STEEL PANELS SLIDING!

9

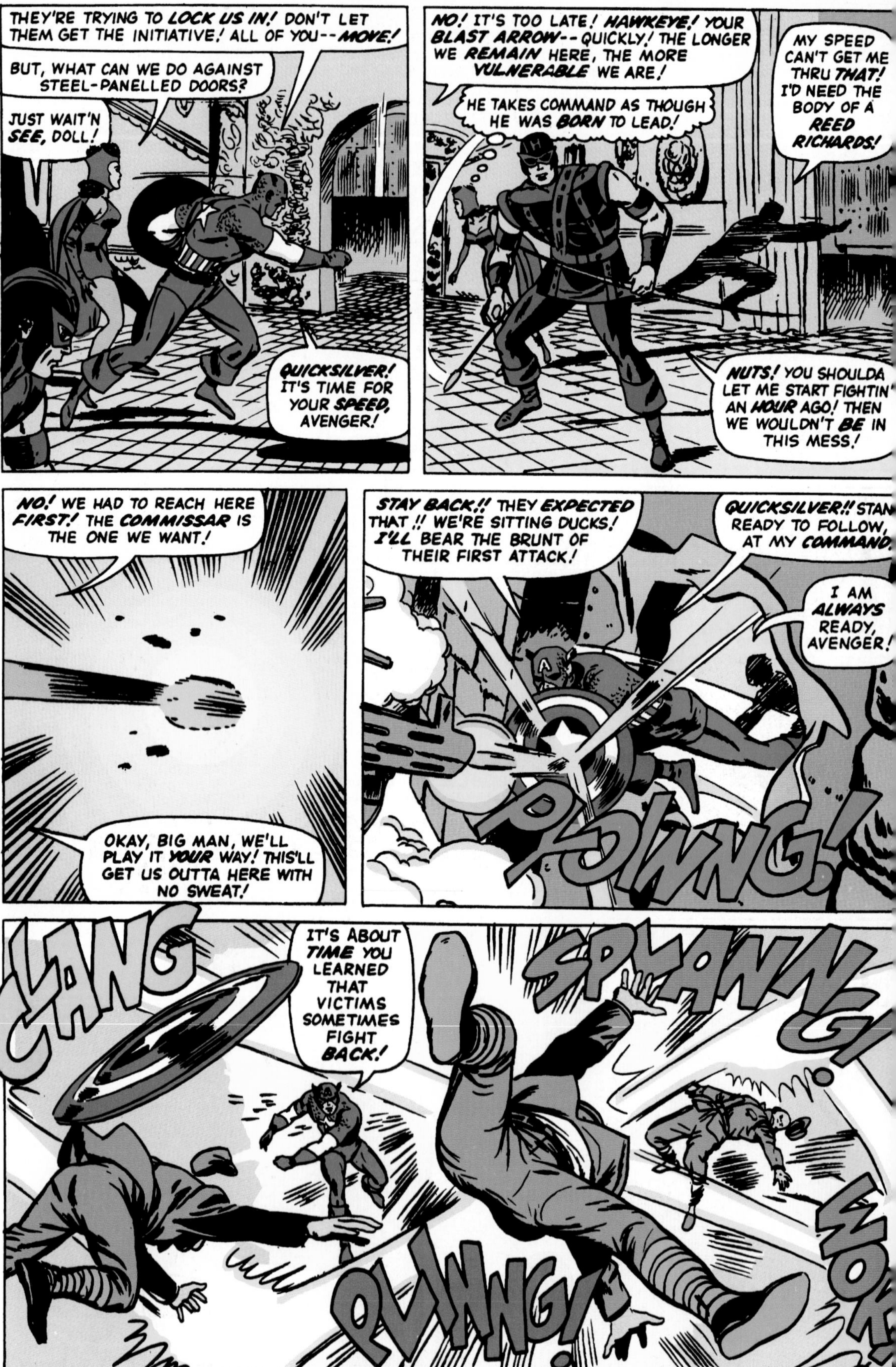
THEY'RE TRYING TO LOCK US IN! DON'T LET THEM GET THE INITIATIVE! ALL OF YOU--MOVE!
BUT, WHAT CAN WE DO AGAINST STEEL-PANELLED DOORS?
JUST WAIT'N SEE, DOLL!
QUICKSILVER! IT'S TIME FOR YOUR SPEED, AVENGER!
NO! IT'S TOO LATE! HAWKEYE! YOUR BLAST ARROW--QUICKLY! THE LONGER WE REMAIN HERE, THE MORE VULNERABLE WE ARE!
HE TAKES COMMAND AS THOUGH HE WAS BORN TO LEAD!
MY SPEED CAN'T GET ME THRU THAT! I'D NEED THE BODY OF A REED RICHARDS!
NUTS! YOU SHOULDA LET ME START FIGHTIN' AN HOUR AGO! THEN WE WOULDN'T BE IN THIS MESS!
NO! WE HAD TO REACH HERE FIRST! THE COMMISSAR IS THE ONE WE WANT!
OKAY, BIG MAN, WE'LL PLAY IT YOUR WAY! THIS'LL GET US OUTTA HERE WITH NO SWEAT!
STAY BACK!! THEY EXPECTED THAT!! WE'RE SITTING DUCKS! I'LL BEAR THE BRUNT OF THEIR FIRST ATTACK!
QUICKSILVER!! STAN READY TO FOLLOW, AT MY COMMAND
I AM ALWAYS READY, AVENGER!
PYOINNG!
CLANG
IT'S ABOUT TIME YOU LEARNED THAT VICTIMS SOMETIMES FIGHT BACK!
SPLANNG!
PLINNG!
WOK!

AND *NOW*, QUICKSILVER-- *NO*!! STAY WHERE YOU *ARE*! THERE ARE *MORE* OF THEM, COMING FROM *BEHIND*!!

BE THAT AS IT MAY, CAPTAIN AMERICA, THEIR GUNS SHALL NOT HARM YOU!

--NOT WHEN I CAN JAM THEIR BARRELS WITH A SIMPLE, QUICK-ACTING *HEX*!

OUR GUNS ARE *DEFECTIVE*! THEY WILL NOT *FIRE*!

BUT *OTHERS* ARE COMING! I CANNOT PUT A *HEX* ON THEM ALL!

CAP! LOOK OUT! THERE'S A *BAZOOKA* BEHIND YOU!

IF ONLY HE HADN'T ORDERED *US* TO REMAIN *BEHIND*! NO *TIME* FOR MY ARROWS NOW!

WHOOSH!

HE HURLED HIMSELF *CLEAR* --HIS TIMING WAS *PERFECT*!

NOW, QUICKSILVER--*BEFORE* HE CAN RELOAD!! *PLAN SEVEN*, AVENGER!!

THEN, WITH MOST OF THE *RED* GUNS INOPERATIVE, *QUICKSILVER* STREAKS PAST THE DAZED GUARDS LIKE AN AVENGING WRAITH, PUTTING EACH OUT OF ACTION IN HIS TURN!

THOK!

WUP!

BUK!

BLAP!

ALL PRESENT AND ACCOUNTED FOR, CAP!

11

SECONDS LATER...

ONCE AGAIN WE HAVE WRESTED VICTORY FROM DEFEAT, UNDER YOUR LEADERSHIP, CAP!

I'M AFRAID WE'RE A LONG WAY FROM VICTORY, WANDA! WE'VE MERELY MANAGED TO SAVE OUR NECKS FOR THE TIME BEING!

BOY! YOU'RE JUST A BIG, BOLD, BUNDLE OF CONFIDENCE TODAY, CHUM!

AT ANY RATE, WHAT DO WE DO NEXT?

OUR MAIN OBJECTIVE IS TO CONTACT THE UNDER-GROUND LEADERS WHO ASKED FOR OUR HELP! UNLESS--!

I KNOW WHAT YOU'RE THINKING, CAP! UNLESS THERE ISN'T ANY UNDERGROUND! UNLESS WE WERE DUPED!

AND, IF IT IS JUST A TRAP, IT PROVES THAT YOU'RE NOT SO-- HEY!

THAT STONE BLOCK IN THE FLOOR SWUNG OPEN! WANDA JUST FELL THRU!

PIETRO! CAP! HAWKEYE! --HELP!

BUT, BEFORE ANYONE CAN MAKE A MOVE...

IT SWUNG CLOSED AGAIN! WE'VE GOT TO GET HER OUT OF THERE!

STAND BACK! MY BLAST ARROW WILL DO THE TRICK!

NO! DON'T DO IT, HAWKEYE!

YOU MIGHT CAUSE A CAVE-IN! WE DON'T KNOW HOW THE DUNGEON BELOW IS CONSTRUCTED!

BUT, THE LONGER WE WAIT, THE LONGER SHE-- LISTEN!

A SCREAM!! IT'S FROM WANDA!

EEEE

160

HEY! WAIT FOR US, WINKLE-TOES!

NOTHING CAN SLOW HIM DOWN NOW, HAWKEYE! NOT WITH HIS SISTER IN DANGER!

I'M COMING, WANDA! AFTER HAVING SURVIVED SO MANY BATTLES WITH THE X-MEN--

--I COULDN'T BEAR ANY HARM COMING TO YOU NOW!

I AM AS YET UNHARMED, PIETRO! BUT I FIND MYSELF HELPLESS!

HAMPERED BY A BLINDFOLD, I CANNOT USE MY HEX POWER!

BUT WE STILL HAVE OUR POWER! TO MY SIDE, AVENGERS!

SO! SHE'S IMPRISONED BELOW! MY SHIELD MIGHT PRY THOSE BARS LOOSE!

SAVE YOUR BREATH, PAL! MY ARROW CAN DO IT FASTER!

WELL, DON'T JUST STAND THERE, HAWKEYE!

RELAX, QUICK STUFF! THIS IS DUCK SOUP FOR ME!

ALL I NEED DO IS STRIKE A FLARE ARROW AGAINST THE STONE WALL-- LIKE A MATCH!

AND ITS CONCENTRATED HEAT WILL MELT THOSE BARS LIKE BUTTER!

FSSSZZZZZZZ

BUT, BEHIND THE AVENGERS, A FALSE SLAB OF ROCK SLIDES BACK, AS VAPORS OF COLORLESS, ODORLESS GAS SILENTLY SEEP INTO THE GLOOMY CORRIDOR...

UNTIL... GETTING GROGGY-- SOMETHING WRONG-- CAN'T KEEP MY EYES OPEN--!

MY HAND'S GETTING NUMB-- HARD TO HOLD ARROW--!

I FEEL LIKE A MAN IN A TRANCE! GETTING HARD TO SEE--!

13

161

SECONDS LATER... IT'S A FORM OF *SLEEP GAS!!* HOLD YOUR BREATHS-- THE LESS YOU INHALE-- THE LESS TIME YOU'LL STAY UNDER-- HOLD YOUR BREATHS-- HOLD YOUR-- ;UHHH;..

LUCKILY, THE OTHER TWO AVENGERS HEAR CAP'S WARNING IN TIME-- THUS, THE SLEEP GAS HARMS THEM LESS THAN IT NORMALLY MIGHT! AND, WHEN THEY AWAKEN...

THEY'VE *MOVED* US!! WE'RE IN ANOTHER HUGE CHAMBER....!

CAP! LOOK-- OVER *THERE!*

THE MIGHTY *AVENGERS!!* HA! YOU BLUNDERED INTO MY TRAP LIKE WITLESS FOOLS!

IMPERIALIST DOGS! BOW YOUR HEADS IN THE PRESENCE OF-- THE *COMMISSAR!*

SO, IT *WAS* A TRAP! AND WE STUMBLED BLINDLY INTO IT!

BETTER STAND *BACK,* BIG MAN! YOU'LL NEED A LOT OF *FALLING ROOM* WHEN WE PLOW *INTO* YOU!

HE CAN'T THINK HIS ENORMOUS SIZE *ALONE* WILL BEAT US! THERE MUST BE *MORE* TO THIS TRAP THAN WE SUSPECT!

...ND, IF HE *HAS* ANY-
THING UP HIS SLEEVE,
WE'LL SOON FIND *OUT!*
STAND BY, WHILE I
TACKLE HIM!

HOW COME IT'S ALWAYS
YOU?? WHAT DO YOU
WANT-- A TEAM OF
AVENGERS, OR A
CHEERING GALLERY??

BUT, BEFORE THE RED-WHITE-AND-BLUE AVENGER
CAN ANSWER HAWKEYE, OR MAKE ANY OTHER *MOVE*...

HALT! COME NO FURTHER, IF YOU WISH THE MASKED
FEMALE TO REMAIN ALIVE!

HE MEANS MY *SISTER!* DON'T
MOVE! DON'T TAKE ANY
CHANCES WITH HER SAFETY!

EASY, QUICKSILVER!
I WON'T JEOPARDIZE
WANDA'S LIFE!

SPEAK YOUR *PIECE*,
COMMISSAR--AND BE
QUICK ABOUT IT!

THERE IS MY PRISONER-- COMPLETELY HELPLESS
WITHIN AN UNBREAKABLE GLASS CAGE! AT ONE
COMMAND FROM ME, MAJOR HOY WILL PRESS
A BUTTON, SLAYING HER *INSTANTLY!*

--UNLESS YOU
AGREE TO THE
TERMS I NOW
PROPOSE!

AND, THOSE TERMS ARE
--THAT YOU EACH *BATTLE*
ME, ONE AT A TIME!

FIRST, YOU MUST SET MY
SISTER *FREE!*

NOT UNTIL
THE BATTLE
IS *ENDED!*

DON'T
WORRY,
PIETRO! HE
WON'T DARE
HARM HER
WHILE WE
LIVE!

THEN, I
ACCEPT
HIS
CHALLENGE!

WILD HORSES COULDN'T
KEEP ME FROM TACK-
LING HIM!

YOU *HAVE*
YOUR ANSWER,
COMMISSAR!

AH, SO! I HAVE TAKEN THE LIBERTY OF BRINGING A DELEGATION
OF TOWNSPEOPLE TO *WITNESS* OUR FIGHT-- SO THEY MAY *SEE* HOW
WEAK AND INFERIOR YOU CAPITALISTS REALLY ARE!

SO *THAT'S* YOUR MOTIVE!
YOU HOPE TO WIN A *PROPAGANDA*
VICTORY! I SHOULD HAVE
GUESSED!

REMAIN HERE, WHILE
I CHANGE INTO MY
COMBAT ATTIRE!

ALAS! THEY WHO CALL
THEMSELVES *AVENGERS*
WILL BE DEFEATED AS ALL
THE OTHERS *BEFORE* THEM!

15

IS THIS A *GAG?* YOU CALL THAT BAGGY-LOOKING PAIR OF *DIAPERS* YOUR "COMBAT ATTIRE"?!!

FOR THAT TAUNTING REMARK, I CHOOSE *YOU* TO BE MY FIRST VICTIM, CAPTAIN AMERICA!

I SHALL CRUSH YOU LIKE THE *FLEA* YOU ARE!

DON'T *BET* ON IT, BRIGHT EYES! I'M *ONE* FLEA WHO'S GOT A *STING!*

BXUNNG!

IT'S LIKE STRIKING A *MOUNTAIN!* HE DOESN'T SEEM TO *FEEL* IT!

THEN, REGAINING HIS SHIELD, CAP MAKES A PRODIGIOUS *LEAP,* PUTTING EVERY OUNCE OF HIS MAGNIFICENT FIGHTING STRENGTH AND SKILL INTO ONE SHATTERING, ROUNDHOUSE RIGHT--!

IT ISN'T *POSSIBLE!* HE DIDN'T EVEN BAT AN EYE! AND MY FIST FEELS AS THOUGH IT HIT A *STEAM ROLLER!*

NOW THAT OUR AUDIENCE HAS SEEN HOW EASILY I STAND UP TO YOUR STRONGEST ATTACK, I SHALL SHOW THEM HOW THE *COMMISSAR* STRIKES BACK--!

FIRST, I RELIEVE YOU OF YOUR USELESS *SHIELD--!*

PROVING HOW DEFENSE-LESS YOU ARE AGAINST MY POWER!

--UHHH!-- HOW DOES HE *DO* IT? SIZE ALONE CAN'T BE THE ANSWER!

THEN, ONE SIMPLE *BEAR HUG* WILL OVERCOME THE MUCH-VAUNTED CAPTAIN AMERICA!

CAN'T *REACH* HIM-- CAN'T CATCH MY BREATH--!

LET HIM *GO,* COMMISSAR! TRY *ME* NEXT--!

DO NOT BE IMPATIENT, HAWKEYE! I HAD *PLANNED* THAT YOU WOULD BE MY SECOND VICTIM!

NOW EFFORTLESSLY THE COMMISSAR TOSSES ASIDE THE DEFEATED AVENGER!

CAPTAIN AMERICA HAS NEVER BEEN SO HUMBLED BEFORE!

BUT, CAN THE *OTHER* AVENGERS FARE *BETTER?*

YOUR *ARROWS* DO NOT FRIGHTEN ME, HAWKEYE! I SHALL PUT THEM *ALL* TO SHAME!

STAY BACK, QUICK-SILVER! I'M GONNA MAKE HIM *EAT* THOSE WORDS!

ONE STUN-BLAST ARROW IS ALL IT'LL TAKE!

HE SWATTED THE ARROW ASIDE LIKE A *TOY!* BUT *HOW??* AT THAT RANGE, IT TRAVELS WITH THE SPEED OF A *BULLET!*

WHIT!

BEGINNER'S LUCK CAN'T STRIKE *TWICE,* CHUBBINS,! NOW CHEW ON *THIS* FOR A WHILE!

THWANNG!

HOW MANY *MORE* ARROWS HAVE YOU, DOOMED ONE? I CAN FEND OFF SUCH PUNY WEAPONS ALL *DAY!*

OH, *NOO--!*

SOMETHING'S *WRONG!* MY ARROWS DIDN'T HAVE THE RIGHT *HEFT* TO THEM--!

THERE'S ONLY *ONE* ANSWER-- THEY WERE *TAMPERED* WITH WHILE WE WERE UN-CONSCIOUS!

17

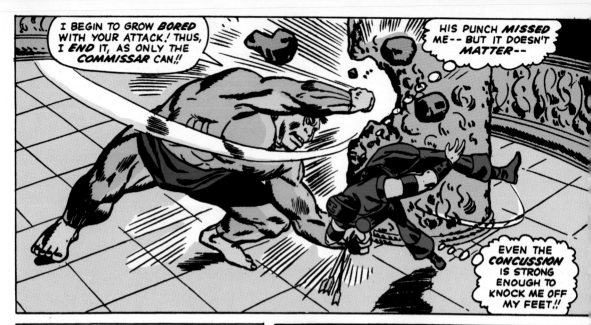

I BEGIN TO GROW *BORED* WITH YOUR ATTACK! THUS, I *END* IT, AS ONLY THE *COMMISSAR* CAN!!

HIS PUNCH *MISSED* ME-- BUT IT DOESN'T *MATTER*--

EVEN THE *CONCUSSION* IS STRONG ENOUGH TO KNOCK ME OFF MY FEET!!

THEN, SEIZING THE STUNNED AVENGER, THE GIGANTIC RED WARRIOR DELIVERS TWO WELL-PLACED KARATE CHOPS, AND...

BY THE TIME YOU WAKE UP, I SHALL HAVE DISPOSED OF YOUR *THIRD* COMRADE JUST AS EASILY!

PERHAPS *NOT,* EVIL ONE! BEFORE *QUICKSILVER* CAN BE DEFEATED--

--HE MUST FIRST BE *CAUGHT!*

GRABBING A THICK, HANGING *DRAPE* WITH LIGHTNING SPEED, QUICKSILVER TRIES A NEW ATTACK--!

ONCE I GET MY *HANDS* ON YOU--!

TRUE, MY STRENGTH IS NOT THE EQUAL OF *YOURS*--

BUT, IF I CAN ENTANGLE YOU IN THIS SWIRLING DRAPE--!

CAN IT *BE* THAT THE COMMISSAR HAS FINALLY MET HIS MATCH?

THE AVENGER MOVES WITH THE SPEED OF THE *WIND!*

NO! HIS TACTIC IS *USELESS!* SEE WHAT THE COMMISSAR DOES *NOW*--!

16

FOOL! ALL I NEED DO IS GRAB ONE END OF THE DRAPE IN MY OWN HANDS--

--AND SWING YOU *TO* ME LIKE A PUPPET!

I FAILED! HIS STRENGTH IS TOO GREAT!

BUT, I STILL HAVE MY *SPEED!* PERHAPS, BY GRABBING HIS SWORD IN A SURPRISE ATTACK--!

ENOUGH! LET US *END* THIS FARCE, HERE AND NOW!

HE DIDN'T EVEN *TOUCH* ME--- AND YET, I'M HURLED TO THE GROUND--!!

AT THAT INSTANT, THE SAME THOUGHT STRIKES **CAPTAIN AMERICA**-- *AS HE REALIZES...*

WE'VE BEEN FIGHTING THE *WRONG MAN!*

HAVE I NOT *PROVEN* THE SUPERIORITY OF COMMUNISM?? SINGLE-HANDED, I HAVE BEATEN EACH OF THE AVENGERS!

NOT *YET* YOU HAVEN'T--!

THERE IS STILL THE *GIRL!* SHE *TOO* IS AN AVENGER.! OR DO YOU FEAR *HER* POWER?

SO! YOU WISH TO *CONTINUE* YOUR HUMILIATION! *SET THE FEMALE FREE!* THE COMMISSAR FEARS *NO ONE!*

NO! HE MUSTN'T MATCH HIS STRENGTH AGAINST *HER!* NOT AGAINST MY *SISTER!*

QUIET, QUICKSILVER! TRUST ME --I KNOW WHAT I'M DOING!

LISTEN CLOSELY, WANDA--THERE ISN'T MUCH TIME! WE HAVE ONLY *ONE* CHANCE--!

YOU HAVE NOTHING TO FEAR--THE *SCARLET WITCH* WILL NOT FAIL YOU!

THEN, AFTER CAP HAS WHISPERED HIS BRIEF INSTRUCTIONS...

LET US *BEGIN,* COMMISSAR--!

GRACEFULLY BACKING AWAY FROM THE ONRUSHING GIANT, WANDA SOFTLY MURMURS...

WHY DOES *MAJOR HOY* DISAPPEAR BEHIND THOSE DRAPES WHILE *YOU* DO THE FIGHTING?

IT IS NO CONCERN OF *YOURS,* WOMAN!

19

AH, BUT IT *IS!* LET ME BURN THE DRAPES *AWAY* WITH MY *HEX POWER,* AND SEE WHAT IS REVEALED *BEHIND* THEM!

HOW *INTERESTING!* AN ELABORATE *CONTROL PANEL!* FOR *WHAT,* I WONDER?

STAND AWAY FROM THERE! I'LL *KILL* YOU FOR THAT!! THAT IS *MY SECRET!*

NOT ANY *MORE,* IT ISN'T!

NOT WHEN A SIMPLE HEX CAN MAKE IT ALL GO *BOOM BOOM!*

THUS, WITH A SIMPLE GESTURE, THE SCARLET WITCH *DESTROYS* THE CONTROL PANEL--!

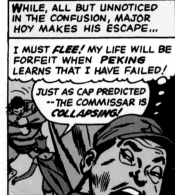

WHILE, ALL BUT UNNOTICED IN THE CONFUSION, MAJOR HOY MAKES HIS ESCAPE...

I MUST *FLEE!* MY LIFE WILL BE FORFEIT WHEN *PEKING* LEARNS THAT I HAVE FAILED!

JUST AS CAP PREDICTED --THE COMMISSAR IS *COLLAPSING!*

FOR, WITH THE CONTROL PANEL SHATTERED, THE CURRENT HAS SHORT-CIRCUITED THE FANTASTIC *ROBOT!!*

BEHOLD! THE COMMUNISTS *DECEIVED* US! THE TYRANT WAS MERELY A *ROBOT!*

ALTHOUGH HE WAS MADE TO BE SUPERIOR TO FLESH AND BLOOD, THE AVENGERS *DEFEATED* HIM!

THEY HAVE FREED US FROM THE TYRANNY OF THE *COMMISSAR!*

BY EXPOSING THEIR DECEPTION, WE HAVE CAUSED THEM TO *LOSE FACE!* THIS IS THE WORST FATE THAT CAN BEFALL THEM!

BUT, BE ALWAYS ON YOUR *GUARD!* THEIR GOAL IS NOTHING LESS THAN TOTAL WORLD CONQUEST, AND WORLD ENSLAVEMENT!

ONLY CONSTANT VIGILANCE AND DEVOTION TO FREEDOM CAN STOP THEM!

AND REMEMBER --THE *AVENGERS* ALWAYS STAND READY TO DO THEIR PART!

CAP, DID YOU TAKE *LESSONS* ON HOW TO BE A CORNBALL, OR DOES IT COME NATURAL?

SORRY, HAWKEYE! GUESS I GOT CARRIED AWAY BY MY OWN CONVICTIONS!

WITH CONVICTIONS SUCH AS *THOSE,* ONE HAS A *RIGHT* TO BE CARRIED AWAY!

AND, SPEAKING OF BEING CARRIED AWAY, I HOPE WANDA DOES NOT EXPECT SUCH SERVICE UPON HER RETURN TO AMERICA WITH US!

The End

BUT, THE *AVENGERS* WILL HAVE A FAR GREATER PROBLEM TO FACE WHEN THEY RETURN TO THE STATES! A PROBLEM WHICH NEITHER THEY, NOR YOU, ARE LIKELY EVER TO FORGET! LET'S TRY TO SOLVE IT TOGETHER, NEXT ISSUE!

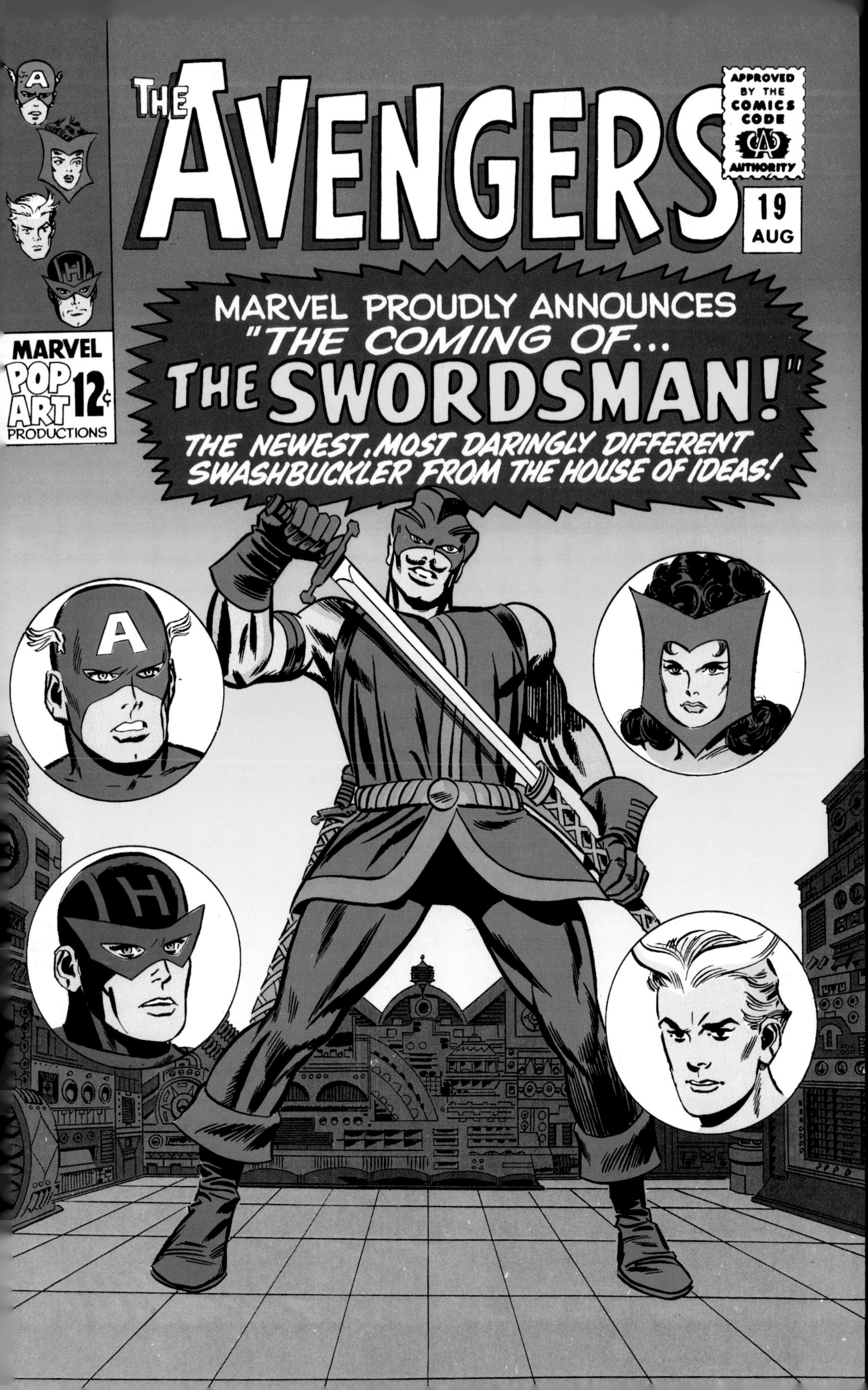

THE AVENGERS
APPROVED BY THE COMICS CODE AUTHORITY
19
AUG
MARVEL POP ART PRODUCTIONS 12¢
MARVEL PROUDLY ANNOUNCES
"THE COMING OF...
THE SWORDSMAN!"
THE NEWEST, MOST DARINGLY DIFFERENT SWASHBUCKLER FROM THE HOUSE OF IDEAS!

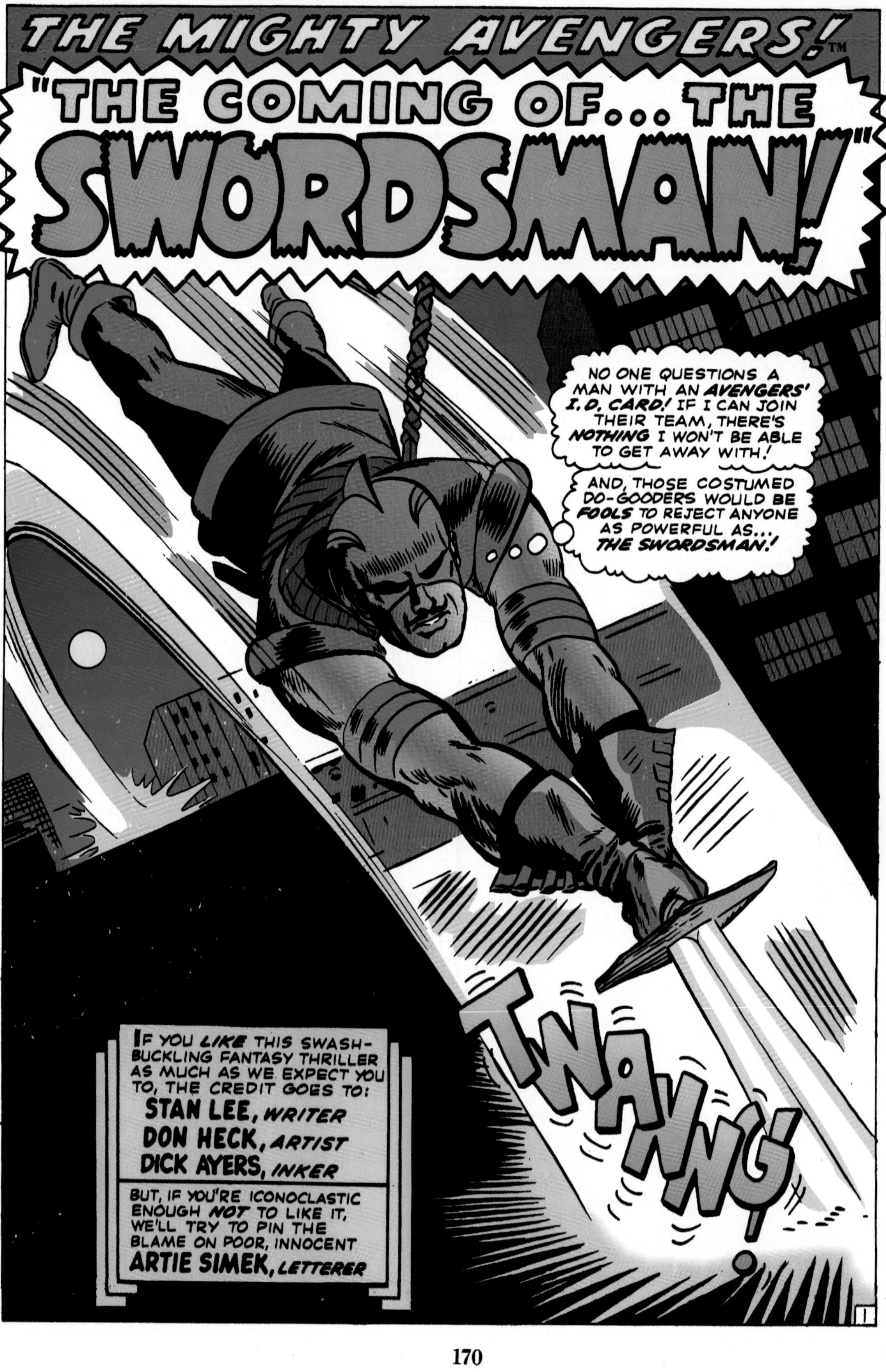
THE MIGHTY AVENGERS!
"THE COMING OF... THE SWORDSMAN!"
NO ONE QUESTIONS A MAN WITH AN AVENGERS' I.D. CARD! IF I CAN JOIN THEIR TEAM, THERE'S NOTHING I WON'T BE ABLE TO GET AWAY WITH!
AND, THOSE COSTUMED DO-GOODERS WOULD BE FOOLS TO REJECT ANYONE AS POWERFUL AS... THE SWORDSMAN!
TWANNG!
IF YOU LIKE THIS SWASH-BUCKLING FANTASY THRILLER AS MUCH AS WE EXPECT YOU TO, THE CREDIT GOES TO:
STAN LEE, WRITER
DON HECK, ARTIST
DICK AYERS, INKER
BUT, IF YOU'RE ICONOCLASTIC ENOUGH NOT TO LIKE IT, WE'LL TRY TO PIN THE BLAME ON POOR, INNOCENT ARTIE SIMEK, LETTERER
1

AT AVENGERS HQ., *SOMEBODY'S* GOT TO "*MIND THE STORE*", AND SO...

I AM *BORED* WITH THIS BUSINESS OF BEING *ON CALL!* I CRAVE *ACTION,* WANDA-- NOT THIS ENDLESS WAITING AROUND!

YOU WERE ALWAYS AN IMPATIENT ONE, PIETRO, MY BROTHER!

BUT THEN, AS IF IN ANSWER TO QUICKSILVER'S COMPLAINT...

LOOK! THE *ALARM SIGNAL!!*

THERE IS AN *INTRUDER* ON THE PREMISES!

A MAN IN COSTUME --CARRYING A *SWORD!* *HALT!* IN THE NAME OF THE *AVENGERS!*

WELL! IT'S ABOUT *TIME* SOMEONE SHOWED UP!

YOU WERE ORDERED TO *HALT!* NOW I'LL--*WHA--??!*

BACK!! NOBODY *ORDERS* THE *SWORDSMAN!*

THEN, INFURIATED BY THE STRANGER'S EFFRONTERY, QUICKSILVER BLAZES INTO ACTION WITH THE DAZZLING SPEED WHICH HAS MADE HIS NAME RENOWNED THRUOUT THE GLOBE!

HOLD YOUR TONGUE! YOU SPEAK TO AN *AVENGER!*

THAK!

DUCK, QUICKSILVER! EVEN YOUR *SPEED* IS NO MATCH FOR MY *BLADE!*

I SHOULD NOT HAVE PULLED MY PUNCH! HE IS MORE *DANGEROUS* THAN I GUESSED!

HIS WEAPON SPINS LIKE A *PROPELLER!*

2

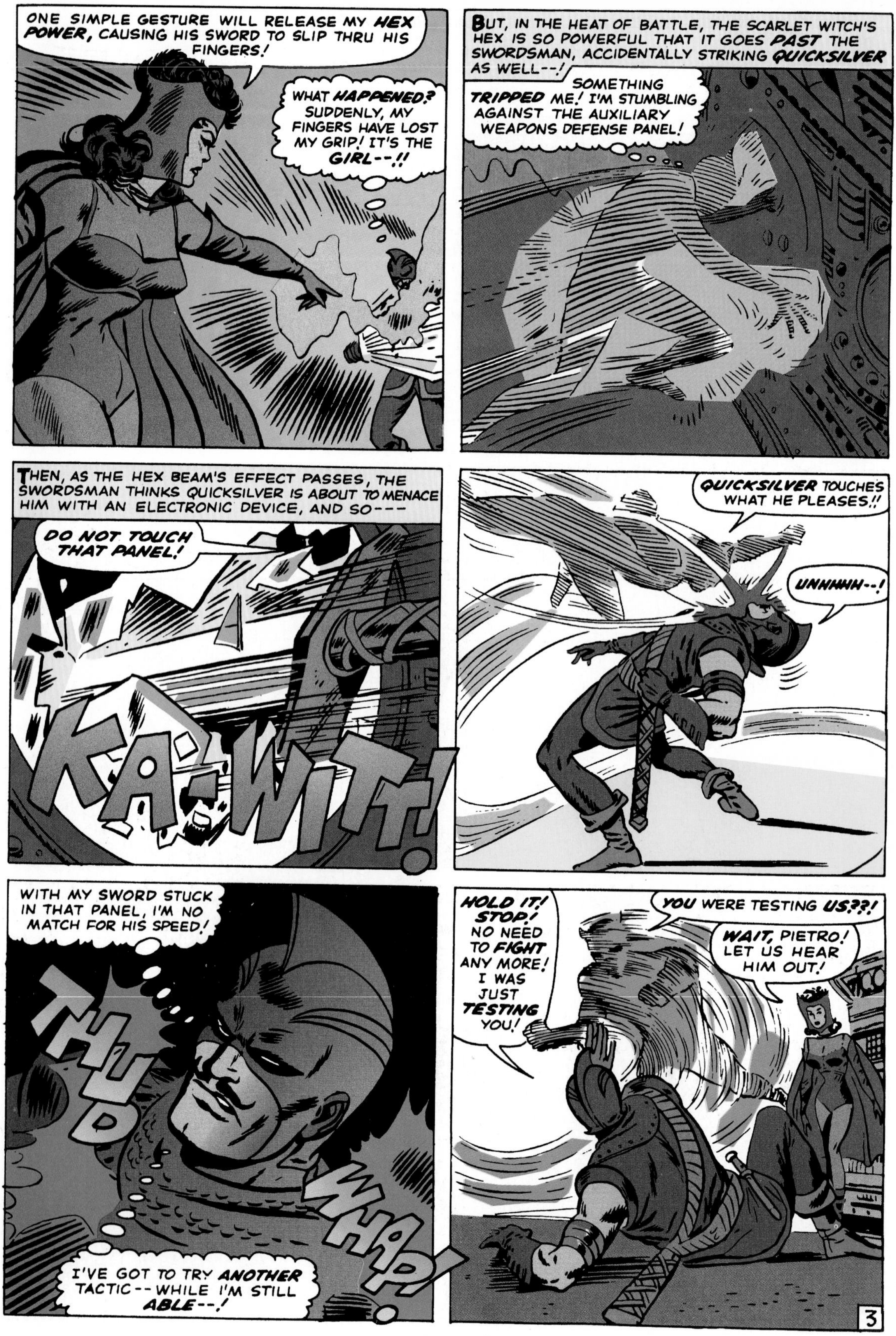
ONE SIMPLE GESTURE WILL RELEASE MY HEX POWER, CAUSING HIS SWORD TO SLIP THRU HIS FINGERS!
WHAT HAPPENED? SUDDENLY, MY FINGERS HAVE LOST MY GRIP! IT'S THE GIRL--!!
BUT, IN THE HEAT OF BATTLE, THE SCARLET WITCH'S HEX IS SO POWERFUL THAT IT GOES PAST THE SWORDSMAN, ACCIDENTALLY STRIKING QUICKSILVER AS WELL--!
SOMETHING TRIPPED ME! I'M STUMBLING AGAINST THE AUXILIARY WEAPONS DEFENSE PANEL!
THEN, AS THE HEX BEAM'S EFFECT PASSES, THE SWORDSMAN THINKS QUICKSILVER IS ABOUT TO MENACE HIM WITH AN ELECTRONIC DEVICE, AND SO---
DO NOT TOUCH THAT PANEL!
KA-WITT!
QUICKSILVER TOUCHES WHAT HE PLEASES!!
UNHHHH--!
WITH MY SWORD STUCK IN THAT PANEL, I'M NO MATCH FOR HIS SPEED!
THUD
WHAP!
I'VE GOT TO TRY ANOTHER TACTIC--WHILE I'M STILL ABLE--!
HOLD IT! STOP! NO NEED TO FIGHT ANY MORE! I WAS JUST TESTING YOU!
YOU WERE TESTING US??!
WAIT, PIETRO! LET US HEAR HIM OUT!
3

I WANT TO **JOIN** YOUR GROUP--BUT FIRST, I HAD TO BE CERTAIN YOU ARE AS GOOD AS THEY **SAY** YOU ARE!

NOW I'M CLOSE ENOUGH TO SEIZE MY SWORD, AND PAY HIM **BACK** FOR THOSE TAUNTING BLOWS!

BUT, BEFORE JOINING, THE SLATE MUST BE WIPED CLEAN! I **OWE** YOU THIS, FOR STRIKING ME!

UHHHHH--!

WHAP!

IF YOUR COWARDLY BLOW HAS INJURED MY BROTHER, YOU'LL PAY **DEARLY** FOR IT--!

RELAX, LITTLE LADY! I JUST TAUGHT HIM A LESSON WITH THE FLAT OF MY BLADE!

IT'LL TEACH HIM NOT TO BE SO **TRUSTING** NEXT TIME! HE SHOULD BE **GRATEFUL** TO ME!

FOR THE **SWORDSMAN** ALWAYS HAS THE LAST WORD!

YOU'LL **NEVER** BE AN AVENGER--FOR YOU ARE LACKING IN **HONOR!!**

AS FOR THE LAST WORD, **THAT** IS A WOMAN'S PREROGATIVE -- AS YOU SHALL **SEE!**

STOP! DON'T FORCE ME TO DEFEND MYSELF AGAINST **YOU!!**

4

THERE *IS* NO DEFENSE AGAINST THE SCARLET WITCH'S *HEX!*

AT THAT MOMENT, THE DRAMATIC FIGURE OF THE AVENGERS' "LEADER PRO TEM" RACES ONTO THE SCENE LIKE A RED-WHITE-AND BLUE GLADIATOR!

I *THOUGHT* I HEARD SOMETHING GOING ON DOWN HERE!

WHY DIDN'T YOU *CALL* ME, WANDA?

THERE WAS NO NEED TO DISTURB *CAPTAIN AMERICA*--!

NO, I GUESS NOT! IT LOOKS AS THOUGH YOU HAVE THE SITUATION WELL IN HAND!

NOW, SUPPOSE YOU CLUE ME IN TO WHAT HAPPENED! WHO'S THE SLUMBERING STRANGER?

HE CALLS HIMSELF THE *SWORDSMAN!* THAT IS ALL WE KNOW OF HIM! AND YET---

--THERE IS AN AURA OF SUBTLE *EVIL* ABOUT HIM --I CAN *SENSE* IT!

THE *SWORDSMAN,* EH? LET'S CHECK HIM OUT ON OUR MICRO-TAPE IDENTITY FILE!

IF HE HAS ANY SORT OF *RECORD,* WE'LL FIND OUT ABOUT IT *NOW!*

SECONDS LATER...

HE *DARED* TRY TO JOIN OUR RANKS?!! HE'S KNOWN IN ALMOST EVERY NATION IN EUROPE AS ONE OF THE MOST DANGEROUS ADVENTURERS OF ALL! HE'S BEEN *EXILED* FROM A DOZEN COUNTRIES!

5

BUT, BEFORE ANOTHER WORD CAN BE SAID, A SURGICAL STEEL BLADE SLASHES OUT...

WHITT

THE SWORDSMAN *RECOVERED!* HE CUT THE ELECTRIC LIGHT WIRES!

HE'S *ESCAPING!* QUICK--HIT THE EMERGENCY LIGHTING SWITCH!

BUT, BY THE TIME THE LIGHTS GO ON AGAIN...

HE'S *GONE!*

I'LL CATCH HIM WITH EASE!

IT WON'T BE THAT SIMPLE! HE'LL LOSE HIMSELF IN THE NIGHT! HE COULD BE *ANYWHERE* BY NOW!

BUT YOU'VE BOTH BEEN GETTING RESTLESS-- YOU COULD *USE* A LITTLE ACTION! SO, TRY TO FIND HIM IF YOU WISH!

I'LL STAY AND MIND THE STORE!

VERY WELL! COME, PIETRO--!

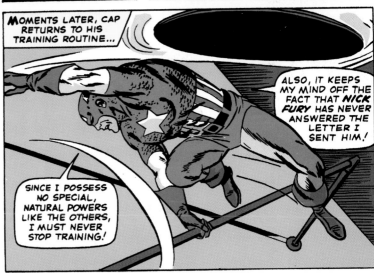

MOMENTS LATER, CAP RETURNS TO HIS TRAINING ROUTINE...

ALSO, IT KEEPS MY MIND OFF THE FACT THAT *NICK FURY* HAS NEVER ANSWERED THE LETTER I SENT HIM!

SINCE I POSSESS NO SPECIAL, NATURAL POWERS LIKE THE OTHERS, I MUST NEVER STOP TRAINING!

THE LETTER ASKING TO JOIN HIS SECRET, COUNTER-INTELLIGENCE UNIT!

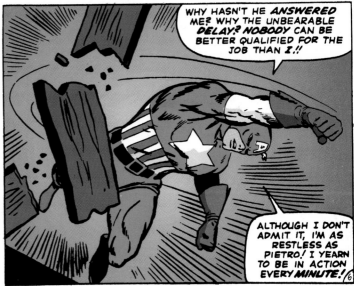

WHY HASN'T HE *ANSWERED* ME? WHY THE UNBEARABLE *DELAY?* NOBODY CAN BE BETTER QUALIFIED FOR THE JOB THAN *I.!!*

ALTHOUGH I DON'T ADMIT IT, I'M AS RESTLESS AS PIETRO! I YEARN TO BE IN ACTION EVERY *MINUTE!* 6

WELL WELL! WHAT ARE YA TRYIN' TO DO, GLAMOR-PANTS --WRECK THE PLACE?

NOT QUITE, HAWKEYE! BUT YOU MIGHT HAVE WANTED TO IF YOU'D BEEN HERE A FEW MINUTES SOONER!

WE HAD AN UNEXPECTED VISITOR--CALLED THE SWORDSMAN!

THE SWORDSMAN! NO! IT CAN'T BE HIM!!

WHY? HAVE YOU HEARD OF HIM?

I'VE MORE THAN HEARD OF HIM--!

HE'S THE ONE MAN-- IN ALL THE WORLD-- I USED TO FEAR!

BETTER START AT THE BEGINNING, AVENGER!

YEAH! IT'S ABOUT TIME I GOT IT OFF MY CHEST!

"I NEVER KNEW MY PARENTS! I WAS AN ORPHAN! AS A KID, I HUNG AROUND CIRCUSES AND CARNIVALS--THAT'S WHERE I MET HIM!"

SO, YOU WANNA JOIN THE CARNEY, HUH? OKAY, I CAN USE AN ASSISTANT!

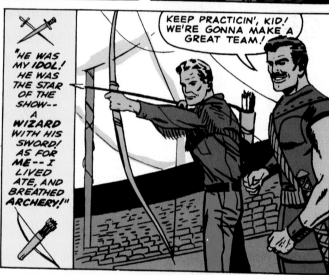

"HE WAS MY IDOL! HE WAS THE STAR OF THE SHOW-- A WIZARD WITH HIS SWORD! AS FOR ME-- I LIVED ATE, AND BREATHED ARCHERY!"

KEEP PRACTICIN', KID! WE'RE GONNA MAKE A GREAT TEAM!

BUT NEVER FORGET WHICH ONE OF US IS THE MASTER!

SOME DAY I'LL BE AS GOOD WITH MY BOW AS YOU ARE WITH YOUR SWORD! YOU'LL SEE!

DON'T TRY IT, KID! DON'T EVER TRY IT! I'M WARNING YOU-- IT WON'T BE HEALTHY!

7

"BUT, A SHORT TIME LATER, SOMETHING EVEN *UNHEALTHIER* HAPPENED--I SAW A SIGHT I SHOULDN'T HAVE SEEN--!"

DID YOU HEAR ABOUT THE PAYMASTER BEING *ROBBED,* AND--*WHA-?*? WHERE'D YOU GET ALL THAT *MONEY*??

YOU LITTLE *PUNK!* I *WARNED* YA NEVER TO COME IN HERE WITHOUT *ASKING* FIRST!!

"THAT WAS THE FIRST TIME I REALIZED THAT EVEN AN *IDOL* CAN HAVE FEET OF CLAY! FOR, *MY IDOL* WAS NOTHING BUT A *THIEF!*"

WHAT ARE YA *STARIN'* AT?? THE MONEY'S RIGHTFULLY *MINE! I'M* THE STAR OF THE SHOW! WITHOUT ME, THEY'D HAVE GONE BROKE *LONG* AGO!

BUT, YOU DIDN'T HAVE TO *STEAL* IT!!

SHUDDUP! NOW THAT YOU *KNOW,* YOU'RE IN IT WITH ME! YOU'RE MY *PARTNER* NOW!

YOU DIDN'T THINK I WASTED ALL THAT TIME *TEACHIN'* YOU FOR MY *HEALTH,* DID YOU? *THIS* IS WHAT I ALWAYS PLANNED!

MY SWORD AND YOUR BOW-- NOBODY'LL *EVER* CATCH US!!

"BITTER AND DISILLUSIONED, I BROKE AWAY FROM HIM! I DIDN'T KNOW WHERE I WAS RUNNING TO-- I JUST HAD TO GET *AWAY--!*"

SO! YOU'RE TOO *GOOD* FOR ME, HUH? YOU'RE TURNIN' YOUR *BACK* ON ME NOW, ARE YOU?

I'M *LEAVING!* I'M GETTING *OUT* OF HERE!

THIS IS YOUR *LAST CHANCE!* NEXT TIME I THROW MY SWORD LIKE A BOOMERANG, I WON'T TRY TO *MISS!*

I'LL SWING UP TO THE *HIGH WIRE!* HE WON'T GET ME *THERE!*

IT'S NO USE! HE'S *STILL* FOLLOWING! HE'S CLIMBING TO THE PLATFORM BEHIND ME!

I CAN'T *RUN* ANY FURTHER!

"AND, IN THAT MOMENT, I BECAME -- A MAN!"

I'VE GOT TO STAND AND FIGHT!

IF I CAN JUST SHOOT HIS SWORD FROM HIS HAND--!

"THOUGH I HIT HIS BLADE, IT WAS LIKE HITTING A PROPELLER! I COULDN'T SHAKE HIS GRIP!"

"AND THEN, WITH ONE LIGHTNING-LIKE THRUST--"

"--HE ENDED THE BATTLE!"

HE LEFT ME FOR DEAD, NOT KNOWING THE ROPE HAD BROKEN MY FALL!

THAN HE PROBABLY DOESN'T SUSPECT HAWKEYE IS THAT BOY FROM HIS PAST!

BUT NOW, WE SUDDENLY SWITCH OUR SCENE TO WASHINGTON, D.C., TO SOLVE A VEXING MYSTERY...

FURY'S OFFICE HAS BEEN DESERTED FOR DAYS!

USE THE GAMMA-LENS! PERHAPS THERE'S A CLUE--!

I SEE A LETTER ON HIS DESK -- FROM THE AVENGERS!

The AVENGERS
AIR MAIL
SPECIAL 1ST
Col. Nick Fury
Pentagon
Wash., D.C.

WE MUST RETRIEVE IT! IT MAY LEAD US TO FURY!

EVER SINCE HE LEFT THE C.I.A. TO TAKE OVER LEADERSHIP OF SHIELD,* OUR MISSION HAS BEEN TO DESTROY HIM!

BUT, SO FAR HYDRA* HAS BEEN UNABLE TO FIND HIS NEW SECRET HEAD-QUARTERS!

THAT'S WHY WE'VE BEEN SPYING ON HIS OLD OFFICE-- HOPING FOR A LEAD!

*IT'S ALL SPELLED OUT FOR YOU IN STRANGE TALES #135 AND 136-- STAN.

AND, THAT LETTER FROM THE AVENGERS MIGHT BE WHAT WE WANT! AIM THE DISPLACER RAY AT IT!

NOW, LET ME SLIP MY BLASTED HOOD OFF, SO I CAN SEE BETTER! THAT'S IT-- DON'T MOVE! HERE GOES!

9

THE BEAM IS INVISIBLE! NO ONE IN THE STREET WILL NOTICE IT PASSING INTO FURY'S WINDOW!

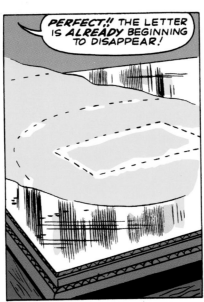

PERFECT!! THE LETTER IS ALREADY BEGINNING TO DISAPPEAR!

YOU MAY SWITCH THE RAY OFF! IT'S GONE!

HOW CAN ANY FORCE DEFEAT HYDRA WHEN WE POSSESS INSTRUMENTS SUCH AS THIS?

ONCE FURY IS BEATEN, NOBODY EVER SHALL STOP US!

NOW, AT THE PRESS OF A BUTTON, THE LETTER REMATERIALIZES HERE IN MY HAND!

IT'S DATED WEEKS AGO! IT'S FROM CAPTAIN AMERICA, REQUESTING A CHANCE TO WORK WITH FURY! FURY NEVER RECEIVED THE LETTER!

BUT IT TELLS US NOTHING! IT'S USELESS TO US!

THEN, IN HIS ANGER AND FRUSTRATION, THE AGENT OF HYDRA, CRUMPLES THE LETTER IN A FIT OF RAGE...

WE HAVE FAILED AGAIN!

AND SO, UNKNOWN TO CAPTAIN AMERICA, THE FATEFUL LETTER HE HAD SENT COL. FURY NEVER REACHES ITS GOAL! INSTEAD, IT IS VEHEMENTLY TOSSED THRU AN OPEN WINDOW IN THE NATION'S CAPITOL...

...ONLY TO LAND, A CRUMPLED MASS, ON THE STREET BELOW-- WHERE FATE ONCE AGAIN STEPS IN...!

HEY-- WHAT'S THAT?

10

A SHORT TIME LATER, AS A PENNY-ANTE CARD GAME IS IN PROGRESS IN A SLEAZY SECTION OF THE SPRAWLING CITY...

DID YOU GUYS HEAR ABOUT THE DOUGH THE *SWORDSMAN* IS OFFERIN'??

NO! FILL US IN, BLACKIE-- WHAT'S THE ANGLE?

I HEARD HE'LL PAY A COOL *GRAND* TO ANYONE WHO CAN GIVE 'IM A LEAD ON HOW TO *TRAP AN AVENGER!*

CHEEE! HE MIGHT AS WELL ASK FER A LEAD ON HOW TA CRACK FORT KNOX!

NO ONE CAN-- *HEY!* WAIT A MINNIT!!!

I JUST THOUGHT OF A *LETTER* I FOUND--!

HUH? WHAT'S *THAT* GOTTA DO WITH THE SWORDSMAN?

NONE OF YER BUSINESS!! DEAL ME *OUTTA* THIS HAND, GENTS! I GOT *THINGS* TA DO!

MINUTES LATER...

I FIGGER THIS *LETTER'LL* BE WORTH A THOUSAND CLAMS TO YA, SWORDSMAN!

I'LL BE THE JUDGE OF THAT! *GIVE* IT TO ME!

HEY! WAIT A MINNIT! YOU CAN'T--!!

CAN IT BE YOU DON'T *TRUST* ME, LITTLE MAN?

N-NO! I DIDN'T MEAN *THAT* --HONEST!!

AHHH! SO *CAPTAIN AMERICA* WANTS TO JOIN NICK FURY'S ORGANIZATION, EH? THIS *COULD* BE WHAT I WANT!

THEN-- I'LL *GET* MY DOUGH??

SURE-- AFTER I'VE *TRAPPED* HIM!

NOW, *GET OUT!* YOU'VE *SERVED* YOUR PURPOSE!

AND SO, THE NEXT DAY...

I GOT MY ANSWER!! FURY WANTS ME! AT LAST!!

WHAT ABOUT YOUR DUTIES HERE, WITH THE AVENGERS?

I'LL STILL BE ON CALL, WHEN YOU NEED ME! BUT, AT LEAST-- I'LL BE IN ACTION ALL THE TIME NOW!

I DO NOT LIKE IT! WHAT GIVES YOU THE RIGHT TO BE A PART-TIME AVENGER?

EASY, PIETRO! DO NOT ANGER HIM!

MY ENTIRE LIFE GIVES ME THE RIGHT, MISTER! WHEN YOU CAN POINT TO A RECORD LIKE MINE, THEN I'LL DISCUSS IT FURTHER WITH YOU!

NOW I KNOW WHY YOU USUALLY WEAR A MASK! IT'S TO HIDE YOUR SWELLED HEAD!

KEEP OUT OF THIS, HAWKEYE!

NEVER HAVE I SEEN HIM SO COLD-- SO GRIM--!

VERY WELL --WE CANNOT FORCE YOU TO STAY!

REMEMBER-- I'M NOT LEAVING THE AVENGERS! I'M JUST PICKING UP SOME THREADS-- THE THREADS OF A LIFE THAT ONCE WAS MINE!

Y'KNOW, IN A WAY THIS COULD BE THE BEST THING FOR ALL OF US!

INDEED IT COULD, HAWKEYE!

I KNOW WHAT THEY'RE THINKING! IF CAPTAIN AMERICA LEAVES, EACH OF THEM HOPES THAT HE WILL BECOME OUR LEADER!

BUT, FATE HAS A WAY OF TAKING A HAND WHEN LEAST EXPECTED! A FEW HOURS LATER, NOT FAR AWAY, WE FIND...

I'LL HAVE 'ER OPEN IN ANOTHER COUPLEA MINUTES!

OKAY, OKAY! STEP ON IT! WE AINT GOT ALL NIGHT!

12

FINALLY...

SO FAR, SO GOOD! NOW LET'S HIGHTAIL IT OUTTA TOWN!

LISTEN! DID YOU HEAR SOMETHIN' ??

NAH! IT'S YER NERVES! YOU'RE JUST JUMPY!

JUMPY, AM I? WHAT DO YA CALL THAT??!

A FLARE!! LIGHTIN' UP THE WHOLE ALLEY! IT MUST BE THE COPS!

YER NUTS! SINCE WHEN DO COPS SHOOT ARROWS?!!

JUST OUR BLASTED LUCK! IT--IT'S GOTTA BE-- HAWKEYE!!

THWIP!

WE CAN'T GET CAUGHT NOW! WE'RE BOTH TWO-TIME LOSERS! I'LL TAKE CARE OF 'IM!

YOU AND WHAT OTHER ARMY, DUMBO?? I CAN HANDLE PUNKS LIKE YOU WITH MY EYES CLOSED!

CRAK!

THAT'LL HOLD YOU TILL THE COPS COME! AND NOW I'LL PLAY PATTYCAKE WITH YOUR PLAYMATE IN THE GETAWAY CAR!

ONE BLAST ARROW IS ALL IT'LL TAKE!

OKAY, CHUCKLES--YOU CAN COME OUT NOW! THAT'S A GOOD LITTLE FELLA!

WHOOM!

13

WHOOPS! HOLD IT! I'M NOT **DONE** WITH YOU YET!

THWP!

NOW LET'S YOU'N ME HAVE A NICE LITTLE TALK--!

IT'S **HAWKEYE**! I MIGHTA **KNOWN**!

HE MUSTA FOUND OUT ABOUT THE **LETTER** I SOLD TO THE **SWORDSMAN**!!

I DIDN'T **MEAN** TO HELP THE SWORDSMAN TRAP CAPTAIN AMERICA--HONEST! YA GOTTA **BELIEVE** ME!

WHAT?!!

THAT LETTER--IT MUSTA BEEN A **PHONY**!

MINUTES LATER...

GOOD WORK, HAWKEYE!

SO WHERE'S MY JUNIOR G-MAN BADGE?!!

THEN, AS THE AMAZING ARCHER DEPARTS...

GLAMOR PANTS IS WALKIN' RIGHT INTO SOME KINDA **TRAP**! BUT, HE **ASKED** FOR IT!

WHY SHOULD **I** BUTT IN! HE'S A BIG BOY NOW!

AND YET, EVEN IF HE **AIN'T** MY FAVORITE PIN-UP--

-- I'M STILL AN **AVENGER**!!

AND SO...

WANDA! PIETRO! WE'VE GOTTA FIND CAP! WE'VE GOTTA **WARN** HIM!

THEN, AFTER A QUICK EXPLANATION...

YOU'RE TOO LATE! HE HAD TOO MUCH OF A START! HE'S **GONE**!

HOW CAN WE HELP HIM IF WE DON'T KNOW WHERE HE **IS**??

WELL, WE CAN'T JUST **STAND** HERE!

MEANWHILE, IN ANOTHER PART OF TOWN...

I **KNOW** THE GOVERNMENT IS TRYING TO SAVE MONEY-- BUT **THIS** IS RIDICULOUS!

THIS **CAN'T** BE THE OFFICE OF COL. FURY!

I WONDER WHY HE'D PICK A RUN-DOWN WAREHOUSE AS A CONFERENCE SITE?

HANDL WITH CAR

14

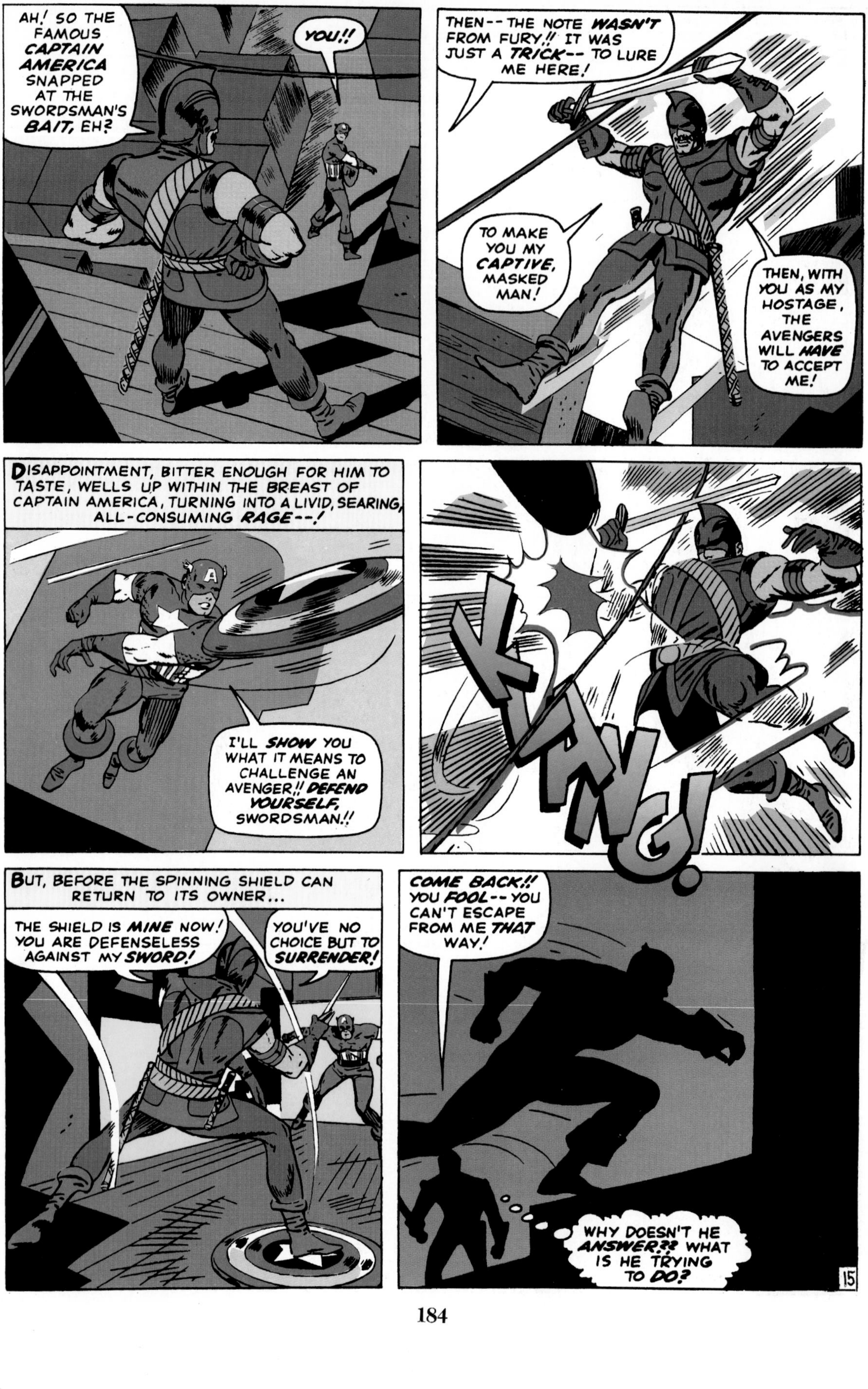
AH! SO THE FAMOUS CAPTAIN AMERICA SNAPPED AT THE SWORDSMAN'S BAIT, EH?
YOU!!
THEN--THE NOTE WASN'T FROM FURY!! IT WAS JUST A TRICK-- TO LURE ME HERE!
TO MAKE YOU MY CAPTIVE, MASKED MAN!
THEN, WITH YOU AS MY HOSTAGE, THE AVENGERS WILL HAVE TO ACCEPT ME!
DISAPPOINTMENT, BITTER ENOUGH FOR HIM TO TASTE, WELLS UP WITHIN THE BREAST OF CAPTAIN AMERICA, TURNING INTO A LIVID, SEARING, ALL-CONSUMING RAGE--!
I'LL SHOW YOU WHAT IT MEANS TO CHALLENGE AN AVENGER!! DEFEND YOURSELF, SWORDSMAN!!
KLANG!
BUT, BEFORE THE SPINNING SHIELD CAN RETURN TO ITS OWNER...
THE SHIELD IS MINE NOW! YOU ARE DEFENSELESS AGAINST MY SWORD!
YOU'VE NO CHOICE BUT TO SURRENDER!
COME BACK!! YOU FOOL--YOU CAN'T ESCAPE FROM ME THAT WAY!
WHY DOESN'T HE ANSWER?? WHAT IS HE TRYING TO DO?
15

A SECOND LATER, THE SWORDSMAN **HAS** HIS ANSWER...

STILL THINK I'M DEFENSELESS NOW?

BAH! KICKING THOSE CARTONS DOWN AT ME ISN'T GOING TO **SAVE** YOU!

NO, BUT IT'LL KEEP YOU OFF-BALANCE LONG ENOUGH FOR ME TO DO-- THIS!

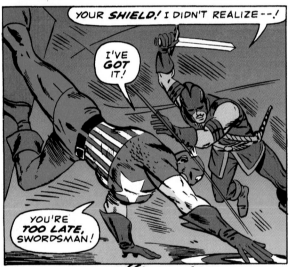

YOUR **SHIELD!** I DIDN'T REALIZE--!

I'VE **GOT** IT!

YOU'RE **TOO LATE**, SWORDSMAN!

UNHHHH!

YOUR **SWORD** CAN'T STOP ME NOW!

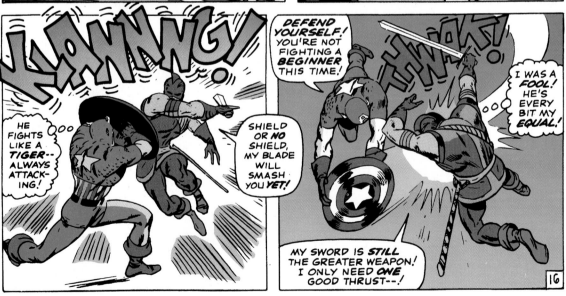

KLANNNG!

HE FIGHTS LIKE A **TIGER**-- ALWAYS ATTACK-ING!

SHIELD OR **NO** SHIELD, MY BLADE WILL SMASH YOU **YET!**

DEFEND YOURSELF! YOU'RE NOT FIGHTING A **BEGINNER** THIS TIME!

THWOK!

I WAS A **FOOL!** HE'S EVERY BIT MY **EQUAL!**

MY SWORD IS **STILL** THE GREATER WEAPON! I ONLY NEED **ONE** GOOD THRUST--!

16

185

AT THAT VERY MOMENT, TENSION RUNS HIGH AT AVENGERS HQ....

YOU **MUST** LOCATE HIM, PIETRO! HE MAY **NEED** US!

I'M **TRYING**, WANDA-- BUT I CAN REACH HIM ON NONE OF OUR NORMAL WAVELENGTHS!

WE'LL HAVE TO TRY SOMETHING **ELSE!**

INDEED? WHAT WOULD **YOU** SUGGEST, SMART ONE??

HOLD YOUR **TEMPER**, MY BROTHER!

GET THAT **CHIP** OFF YOUR SHOULDER AND TRY YOUR **TRACER BEAM**, SPEEDY!

THE **TRACER BEAM!** OF **COURSE!**

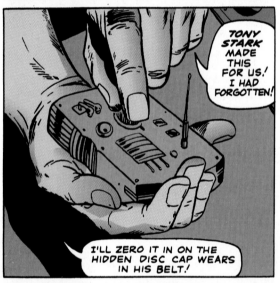

TONY STARK MADE **THIS** FOR US! I HAD FORGOTTEN!

I'LL ZERO IT IN ON THE HIDDEN DISC CAP WEARS IN HIS BELT!

SCANT SECONDS LATER...

NOW, ALL WE HAVE TO DO IS LET THE SIGNAL BEAM LEAD US TO HIM!

I HOPE WE WON'T BE-- TOO LATE!

AND, AS THE AVENGERS SPEED TO THE WAREHOUSE...

NO **WONDER** HIS FAME IS WORLD-WIDE! USING NOTHING BUT THAT SHIELD, HE'S MORE DANGEROUS THAN A REGIMENT!

THIK!

BUT, **THIS** WILL STOP HIM NOW!

HE LED ME INTO A **TRAP!** BY CUTTING THAT ROPE, HE RELEASED A PILE OF METAL CASING ABOVE ME!

17

BUT, A BATTLE-WISE AVENGER KNOWS WHEN TO FIGHT, WHEN TO RUN, --AND WHEN TO *TAKE COVER* WHILE WAITING OUT AN ATTACK--!

MY SHIELD WILL PROTECT ME -- BUT NOW *HE'LL* SEIZE THE INITIATIVE AGAIN!

AND, CAP IS *RIGHT!* FOR, SECONDS LATER...

HE'S HEADING FOR ME IN THAT MECHANIZED HYDRAULIC LIFT-- TRYING TO BURY ME UNDER THOSE TWO-TON CRATES!!

WITH SPLIT-SECOND TIMING, THE RED-WHITE-AND-BLUE AVENGER EXECUTES THE TYPE OF DAZZLING MANEUVER WHICH HAS MADE HIM A LIVING LEGEND IN HIS OWN TIME!

BUT, I'VE GOT *OTHER* PLANS --AND THE *TRAINING* TO CARRY THEM *OUT!*

IT'S THE END OF THE LINE, SWORDSMAN! YOU JUST LOST YOUR DRIVER'S LICENSE!

YOU--!

BUT, BEFORE CAP CAN GRAB THE CONTROLS, THE SOLID STEEL MACHINE PLOWS INTO A SECTION OF WEIGHTED CRATES, AND...

BAROOM!

WHAT A STROKE OF *LUCK* FOR ME! I'M PROTECTED BY BEING INSIDE THIS CAB -- BUT *HE* ISN'T!!

18

187

YOU FOUGHT *WELL*, CAPTAIN AMERICA-- BUT LADY LUCK WAS IN *MY* CORNER TODAY!

UNLESS I MISS MY GUESS, YOUR FELLOW AVENGERS WILL BE HERE BEFORE LONG!

WHAT A PITY THEY'LL BE *TOO LATE!*

WE'LL REACH THE ROOF WITHIN SECONDS--AND THEN, *NOTHING* CAN SAVE YOU!

THEN, ALMOST BEFORE THE SWORDSMAN'S MOCKING VOICE CAN FADE...

THERE'S BEEN A *BATTLE!* THIS PLACE IS A SHAMBLES!

THEN-- HE'S *BEEN* HERE!

YOU CAN SAY *THAT* AGAIN! THERE'S HIS *SHIELD*, IN THE RUBBLE!

AND YOU KNOW *HIM!* HE'D *NEVER* LEAVE THAT HUNK OF TIN BEHIND, UNLESS-- HE WAS *HELPLESS!*

QUICKLY, PIETRO! YOU HAD BETTER RACE AROUND AND TRY TO-- *PIETRO!*

I HAVE ALREADY *DONE* IT, WANDA! HE IS NOWHERE INSIDE THIS BUILDING!

YOU'RE BLAMED *RIGHT* HE ISN'T! *I* SEE HIM!! *LOOK*-- HE'S UP *THERE!*

OH, *NO--!*

DON'T *MOVE*, QUICKSILVER! DON'T REACH FOR AN ARROW, HAWKEYE! DON'T TRY A *HEX*, WITCH! *I* HOLD THE HIGH CARD NOW!

ONE PROD OF MY BLADE, AND CAPTAIN AMERICA PLUNGES TO HIS DOOM!

19

IF YOU VALUE HIS LIFE, YOU HAVE *TEN SECONDS* IN WHICH TO MAKE *ME* THE NEW *LEADER* OF THE AVENGERS!

DON'T DO IT! MY LIFE MEANS *NOTHING!* IT'S THE *TEAM* THAT MATTERS!

BUT--WE *CAN'T* LET YOU DIE!

REMEMBER YOUR *VOWS!* YOU MUST OBEY WITHOUT QUESTION! YOU *HEARD* MY COMMAND--!

THERE MUST BE *NO* SURRENDER!

THEY'LL *SURRENDER!* ONLY THREE SECONDS REMAIN! THEY WON'T LET YOU DIE--!

I *WANTED* TO BE RID OF HIM!! BUT--NOT LIKE *THIS!*

THERE'S NO WAY TO SAVE HIM--THERE'S NO *TIME*--!

NO MATTER *WHAT* HE SAYS--WE *MUST* ACCEPT THE SWORDSMAN'S TERMS!

LOOK! WHA--WHAT *HAPPENED??!*

YOU *FOOL!* NOTHING CAN SAVE YOU *NOW!*

WE'RE *TOO LATE!* THE SWORDSMAN *PUSHED* HIM!

20

NO! HE *DIDN'T!* I *SAW* IT! CAP *JUMPED!*

HE DID IT FOR--*US!*

SO THAT WE WOULDN'T SURRENDER!

AND SO, THE NEW *AVENGERS* FACE THEIR FIRST IMPENDING TRAGEDY! YET, SOMETIMES THE FLAMES OF *GLORY* CAN RISE FROM THE ASHES OF DEFEAT! DON'T DARE MISS OUR GRIPPING SEQUEL NEXT ISSUE--THE TALE HISTORY WILL LONG REMEMBER AS--*"VENGEANCE IS OURS!"*

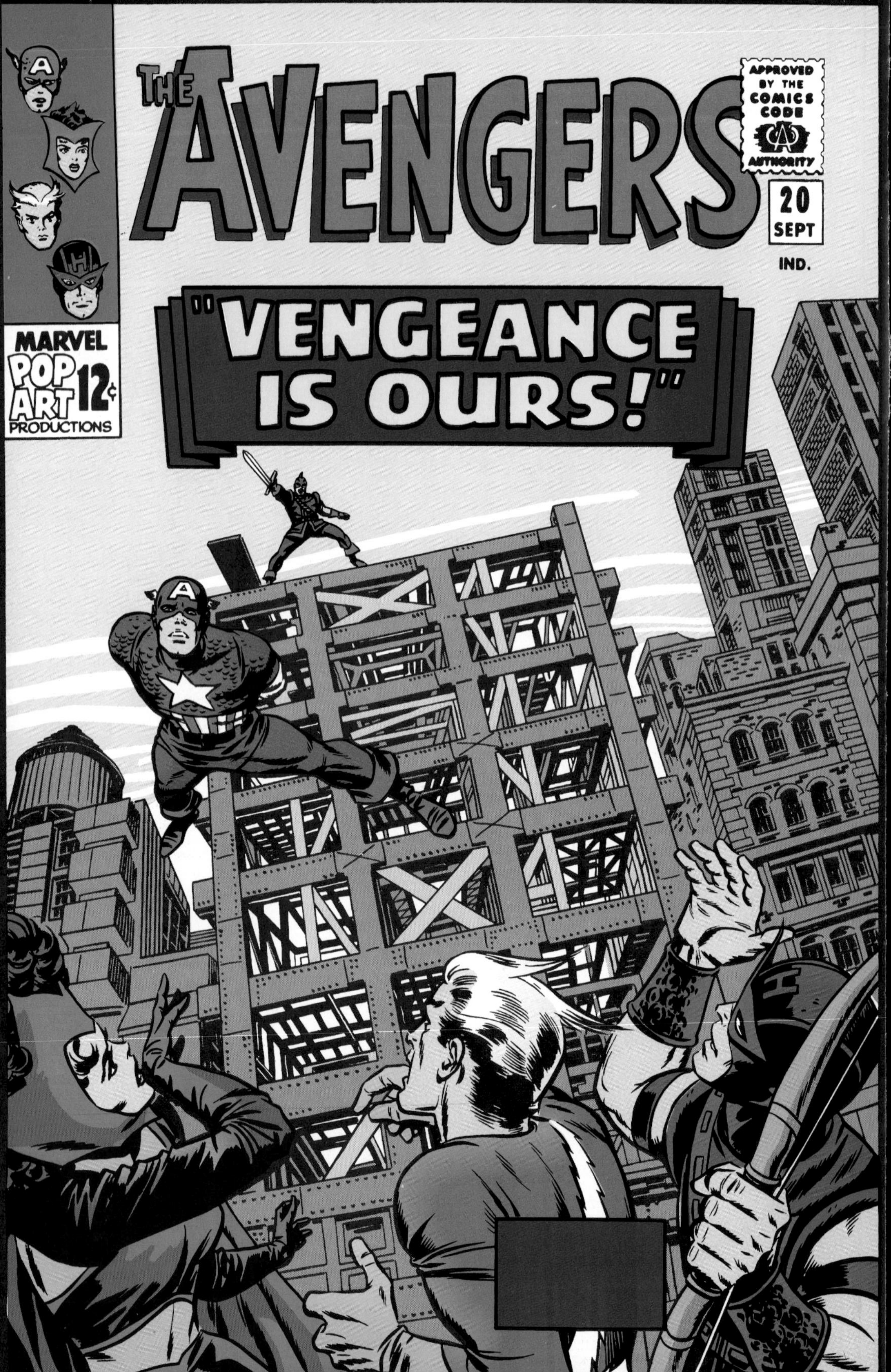
THE AVENGERS
APPROVED BY THE COMICS CODE AUTHORITY
20
SEPT
IND.
MARVEL POP ART PRODUCTIONS 12¢
"VENGEANCE IS OURS!"

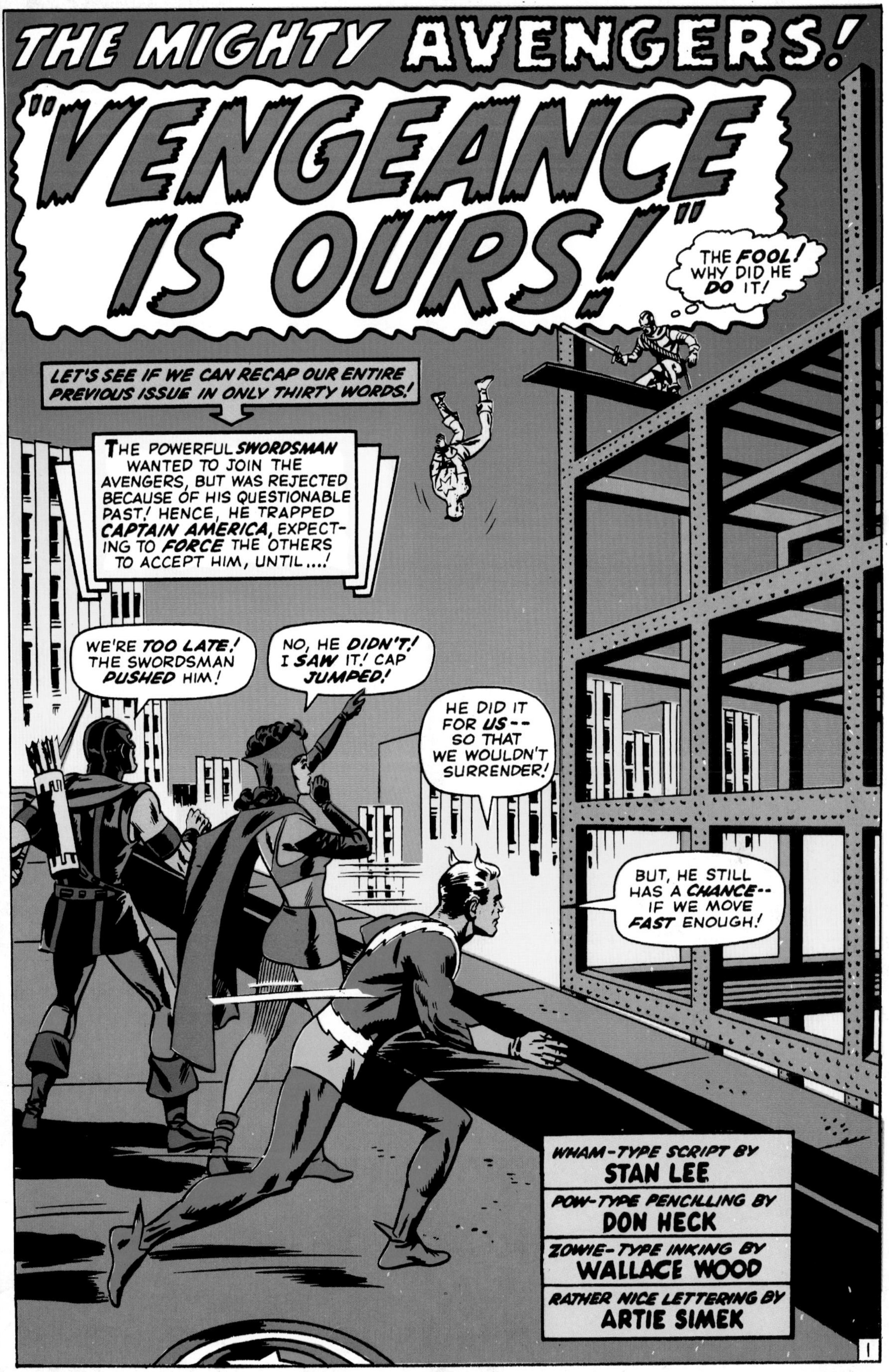
THE MIGHTY AVENGERS!
"VENGEANCE IS OURS!"
THE FOOL! WHY DID HE DO IT!
LET'S SEE IF WE CAN RECAP OUR ENTIRE PREVIOUS ISSUE IN ONLY THIRTY WORDS!
THE POWERFUL SWORDSMAN WANTED TO JOIN THE AVENGERS, BUT WAS REJECTED BECAUSE OF HIS QUESTIONABLE PAST! HENCE, HE TRAPPED CAPTAIN AMERICA, EXPECTING TO FORCE THE OTHERS TO ACCEPT HIM, UNTIL....!
WE'RE TOO LATE! THE SWORDSMAN PUSHED HIM!
NO, HE DIDN'T! I SAW IT! CAP JUMPED!
HE DID IT FOR US-- SO THAT WE WOULDN'T SURRENDER!
BUT, HE STILL HAS A CHANCE-- IF WE MOVE FAST ENOUGH!
WHAM-TYPE SCRIPT BY STAN LEE
POW-TYPE PENCILLING BY DON HECK
ZOWIE-TYPE INKING BY WALLACE WOOD
RATHER NICE LETTERING BY ARTIE SIMEK
1

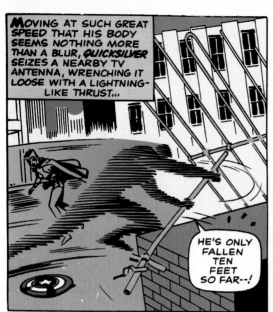

MOVING AT SUCH GREAT SPEED THAT HIS BODY SEEMS NOTHING MORE THAN A BLUR, *QUICKSILVER* SEIZES A NEARBY TV ANTENNA, WRENCHING IT LOOSE WITH A LIGHTNING-LIKE THRUST...

HE'S ONLY FALLEN TEN FEET SO FAR--!

THEN, SPINNING AROUND LIKE A HUMAN TORNADO, THE MUTANT MASTER OF SPEED CREATES A POWERFUL, ARTIFICIAL *WIND GUSHER* OF INCREDIBLE FORCE...

I CAN ONLY KEEP THIS UP FOR ANOTHER FEW SECONDS...

BUT, IT WILL GIVE THE *OTHERS* TIME TO ACT!

QUICKSILVER DIDN'T DISAPPOINT ME! THIS VORTEX OF AIR IS SLOWING MY FALL!

NOW, IF THE *OTHERS* COME THRU--!

AND, *ONE* OF THE "OTHERS" IS ALREADY PRIMED FOR ACTION...!

I'VE GOTTA *HAND* IT TO 'IM! HE'S TRYING TO HOLD *STILL*-- KNOWING WHAT I'M GONNA DO!

MY HANDS-- THEY'RE *FREE!*

THTT!

HAWKEYE *DID* IT!

QUICKSILVER IS *WEAKENING!* ONLY THE SCARLET WITCH'S *HEX* CAN SAVE CAP *NOW!*

I *DID* IT! I CAUSED THOSE *RIVETS* TO POP OUT, LOOSENING THE GIRDER ALONGSIDE OF HIM!

TH/KK!

THKK!

THKK!

THTT!

TSSS!

2

192

PERFECT! THAT GIRDER DROPPED RIGHT IN PLACE!

NOW, WITH MY HANDS FREE, FOR BALANCE...

...AND, A CHANCE TO SOMERSAULT TO SAFETY...

--I'M BACK IN THE FIGHT AGAIN!

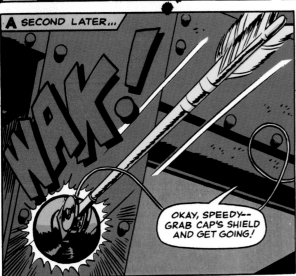

A SECOND LATER...

WAK!

OKAY, SPEEDY-- GRAB CAP'S SHIELD AND GET GOING!

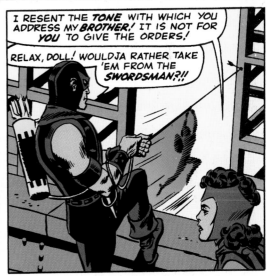

I RESENT THE TONE WITH WHICH YOU ADDRESS MY BROTHER! IT IS NOT FOR YOU TO GIVE THE ORDERS!

RELAX, DOLL! WOULDJA RATHER TAKE 'EM FROM THE SWORDSMAN?!!

GOOD WORK QUICKSILVER! I HAD A HUNCH YOU THREE WOULDN'T FAIL ME!

YOU CHOSE A DANGEROUS WAY TO PLAY THAT HUNCH, AVENGER!

MEANWHILE, MANY FEET ABOVE, THE SWASH- BUCKLING SWORDSMAN WATCHES WITH COLD, UNBLINKING EYES--!

THEY'RE FAR MORE DANGEROUS THAN I THOUGHT! INDIVIDUALLY, EACH ONE IS AN ENEMY TO BE RESPECTED--

BUT, AS A TEAM, THEY'RE PRACTICALLY UNBEATABLE!

3

I'M NOT AFRAID TO TACKLE ANYTHING THAT *LIVES*-- BUT, EVEN FOR THE *SWORDSMAN*, THERE'S A TIME TO *REST* AND LICK YOUR WOUNDS!

I'LL HOLD THEM AT BAY LONG ENOUGH TO MAKE MY ESCAPE!

HIS SWINGING SWORD IS JUST *RIPE* FOR ANOTHER *HEX!*

I CAN HARDLY *SEE* HIM FOR THE SUDDEN *BLUR*--!

--*UHHH*--! WHERE DID THAT *GIRDER* POP UP FROM??

KLANG!

YOU WILL SEE HIM *NOW!*

THAT SUDDEN RUSH OF WIND-- THAT SHADOWY, SPEEDING FORM-- IT'S *QUICKSILVER!*

AND *NOW,* SWORDSMAN, YOU'LL LEARN WHAT IT *MEANS* TO ATTACK THE *AVENGERS!!*

MELODRAMATIC PHRASES DON'T FRIGHTEN *ME,* SON! I'VE NEVER SEEN *ANYONE* I COULDN'T BEAT! MY *BLADE* WILL SLOW YOU DOWN!

WHIT T!

WH-WHERE'D HE *GO??* I DON'T-- OH!

THERE YOU ARE! DIDN'T THINK I'D *SEE* YOU, EH?

THAT *PLANK?* NO TIME TO *DODGE* IT--!

ON THE CONTRARY -- I *HOPED* YOU'D SEE ME!

JUST A LITTLE *CLOSER* NOW--!

4

ALTHOUGH I CANNOT OUT-RUN YOUR ATTACK, MY *SWORD* CAN DO MY RUNNING FOR ME!

QUICKSILVER-- *ENOUGH!* LEAVE HIM FOR *ME!* THE PRIVILEGE IS *MINE!*

CAPTAIN AMERICA!

VERY WELL, AVENGER!

TURN, SWORDSMAN! TURN AND *FACE ME!*

T-LINNG!

I'LL DO *MORE* THAN FACE YOU! I'LL MAKE YOU WISH YOU HAD NEVER *HEARD* OF THE SWORDSMAN!

NOT *THAT* WAY, YOU WON'T!!

CLANNG!

NO MATTER WHAT YOUR *SWORD* CAN DO, MY *SHIELD* CAN COUNTER-ACT IT!

AND, ONCE THE POWER OF YOUR SWORD IS GONE, THE *SWORDSMAN* WILL BE *THRU!*

SOMETHING'S *HAPPENING* TO ME! I FEEL *STRANGE* --AS THOUGH I'M LOSING CONTROL--!

NO, YOU DON'T! NO TRICK WILL SAVE YOU *NOW!*

ALL OF YOU-- STAY *BACK!* WHATEVER HE TRIES-- *I'LL* HANDLE IT!

IT *ISN'T* A TRICK! HE'S IN *SHOCK*-- LOOK AT HIS *FACE!*

HE'S TURNING PALE-- SOMETHING *IS* WRONG!

LOOK! BEFORE OUR EYES-- HE --HE'S *VANISHING!*

IT ISN'T *POSSIBLE!* HIS ONLY "MAGIC" LIES IN HIS *SWORDSMANSHIP!*

THIS ISN'T *MY* DOING!! IT--MUST BE--ONE OF *YOU!*

5

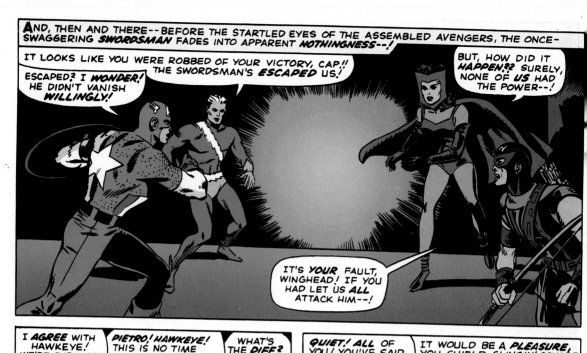

AND, THEN AND THERE--BEFORE THE STARTLED EYES OF THE ASSEMBLED AVENGERS, THE ONCE-SWAGGERING *SWORDSMAN* FADES INTO APPARENT *NOTHINGNESS*--!

IT LOOKS LIKE YOU WERE ROBBED OF YOUR VICTORY, CAP.!! THE SWORDSMAN'S *ESCAPED* US!

ESCAPED? I *WONDER!* HE DIDN'T VANISH *WILLINGLY!*

BUT, HOW DID IT *HAPPEN?* SURELY, NONE OF *US* HAD THE POWER--!

IT'S *YOUR* FAULT, WINGHEAD! IF YOU HAD LET US *ALL* ATTACK HIM--!

I *AGREE* WITH HAWKEYE! WE'RE SUPPOSED TO WORK AS A *TEAM*--AND THAT MEANS *ALL* OF US!

PIETRO! HAWKEYE! THIS IS NO TIME FOR US TO SQUABBLE THIS WAY! WE HAVE TO LEARN WHAT *HAPPENED* TO THE SWORDSMAN!

WHAT'S THE *DIFF?* IF WE *DO* FIND 'IM, CAP'LL PROBABLY BLOW THE BIT AGAIN!

QUIET! *ALL* OF YOU! YOU'VE SAID *ENOUGH!* IF IT'S A *BATTLE* YOU WANT, HAWKEYE--!

IT WOULD BE A *PLEASURE,* YOU SHIELD-SLINGIN' SQUARE --BUT I DON'T PICK FIGHTS WITH *OLDER* MEN!

YOU'RE *BOTH* TOO HOT-TEMPERED! THAT IS WHY *I, QUICKSILVER,* SHOULD BE LEADER!

WITHOUT ANOTHER WORD, CAPTAIN AMERICA TURNS ON HIS HEEL AND HEADS FOR AVENGERS HQ., FOLLOWED BY THE OTHERS--

...NONE OF THEM NOTICING THE EVIL PAIR OF EYES THAT HAVE WATCHED THE ENTIRE INCIDENT--ALTHOUGH THEIR OWNER IS HALF A WORLD AWAY!

...*THE SAME EYES THAT NOW REGARD A MYSTIFIED *SWORDSMAN* WITH DIABOLIC AMUSEMENT....!

WHERE IN BLAZES *AM* I?? AND HOW DID I *GET* HERE?

6

THEN, IN A NEARBY CHAMBER, THE ENERGY FROM A JEWELED *RING* SETS POWERFUL FORCES IN MOTION...

THOSE OVERSIZED *DOORS* ARE SLOWLY SWINGING OPEN.! WHOEVER'S *BEHIND* ALL THIS MUST BE ON THE OTHER SIDE--!

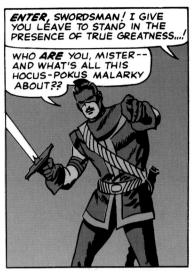

ENTER, SWORDSMAN.! I GIVE YOU LEAVE TO STAND IN THE PRESENCE OF TRUE GREATNESS....!

WHO *ARE* YOU, MISTER-- AND WHAT'S ALL THIS HOCUS-POKUS MALARKY ABOUT??

MEN CALL ME-- THE *MANDARIN.!* AND YOU WILL SOON LEARN THAT THIS IS FAR MORE THAN THE *"MALARKY"* YOU SPEAK OF!

THE *MANDARIN?!!* I ALWAYS THOUGHT OF YOU AS A *LEGEND* --AN OLD WIVES' TALE--!!

THAT IS AS I *WISHED* IT.! IT IS NOT YET TIME FOR THE WORLD TO BE AWARE OF ME-- OR OF MY PLAN FOR COMPLETE DOMINATION OF THIS UNSUSPECTING PLANET!

BUT, AT THIS MOMENT, MY PLANS ARE MORE *MODEST!* I MERELY DESIRE TO DESTROY THE *AVENGERS!* AND I HAVE SELECTED *YOU* TO BE MY AGENT!

WHAT ARE THEY TO *YOU?*

AS A GROUP-- *NOTHING!* BUT, MY MOST HATED ENEMY-- *IRON MAN--* MAY ONE DAY RETURN TO THEM! AND, WHEN HE *DOES* --I WANT *YOU* THERE-- AS A MEMBER OF THE AVENGERS-- TO SMASH HIM FROM *WITHIN!*

THAT IS WHY I DISSIPATED MANY MONTH'S SUPPLY OF MY DELTA ENERGY SOURCE, TO TRANSPORT YOU HERE THRU MOLECULAR TRANSJECTION!

NOW, HAND ME YOUR *SWORD!* I SHALL MAKE CERTAIN *IMPROVEMENTS* UPON IT WHICH WILL MULTIPLY ITS PRESENT POWER A *HUNDRED-FOLD!*

FORGET IT, MANDARIN! YOU PICKED THE *WRONG* BOY THIS TIME!

THE *SWORDSMAN* ISN'T *ANYONE'S* AGENT-- *EVER!*

WHAT! YOU THINK YOU HAVE A *CHOICE??!*

NO ONE RESISTS THE WILL OF THE MANDARIN!

ONLY *IRON MAN* HAS EVER SUCCESSFULLY DEFIED ME.!! AND, FOR THAT FATAL MISTAKE, I HAVE PLEDGED TO *DESTROY* HIM!

NOW, *OBSERVE--!*

AT THE SLIGHTEST TOUCH OF ONE OF MY MYSTIC RINGS, TWO ENERGY SPHERES RISE FROM BENEATH THE FLOORING!

REAL CLEVER, MAC-- BUT PARLOR TRICKS AREN'T MY CUP OF TEA!

DO YOU *STILL* CALL THIS A PARLOR TRICK?

CAN'T HOLD MY SWORD.!! SOMETHING'S PULLING IT FROM ME.!!

8

WITHOUT A SECOND THOUGHT, THE FIGHTING-MAD SWORDSMAN DRAWS A MENACING STILETTO FROM HIS TUNIC, AND CHARGES FORWARD....!

NO ONE TAKES MY SWORD FROM ME WITHOUT FIGHTING TO THE BITTER *END* FOR IT!

WITLESS OCCIDENTAL FOOL! DO YOU THINK TO IMPRESS THE *MANDARIN* WITH SUCH SAVAGE, UNTHINKING TACTICS??!

ALL I NEED DO IS ACTIVATE ANOTHER OF MY *RINGS--!*

AND, YOU SHALL REMAIN THUS HELPLESS, UNTIL YOU REALIZE IT IS TO YOUR OWN ADVANTAGE TO SERVE YOUR MASTER!

MEANWHILE, INSIDE THE NEW YORK MANSION OF MILLIONAIRE TONY STARK, WHICH SERVES AS HEAD-QUARTERS FOR THE MIGHTY *AVENGERS*...

I DON'T LIKE TO AIR MY DIRTY LINEN IN PUBLIC... BUT, NOW THAT WE'RE BEHIND LOCKED DOORS, WHERE WE CAN'T BE OVERHEARD, IF YOU HAVE ANY COMPLAINTS TO MAKE ABOUT MY LEADER-SHIP---

LEADERSHIP?? HAW! *WHAT* LEADERSHIP??!

DON'T *LISTEN* TO HIM, CAP! HE'S SPOILING FOR A FIGHT!

STAY *OUT* OF THIS, WANDA! IT'S BETWEEN *HAWKEYE* AND MYSELF!

YOU'RE BLAMED *RIGHT* IT IS! I'M *SICK* OF THE WAY YOU TRY TO PUSH YOUR WEIGHT AROUND ALL THE TIME! DO YA *READ* ME?

LOUD AND CLEAR, FEATHER-BRAIN!

AND GET YOUR FINGER OUT OF MY FACE BEFORE YOU *LOSE* IT!

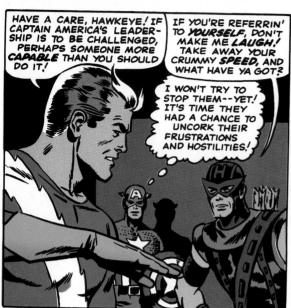

HAVE A CARE, HAWKEYE! IF CAPTAIN AMERICA'S LEADERSHIP IS TO BE CHALLENGED, PERHAPS SOMEONE MORE *CAPABLE* THAN YOU SHOULD DO IT!

IF YOU'RE REFERRIN' TO *YOURSELF*, DON'T MAKE ME *LAUGH*! TAKE AWAY YOUR CRUMMY *SPEED*, AND WHAT HAVE YA GOT?

I WON'T TRY TO STOP THEM--YET! IT'S TIME THEY HAD A CHANCE TO UNCORK THEIR FRUSTRATIONS AND HOSTILITIES!

LET THEM BE, WANDA! PIETRO WON'T APPRECIATE YOUR INTERFERENCE AT A TIME LIKE THIS!

IF YOU ANGER MY BROTHER, YOU *ALSO* ANGER THE *SCARLET WITCH*!

I CAN EVEN BEAT YOUR *SPEED*--WITH ONE OF MY ARROWS!

I THINK *NOT*, BRAGGART! I SHALL *RACE* YOUR ARROW AND PROVE IT!

OKAY, SMART GUY SEE THAT CALENDER ON THE WALL--?

23

--LET'S SEE YOU GET THERE AHEAD OF MY FASTEST ARROW! PUT UP, OR *SHUT* UP!

MAKE YOURSELF *USEFUL*, WING-HEAD! CAN YA SAY "READY, SET, GO" WITHOUT STUMBLING?

FIRE AT *ANY* TIME! IT MATTERS NOT TO ME!

THEN GET IT *OVER* WITH--!

A SPLIT-SECOND LATER, AT CAP'S COMMAND, BOTH THE ARROW AND THE HUMAN STREAK FOR THEIR TARGET IN A BLUR OF LIGHTNING-FAST MOTION...

ooo *GO!*

NOTHING THAT *LIVES* CAN MATCH THE SPEED OF A MASTER'S *ARROW*!

NOTHING--

TWIIANNING

10

--EXCEPT--

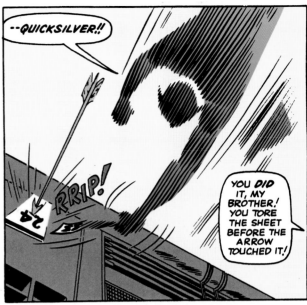

--QUICKSILVER!!

RRRIP!

YOU *DID* IT, MY *BROTHER!* YOU TORE THE SHEET BEFORE THE ARROW TOUCHED IT!

NO *LONGER* WILL HAWKEYE CLAIM THAT *HIS* IS THE GREATER POWER!

WANT TO THROW YOUR *SHIELD* AND HAVE ME RACE IT, CAPTAIN AMERICA?

NO THANKS! I GET THE MESSAGE, PIETRO!

HOW ABOUT *YOU*, LOUD MOUTH?

BIG DEAL! WHAT DOES *ONE RACE* PROVE?

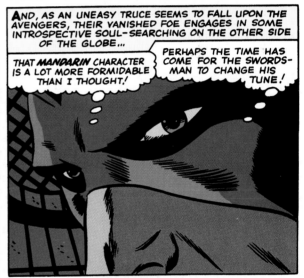

AND, AS AN UNEASY TRUCE SEEMS TO FALL UPON THE AVENGERS, THEIR VANISHED FOE ENGAGES IN SOME INTROSPECTIVE SOUL-SEARCHING ON THE OTHER SIDE OF THE GLOBE...

THAT *MANDARIN* CHARACTER IS A LOT MORE FORMIDABLE THAN I THOUGHT!

PERHAPS THE TIME HAS COME FOR THE SWORDS-MAN TO CHANGE HIS TUNE!

WHY SHOULD I WASTE MY TIME FIGHTING *HIM*, WHEN THE *AVENGERS* ARE THE REAL ENEMY?? IF HE CAN HUMBLE THEM--AS HE CLAIMS--WHY SHOULD I LOOK A GIFT HORSE IN THE MOUTH?!

TIME ENOUGH FOR ME TO TACKLE HIM AGAIN *LATER* --AFTER HE'S SERVED HIS PURPOSE!

OKAY, FU MANCHU --LET'S TALK THINGS OVER!

AH, I SEE YOU HAVE COME TO YOUR SENSES! THAT IS GOOD!

11

201

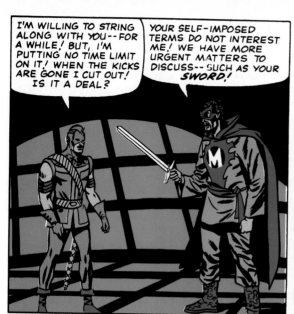

I'M WILLING TO STRING ALONG WITH YOU--FOR A WHILE! BUT, I'M PUTTING NO TIME LIMIT ON IT! WHEN THE KICKS ARE GONE I CUT OUT! IS IT A DEAL?

YOUR SELF-IMPOSED TERMS DO NOT INTEREST ME! WE HAVE MORE URGENT MATTERS TO DISCUSS-- SUCH AS YOUR *SWORD!*

I BELIEVE YOU WILL FIND SOME OF THESE BUTTONS I HAVE ADDED QUITE *INTERESTING!* THEY SHALL MAKE YOU A WORTHY ALLY OF THE *MANDARIN!*

HERE--TAKE IT AND FAMILIARIZE YOURSELF WITH ITS NEW POWERS!

IT WORKS LIKE THOSE *RINGS* OF YOURS! NOW EACH BUTTON ACTIVATES A DIFFERENT BATTLE DEVICE!

AH SO! THE ONE YOU HAVE JUST PRESSED RELEASES BOLTS OF MAN-MADE *LIGHTNING!* AMUSING, IS IT NOT?

BUT, MARK THIS *WELL,* SWORDSMAN... SHOULD YOU EVER ATTEMPT TO USE YOUR BLADE AGAINST *ME,* YOU WILL *REGRET* IT!

THE DEVICES WILL *REVERSE* THEMSELVES --AND IT IS *YOU* WHO WILL BE THEIR TARGET!

YOU COVER ALL THE BASES, DON'T YOU?

INDEED! THE *MANDARIN* LEAVES NOTHING TO CHANCE!

BUT, ENOUGH TALK! YOU WILL COME WITH ME NOW!

IT IS TIME FOR YOU TO RETURN TO THE AVENGERS! AND, *THIS* TIME, YOU SHALL BE *ACCEPTED* AS A MEMBER OF THEIR UNSUSPECTING GROUP!

WHAT MAKES YOU SO *SURE?*

I WILL *SHOW* YOU--!

12

HERE, IN MY HIDDEN CASTLE, I HAVE SPENT *YEARS* DEVELOPING UNDREAMED-OF WONDERS OF SCIENCE!

AND, ONE OF MY GREATEST EFFORTS HAS BEEN THIS INFALLIBLE *MATTER RECREATER!*

Y'KNOW SOMETHING, MISTER--I'M BEGINNING TO WONDER HOW *IRON MAN* EVER MANAGED TO BEAT YOU IN THE PAST!

AN UNFORTUNATE CHOICE OF WORDS, SWORDSMAN! I WOULD PREFER TO SAY HE MERELY *ESCAPED* FROM ME!

NOW, PLEASE OBSERVE...

CLICK!

I HAVE DEVOTED MANY MONTHS TO STUDYING MY ARMOR-CLAD FOE! I KNOW ENOUGH ABOUT HIM NOW TO PERFECTLY *RECREATE* HIS LIFELIKE *IMAGE--*

ZZAT!

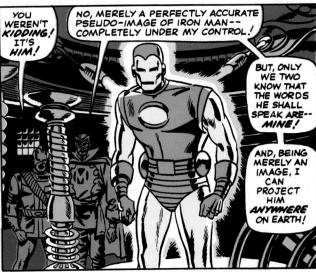

YOU WEREN'T *KIDDING!* IT'S *HIM!*

NO, MERELY A PERFECTLY ACCURATE PSEUDO-IMAGE OF IRON MAN-- COMPLETELY UNDER MY CONTROL*!*

BUT, ONLY WE TWO KNOW THAT THE WORDS HE SHALL SPEAK ARE-- *MINE!*

AND, BEING MERELY AN IMAGE, I CAN PROJECT HIM *ANYWHERE* ON EARTH!

THUS, THE TIME HAS COME FOR US TO RETURN TO THE *AVENGERS* ONCE MORE--AS OUR WONDROUS TALE APPROACHES ITS STARTLING CLIMAX...

LOOK! WE HAVE AN UNEXPECTED *VISITOR!*

I DON'T *GET* IT! HE'S SUPPOSED TO BE BATTLING THE *TITANIUM MAN* IN EUROPE RIGHT NOW!*

HOW DID HE COME *IN?* THE DOORS ARE ALL STILL *LOCKED!*

*NO NEED TO EXPLAIN IT HERE! IT'S ALL IN *SUSPENSE #70*--ON SALE NOW!--STAN.

I *AM* STILL IN EUROPE*!* BUT, BETWEEN ROUNDS, I'M SENDING MY *PROJECTO-IMAGE* TO YOU BECAUSE I HAVE A MESSAGE OF GREAT IMPORTANCE....!

I'LL *BUY* THAT, PARTNER! BUT, YOUR *VOICE* SOUNDS KINDA STRANGE TO ME....!

NATURALLY--THE TONAL QUALITY IS GREATLY DISTORTED DUE TO THE DISTANCE MY IMAGE MUST TRAVEL!

WHAT *IS* YOUR MESSAGE, IRON MAN?

13

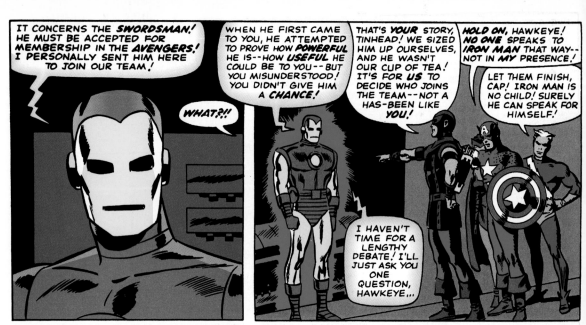

IT CONCERNS THE *SWORDSMAN!* HE MUST BE ACCEPTED FOR MEMBERSHIP IN THE *AVENGERS!* I PERSONALLY SENT HIM HERE TO JOIN OUR TEAM!

WHAT?!!

WHEN HE FIRST CAME TO YOU, HE ATTEMPTED TO PROVE HOW *POWERFUL* HE IS--HOW *USEFUL* HE COULD BE TO YOU--BUT YOU MISUNDERSTOOD! YOU DIDN'T GIVE HIM A *CHANCE!*

THAT'S *YOUR* STORY, TINHEAD! WE SIZED HIM UP OURSELVES, AND HE WASN'T OUR CUP OF TEA! IT'S FOR *US* TO DECIDE WHO JOINS THE TEAM--NOT A HAS-BEEN LIKE *YOU!*

HOLD ON, HAWKEYE! *NO ONE* SPEAKS TO *IRON MAN* THAT WAY-- NOT IN *MY* PRESENCE!

LET THEM FINISH, CAP! IRON MAN IS NO CHILD! SURELY HE CAN SPEAK FOR HIMSELF!

I HAVEN'T TIME FOR A LENGTHY DEBATE! I'LL JUST ASK YOU ONE QUESTION, HAWKEYE...

WHAT WOULD HAVE BECOME OF *YOU* IF WE HAD NOT RELAXED OUR STANDARDS ENOUGH TO ALLOW *YOU* TO JOIN-- EVEN THOUGH YOUR RECORD WAS HARDLY SPOTLESS??

I SEE YOU HAVE NO *ANSWER* TO THAT, MY QUICK-TEMPERED FRIEND!

I CAN REMAIN NO LONGER! BUT, ONCE AGAIN, ON MY WORD AS AN *AVENGER,* I VOUCH FOR THE *SWORDSMAN,* AND I ASK YOU TO ACCEPT HIM FOR MEMBERSHIP!

WELL, IF IT IS ALL RIGHT WITH *CAPTAIN AMERICA....!*

MAYBE I *DO* SHOOT MY MOUTH OFF TOO MUCH!

IRON MAN'S WORD IS GOOD ENOUGH FOR *ME!* THAT SETTLES IT!

WELL, I'LL *BE--!* YOU *DID* IT, MANDY!

THERE! I'VE ERASED THE IMAGE OF IRON MAN! NOW, IT'S *YOUR* TURN....!

YOU MUST REACH THE AVENGERS AT *ONCE*--BEFORE THEY HAVE TIME TO CONSIDER WHAT HAS HAPPENED-- AND TO BECOME SUSPICIOUS--!

YOU SURE FIGURE ALL THE ANGLES...!

THAT IS WHY I AM-- THE *MANDARIN!* AND NOW-- *FAREWELL!*

HE'S SENDING ME BACK THE WAY I *CAME!* WELL, ANYHOW, IT BEATS TAKING A BUS!

14

I'VE GOT TO SAY **ONE** THING FOR THE **MANDARIN**--

HE MAY NOT BE THE GUY I'D MOST LIKE TO BE STRANDED ON A DESERT ISLAND WITH--

--BUT, I'D SURE RATHER HAVE THAT **ORIENTAL** ODDBALL **WITH** ME THAN **AGAINST** ME!

MEANWHILE...

HEY, CAP... I KNOW THAT IRON MAN IS KINDA LIKE AN ELDER STATESMAN AROUND HERE, BUT I THOUGHT WE MADE OUR **OWN** DECISIONS ON THIS TEAM!

LOOK, ROBIN HOOD -- WE'RE A FIGHTING TEAM, NOT A **DEBATING SOCIETY!** THE MATTER'S **SETTLED,** SO GET OFF MY BACK, MISTER!

ARE YOU SURE YOU FOUGHT ON **OUR** SIDE DURING THE WAR? YOU'DA MADE A GREAT **DICTATOR** -- HEY--!

SOMEONE MUST HAVE UNPLUGGED A RAT HOLE! LOOK WHO'S **HERE!**

AT EASE, HAWKEYE! **I'LL** TAKE OVER NOW! STAND ASIDE!

YOU KNOW WHY I'VE RETURNED!

I TOOK THE LIBERTY OF PICKING YOUR LOCK WITH MY SWORD!

THEN, DESPITE SOME MUFFLED GRUMBLING FROM HAWKEYE, THE SWEARING-IN CEREMONY IS QUICKLY COMPLETED...

CONGRATULATIONS, SWORDSMAN! YOU'RE ONE OF US NOW! WELCOME TO THE **AVENGERS!**

GLAD TO BE **WITH** YOU, CAP! MAYBE EVEN GLADDER THAN YOU **THINK!**

NEXT THING Y'KNOW WE'LL BE SWEARIN' IN **DR. DOOM!**

DON'T LET **HAWKEYE** BUG YOU! HE'S NOT TOO EASY TO GET ALONG WITH, BUT, WHEN THE CHIPS ARE DOWN, HE'S ALL **AVENGER!**

HE DOESN'T BOTHER ME! I CAN HANDLE A DOZEN LIKE HIM **ANY** TIME!

I HOPE YOU'LL NEVER HAVE TO **PROVE** THAT STATEMENT!

NOW, COME ON-- I'LL SHOW YOU AROUND....!

BY THE WAY, YOU NEVER TOLD ME WHAT YOUR CONNECTION WITH IRON MAN IS...?

IT'S SORT OF CONFIDENTIAL! I'D BETTER LET **HIM** EXPLAIN IT-- WHEN HE RETURNS!

AND **I'LL** JUST KEEP MY EYE ON YOU TILL THEN, FELLA!

HE'S SUSPICIOUS! EVEN MORE THAN **HAWKEYE!** BUT HE HAS NO **PROOF!**

15

IN THE DAYS THAT FOLLOW, THE SWORDSMAN IS NEVER FAR FROM THE WATCHFUL EYE OF A FELLOW AVENGER, DURING HIS PROBATIONARY PERIOD....!

THEY WATCH ME *CONSTANTLY!* I HAVE NOT YET WON THEIR TRUST! BUT WHAT DOES IT MATTER?

AND THEN, ONE DAY-- DURING A *REST PERIOD--*

THEY'RE NOT *LOOKING!* THIS IS MY CHANCE TO COMPLETE THE MANDARIN'S *TRAP--!*

THIS LITTLE GADGET WILL LOOK LIKE ANOTHER INNOCENT DIAL ON THEIR CONTROL PANEL...

THEY'LL NEVER SUSPECT THAT IT'S A *BOMB*-- CAPABLE OF FINISHING THEM *ALL* WHEN IRON MAN SHOWS UP!

NONE OF THEM SAW ME FASTEN IT TO THE PANEL!

THE *MANDARIN* CAN SET IT OFF BY REMOTE CONTROL AT THE RIGHT MOMENT!

BUT, I WISH I COULD SAVE THE *SCARLET WITCH!* SHE'S TOO *BEAUTIFUL* TO BE HARMED!

LATER THAT NIGHT, A PHANTOM FIGURE AWAKENS THE STARTLED SWORDSMAN...

DO NOT BE ALARMED! THIS IS MERELY A *PROJECTO-IMAGE* OF MYSELF!

I DON'T CARE *WHAT* YOU CALL IT -- I DON'T LIKE UNINVITED GUESTS!! AND THAT GOES FOR *YOU,* TOO!

16

DO NOT BORE ME WITH YOUR PRATTLING! DID YOU PLANT THE BOMB?

SURE! IT WAS A *BREEZE!*

AH, SO! THAT IS *GOOD!*

I AM HERE TO WARN YOU-- I HAVE CHANGED MY PLANS! I AM TOO *IMPATIENT* TO AWAIT THE RETURN OF MY CHOSEN VICTIM!

YOU MUST LEAVE AT *ONCE!* I SHALL SET OFF THE BOMB *TONIGHT!*

NO! YOU'LL KILL THEM *ALL!* HOW COME? WHAT ABOUT *IRON MAN??*

THIS WILL SPEED HIS ARRIVAL! WHEN HE LEARNS OF THEIR FATE, HE WILL COME TO INVESTIGATE--AND *THEN* WE SHALL TRAP HIM!

WAIT! IT'S TOO *SUDDEN!* LET'S TALK IT OVER! WHAT ABOUT THE *GIRL--? MANDARIN!!* HE--HE'S *GONE!*

FOR LONG, TORTUROUS MOMENTS, THE SWORDSMAN STANDS MOTIONLESS--HIS BRAIN SEETHING-- UNTIL--

I NEVER EXPECTED IT TO HAPPEN THIS WAY--!

I *CAN'T* LET HIM DO IT! NOT LIKE *THIS!* NOT WITHOUT A CHANCE!

THUS, WITHIN SECONDS...

I COULD TAKE *PRIDE* IN A VICTORY IN *BATTLE*-- BUT THIS IS *DIFFERENT!*

EVEN AN *ENEMY* DESERVES A FIGHTING CHANCE! THE *SWORDSMAN* CANNOT STOOP TO --ASSASSINATION!!

IT'S COMING UNDONE! *THERE*-- I'VE PRIED IT LOOSE! ONCE IT'S RELEASED FROM THE PANEL, IT CAN NO LONGER BE DETONATED!

SWORDSMAN!! YOU'RE TAMPERING WITH OUR CONTROL PANEL! IN YOUR HAND-- A *NITRO-BOMB!!*

OUR SUSPICIONS WERE *CORRECT!* YOU *WERE* PART OF A PLOT TO DESTROY US!

CAPTAIN AMERICA!!

NO! WAIT! I CAN *EXPLAIN* --!

I'LL **BET** YOU CAN EXPLAIN, MISTER! YOU ALWAYS **WERE** GOOD AT TALKING YOUR WAY OUT OF THINGS! BUT NOW IT'S TOO **LATE!**

DID YOU TAKE US FOR **AMATEURS??** I RAN INTO ENOUGH BOOBY-TRAP BOMBS IN WORLD WAR TWO TO BE ABLE TO **SMELL** ONE A MILE AWAY!

WAIT! IT'S NOT WHAT YOU THINK--! I WASN'T JUST **PLANTING** IT NOW!

STAND WHERE YOU ARE! DON'T MAKE ANY SUDDEN MOVES! **COVER HIM,** HAWKEYE--!

DID YOU THINK I NEEDED YOU TO **TELL** ME THAT, WING-HEAD?!!

NO! YOU'VE GOT TO **LISTEN** TO ME--!

YOU **HEARD** THE MAN!! HE SAID **NO SUDDEN MOVES!!**

BUT, BEFORE HAWKEYE'S BLAST ARROW CAN REACH ITS TARGET, THE SWORDSMAN'S UNCANNY BLADE IS OUT AND FLASHING--!

I'VE GOT TO **FIGHT** THEM! THERE'S NO OTHER WAY!

I CANNOT MAKE THEM BELIEVE ME-- AND I CAN'T **BLAME** THEM! WE CAN **NEVER** UNDERSTAND EACH OTHER!

WHIT!

WE WERE **BORN** TO BE FOES--NOTHING CAN EVER CHANGE THAT!

NOW THAT IT'S OUT IN THE OPEN, I'VE BEEN **WAITING** FOR THIS CHANCE--!

CLANG!

THE SWORD DOESN'T **EXIST** THAT MY **SHIELD** CAN'T PARRY!!

≈UHHHH≈!

NO ONE HAS **EVER** GOTTEN PAST MY SLASHING SWORD BEFORE! NO **WONDER** HE'S BECOME A LIVING LEGEND--!

18

208

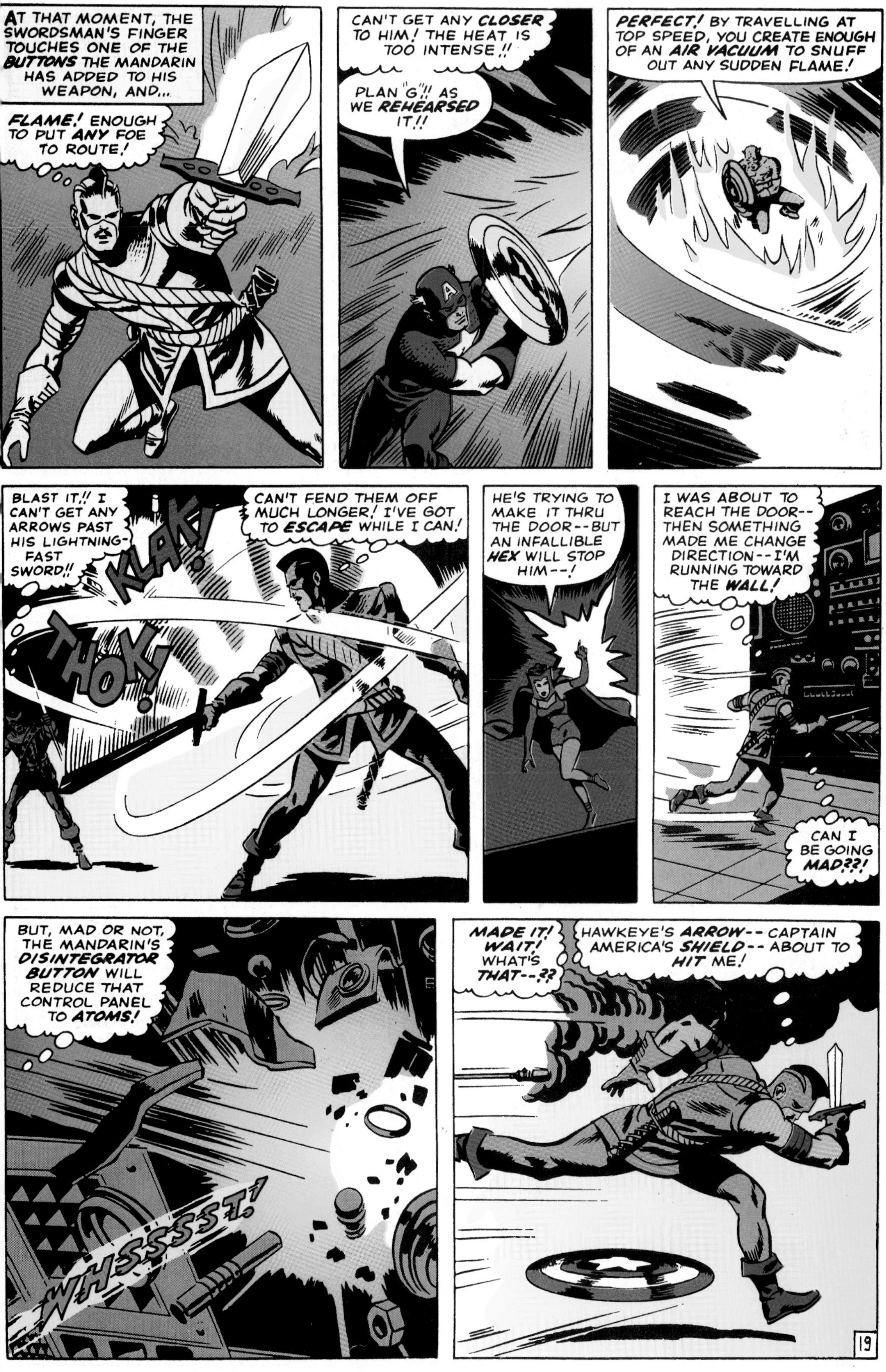
AT THAT MOMENT, THE SWORDSMAN'S FINGER TOUCHES ONE OF THE BUTTONS THE MANDARIN HAS ADDED TO HIS WEAPON, AND...
FLAME! ENOUGH TO PUT ANY FOE TO ROUTE!
CAN'T GET ANY CLOSER TO HIM! THE HEAT IS TOO INTENSE!!
PLAN "G"!! AS WE REHEARSED IT!!
PERFECT! BY TRAVELLING AT TOP SPEED, YOU CREATE ENOUGH OF AN AIR VACUUM TO SNUFF OUT ANY SUDDEN FLAME!
BLAST IT!! I CAN'T GET ANY ARROWS PAST HIS LIGHTNING-FAST SWORD!!
CAN'T FEND THEM OFF MUCH LONGER! I'VE GOT TO ESCAPE WHILE I CAN!
KLAK!
THOK!
HE'S TRYING TO MAKE IT THRU THE DOOR--BUT AN INFALLIBLE HEX WILL STOP HIM--!
I WAS ABOUT TO REACH THE DOOR--THEN SOMETHING MADE ME CHANGE DIRECTION--I'M RUNNING TOWARD THE WALL!
CAN I BE GOING MAD??!
BUT, MAD OR NOT, THE MANDARIN'S DISINTEGRATOR BUTTON WILL REDUCE THAT CONTROL PANEL TO ATOMS!
WHSSSSST!
MADE IT! WAIT! WHAT'S THAT--??
HAWKEYE'S ARROW--CAPTAIN AMERICA'S SHIELD--ABOUT TO HIT ME!
19

BUT, A SUDDEN, MASTERFUL SWEEP OF HIS SWORD DEFLECTS THE FATEFUL SHIELD, CAUSING IT TO STRIKE HAWKEYE'S BOLA ARROW AND RENDER IT USELESS!

BLANG!

THIS GIVES ME A BREATHING SPELL-- BUT ONLY FOR A MATTER OF SECONDS!!

IF I CAN JUST MAKE IT TO THE DOOR THRU ALL THIS FLAME...!

BUT, THE WATCHFUL SCARLET WITCH SENSES THE SWORDSMAN'S INTENT, AND SO--

ONLY THE SLIGHTEST BIT OF MY HEX POWER WILL BE NECESSARY THIS TIME--!

ZAT!

BUT, WANDA SUDDENLY LEARNS, TO HER DISMAY...

I WAS TOO HASTY! I FORGOT THAT A DENSE CLOUD OF STEAM WOULD RESULT FROM MY SETTING OFF THE AUTOMATIC SPRINKLERS!

DON'T LET HIM SNEAK BY UNDER COVER OF ALL THE STEAM!

BUT, WHEN THE VAPORS FINALLY DISSOLVE...

HE'S GONE!

LISTEN! AN EXPLOSION-- FROM OUTSIDE!

THE BOMB HE CARRIED-- DO YOU THINK IT-- GOT HIM??

LET'S HOPE SO, WANDA-- FOR OUR SAKES!

BUT, ON A NEARBY ROOFTOP...

I SUSPECTED THE MANDARIN WOULD TRY SOMETHING LIKE THAT WHEN HE REALIZED I BETRAYED HIM!

LUCKY I THREW THE WHOLE THING INTO THE AIR AS SOON AS I HEARD THE MECHANISM BEGIN TO THROB--!

AND NOW-- IT'S OVER! THE AVENGERS WILL BE OUT TO GET ME-- AND THE MANDARIN TOO!

AND, BACK IN THE ORIENT...

TOO BAD IT HAD TO END THIS WAY! THERE'S SOMETHING ABOUT BEING AN AVENGER-- EVEN A BOGUS ONE-- THAT SEEMS TO GET INTO YOUR BLOOD AND NEVER LET GO!

NEVER AGAIN WILL I TAKE A PARTNER! I FAILED BECAUSE OF THE SWORDSMAN! TO AVENGE MY HONOR, HE TOO MUST BE DESTROYED!

THE END

IF YOU KINDA SUSPECT WE'LL BE SEEING SOME MORE OF THE SWORDSMAN FROM TIME TO TIME, WE MUST ADMIT THERE'S A CHANCE THAT YOU'RE RIGHT! AS FOR MANDY, HE'S HARDER TO FORGET THAN A BEE STING! SO, JOIN US AGAIN NEXT ISH WHEN WE'LL HAVE A WHOLE FLOCK OF SURPRISES WAITING FOR YOU-- ALL WITH THAT SLIGHTLY SENSATIONAL LEE-HECK MAGIC! TILL THEN, FACE FRONT-- AND BE GOOD TO EACH OTHER!

20